Life in Search of Readers:

Reading (in) Chicano/a Literature

Life in Search of Readers

Reading (in) Chicano/a Literature

MANUEL M. MARTÍN-RODRÍGUEZ

UNIVERSITY OF NEW MEXICO PRESS ■ ALBUQUERQUE

For my parents,
Juan (in memoriam) and Modesta,
for their constant encouragement to read
and to cross borders.
For Virginia, Diego, and Alberto,
who have been with me
through the writing of this book.

© 2003 by University of New Mexico Press
First edition
All rights reserved.

———

Library of Congress Cataloging-in-Publication Data

Martín-Rodríguez, Manuel M.
Life in search of readers : reading (in) Chicano/a literature /
Manuel M. Martín-Rodríguez.— 1st ed.
p. cm.
Includes bibliographical references and index.
ISBN 0-8263-3360-5 (cloth : alk. paper)
1. American literature—Mexican American authors—History and
criticism. 2. American literature—Mexican influences. 3. Mexican
Americans—Intellectual life. 4. Authors and readers—United States.
5. Books and reading—United States. 6. Books and reading in
literature. 7. Mexican Americans in literature. I. Title.
PS153.M4 M365 2003
810.9'86872 DC21
2003012773

———

DESIGN: Mina Yamashita

Contents

Acknowledgments

The research and writing of this book have benefited from the following grants and fellowships: A. Whitney Griswold Faculty Award (Yale University), Morse Fellowship (Yale University), Summer Research Support (College of Liberal Arts, Wayne State University), Summer Research Grant (College of Urban, Labor, and Metropolitan Affairs, Wayne State University), and Program to Enhance Scholarly and Creative Activities (Texas A&M University). My most sincere thanks to these institutions for their support.

Parts of the section "*Peregrinos de Aztlán:* In Search of the Forgotten Chicano/a Literary History" (in chapter 2) appeared in Spanish as "En la frontera del lenguaje: Escritores y lectores en *Peregrinos de Aztlán*" in *Bilingual Review/Revista Bilingüe* 19.3 (September–December 1994): 57–70. Parts of the section "Linguistic and Literary Strategies for Addressing a Multicultural Readership" (in chapter 4) were published as "The Act of Reading Chicano/a Texts: Strategies for Creating a Multicultural Readership" in *Language and Literature* XXIV (1999): 17–29. I would like to thank Dr. Gary D. Keller and Dr. Bates L. Hoffer for their kind permission to reproduce these materials here.

Finally, I would like to express my sincere appreciation to the team of editors that have worked with me on this project: Elizabeth Hadas, Karen Taschek, and Evelyn A. Schlatter have been of great help along the way.

Introduction

This book is a reader's book. Its topic (reading), its author (a reader), and its intended recipients (academic and other interested readers) all point toward this often overlooked but most essential element of literary communication. In the field of Chicano/a literature, not much has been written on readers and readerships to date. The relevant studies on the subject will be quoted as appropriate in the following chapters. But those studies, because of size or other limitations, have not attempted to analyze in depth the ways in which Chicano/a literature connects with and is shaped by interaction with its audiences.

The challenge was, then, to reverse that trend and to embrace readerships and response-related issues as the center of a scholarly project. To that end, and through several stages, I started working with a retouched definition I appropriated from one of Tomás Rivera's most influential essays, "Into the Labyrinth: The Chicano in Literature." In that essay, first published in 1971, during a period in which Chicano/a scholars and authors were intent on defining what Chicano/a literature was, Rivera proposed to characterize it as "life in search of form."[1] As a writer, Rivera rightfully emphasized the creative part of the literary process, that of giving form to an experience so as to translate it into art. But urgent as that task was for Chicanos/as in the 1970s, Rivera the reader knew that there was much more to be said about that definition and, as I will discuss in chapter 1, he gave us a coded expansion of his characterization at the end of his celebrated novel . . . *y no se lo tragó la tierra*. As the novel closes, its young protagonist climbs a tree and starts waving to someone he imagines perched on a distant tree. With his hand signals, the boy wants that other person to understand he knows s/he is there. To me, that represented the ultimate poetics of silent communication: reading.

It was this symbolic formulation of the reading process that firmly grabbed my attention in 1990, as I started teaching Rivera's novel to my students at Yale University (where research for this book also started).

As I proposed to them, and as chapter 1 will detail for you, Rivera's novel (his ability to translate life into form) is also the realization that a work of literature has no existence beyond the materiality of its physical components without a reader or a group of readers who would respond to, interact with, and make their own the precise formal arrangement of materials that a text or a book offers them. It was thus that I reformulated Rivera's definition for my own purposes to define Chicano/a literature as "life in search of readers."

In the ensuing years, a clearer structure began taking shape for my project, eventually resulting in this book. In the process, I benefited from the continuous study of the several schools of so-called reception theory, as well as from other theoretical approaches that will be evident throughout the book. Along with the works of Wolfgang Iser, Stanley Fish, Umberto Eco, and Hans R. Jauss, of particular relevance for my project are the ideas of Michel Foucault, Gilles Deleuze and Felix Guattari, Homi Bhabha, and others, both in their own right and in their application to the field of Chicano/a studies that scholars of this literature have undertaken over the years. Needless to say, my work dialogues (both in conformity and in scholarly disagreement) with many of the leading voices in Chicano/a (and other) literary criticism, and they have also helped to shape this book with their insights.

The main claim of this book is that historically, Chicano/a literature has been defined as much by its readers as by its texts and authors. Expanding that main hypothesis, I was interested in researching how writers and audiences interacted in different periods, from colonial times onward. My study reveals that Chicano/a literature has had diverse audiences since its origins in those colonial texts. Consequently, Chicano/a literature has manifested different characteristics based on who its intended readers were, what the material conditions of publication and distribution were like, the linguistic choices available for literary communication, and the geographical mobility of writers and readers. Other factors, both literary and extra-literary, have played a role in shaping Chicano/a literature as well, including class status of its ideal readers (with the attendant effects on leisure time potentially devoted to reading), gender differences in access to both reading and writing, and literary tastes acquired in Mexico or in other countries by readers of Chicano/a literature.

My approach to these questions is not chronological, for reasons that I will explain in more detail in chapter 5, but it can be summarized for now as that I intend to construct a nonteleological discourse on

Chicano/a literature. Furthermore, our present understanding of Chicano/a letters is the result of developments largely taking place in the last forty years, which conditions our reception of any given text beyond its particular date of composition or publication. This extends to our valorization of literary works published before 1959 that, in a sense, belong as much in our time as they do in their respective dates of composition and/or publication. I start, therefore, with the Chicano/a Movement of the 1960s and 1970s, and then I move backward, forward, and sideways as needed.

The book is divided into five chapters that address complementary problematics of Chicano/a literature and its readerships. In chapter 1, "Life in Search of Readers: The Quinto Sol Generation and the Creation of a Chicano/a Readership," I concentrate on the changes brought about by the Chicano/a Movement in the area of literary production and reception. I contend that the creation of Chicano/a owned or controlled presses meant, for the first time in the history of Chicano/a letters, the possibility of conceiving of a Chicano/a readership at the national level. Prior to that movement, and before such an enterprise could be accomplished, Chicano/a authors had depended on local or regional audiences for their works, while much of the cultural transmission had taken place in the folkloric forms of the oral tradition as well. This chapter also analyzes earlier efforts by journalistic associations to transcend the local audiences, as well as the progressive institutionalization of Chicano/a literature in school curricula and in universities and colleges and what those academic changes meant for the success of early presses such as Quinto Sol Publications. The chapter closes with a consideration of the main strategies used by three of the Quinto Sol authors—Rudolfo A. Anaya, Tomás Rivera, and Rolando Hinojosa—to envision and communicate with that new national readership the Movement offered them.

Chapter 2, "Characters as Readers and as Writers: A Metaliterary Reflection on the Reading Process," focuses less on external changes in publishing outlets and on the societal base that would provide writers with an audience. Rather, my interest here is centered on the discourses on reading that are found in Chicano/a literature. To that end, and although I make reference to other texts as well, I concentrate on the two novels that have maximized their use of self-reflexive discourses on readers' response and reception: José Antonio Villarreal's *Pocho* (1959) and Miguel Méndez's *Peregrinos de Aztlán* (1974). These texts contain a wealth of information on how their authors envisioned the task of reading, thus providing their readers with a sort of specular narrative to guide their own activity. At the same time, as critics we can find in those discourses the construction of a poetics of reception that remains essential for our understanding of the role of audiences in Chicano/a literature. Méndez's novel, in addition, is analyzed here as a commentary on the recovery of Chicano/a literary history that will be further discussed in chapter 5. The action in *Pocho*, on the other hand, situates itself in the transition period between the predominance of the oral tradition and the shift toward a pervasive poetics of the written word that, in a sense, announces the major changes in Chicano/a literature to occur in the 1960s and 1970s.

The historical periods analyzed in chapters 1 and 2 were characterized by a patriarchal conception of society and, by implication, of literature that resulted in the displacement and silencing of Chicana writers and readers. Even if Chicana writing and reading is as old as, if not older than, Chicano participation in literature, the time spanning from World War II to the civil rights era was dominated by a masculinist rhetoric that allowed for very few exceptional Chicana voices to be heard and published. This in spite of the fact that, as mentioned in chapter 1, the oldest Chicano/a novel that we know to date was authored by María Amparo Ruiz de Burton (the author, as well, of the first Chicano/a play to which we have references thus far—except for colonial-era dramas) and that the earliest literary characterizations of Chicano/a readers are also centered around women (also explored in chapter 1).

In that context, in chapter three my interest was to analyze how our contemporary Chicana authors and readers have reclaimed that heritage and to discuss the larger role played by Chicanas in literature since the 1980s. "(En)gendering the Reader: Chicana Literature and Its Implied Audience" sets out to accomplish multiple tasks, but the main notions explored can be inferred from the first word in the title: on the one hand, I am interested in discussing how a readership for contemporary Chicana literature is created (or engendered); on the other, I explore how that audience is gendered and why. In this latter sense, chapter 3 branches out into the study of two complementary gender-based discourses in Chicana literature: the gynocentric approach, which privileges a female reader, and the didactic approach, which sets out to educate a male reader. These approaches are not mutually exclusive, and they do not constitute in its entirety any one particular text. Rather, they are to be considered critical categories or tools with which to begin approaching the study of reading (in) Chicana literature. Even if several other authors and their readerships are discussed in the first two sections of this chapter, this segment of the study concentrates on the works of Sandra Cisneros, Gloria Anzaldúa, Ana Castillo, and Erlinda Gonzales-Berry. As in the preceding two chapters, therefore, my approach is not comprehensive but selective of those attributes that can give us a representative entrance to the larger corpus of works available to the reader.

In chapter 4, "Querido Reader: Linguistic and Marketing Strategies for Addressing a Multicultural Readership," I propose to investigate linguistic and extra-linguistic elements involved in and conditioning the interaction between Chicano/a authors and their audiences. To this end, I concentrate on textual strategies utilized and favored by Chicano/a writers in their intracultural, transcultural, or mainstream-bound literary works to address what is now de facto a multicultural readership, composed, in turn, of overlapping segments that may be monocultural and/or monolingual in themselves. I also explore the linguistic and literary consequences of writing for what I call there "the market" (i.e., mainstream cultural circles) or *"la marketa"* (i.e., nontraditional literary publics). Moreover, as I did in chapter 1, with a study of Quinto Sol and other Movimiento presses, and in chapter 3, with the analysis of feminist and other gynocentric presses, in chapter 4 I complement my examination of textual, linguistic, and marketing strategies with a critical consideration of the publishing outlets more recently available for Chicanos/as. The chapter closes with a critical description of certain marketing labels and visual resources used by mainstream presses to promote Chicano/a literature to their broader audiences, including book covers and commercial advertising.

Last but not least, chapter 5 revolves around the question of literary history, particularly as it pertains to the (re)construction of the Chicano/a past through recovery efforts. Numerous previously unknown texts by Chicanos/as are being (re)printed along others that had fallen into oblivion, making Chicano/a literature grow almost as much toward its past as it is expanding toward its future. Paradoxically, a richer knowledge of the Chicano/a literary past complicates the task of writing its history, since—as I explore in chapter 5—traditional parameters employed in literary historiography are of limited use in the case of the Chicanos/as. Therefore, after discussing the problematics of chronology, encyclopedism, and nationalism for (re)writing the history of Chicano/a literature, I advocate a different kind of methodology to be used for this task. My model is based on the concept of the rhizome, as applied to literary theory by Deleuze and Guattari, and it calls for attention to both

continuities and ruptures in cultural transmission, for the inclusion of
reception and reader's response parameters, for a consideration of texts
in their multiple temporalities, for flexibility to adopt local or regional
case scenarios along with transnational analyses, and for attention to
this literature's multicultural and plurilingual existence. This new history
is not based on a "beginning" nor an end, but rather allows the historian
to move freely among different periods as different works of authors
become relevant for readers at those points.

Three additional assertions about my work should be clarified here
as well: first, in this book I read Chicano/a literature not in isolation
from, but in connection with, other minority and nonminority
literatures. I doubt that any real reader has ever limited her or his reading
activity to those books produced by any one human group (regardless,
for a second, of how that group is defined). I believe, therefore, that a
book focusing on Chicano/a literature and its readers should be open
to the potential connections that readerships may bring to their aesthetic
experience when approaching a Chicano/a text. As I propose in the
following pages, we cannot analyze Chicano/a literature without paying
attention to what Chicanos/as read and when. Granted, some of the
external references I will discuss will be based on my own experience as
a reader. In effect, as a trained reader, I may be disposed to (and should
be expected to!) make some associations that go beyond the evident in
reading Chicano/a literature, but whenever I engage in this kind of
comparative analysis, the reader of this book will find a rationale for its
undertaking. In any case, this book will explore many more documented,
and therefore less personal, links and bridges that Chicano/a authors
and readers have extended toward other cultures and literatures.
Chicano/a literature was never produced in isolation from other groups or
experiences, and it was certainly never read as a closed entity either.

Because I am a reader in an authorial position, as far as this book is
concerned, I have tried in the following pages to be as faithful to my
sources as I could. Whenever possible, I have used direct quotes from
those sources so that my audience does not have to read them through
me (not even in the necessarily limited space of a quote). As a corollary,
I have also respected the original language, including linguistic choice,
in those quotes. As I explain at some length in chapter 4, critics and
publishers are responsible for ensuring that English (Only) does not
become the sole linguistic face of Chicano/a literature, and this involves
respecting and promoting its original languages. Precisely because
English-language works enjoy a greater visibility these days, it is

imperative to make sure that immediate accessibility by the larger segment of the audience is not achieved at the expense of linguistic freedom and choice by Chicanos/as. In the following pages, translations (mostly functional ones) have been provided when needed in the endnotes, but all quotes within the text are in their original languages.[2]

Finally, on this same subject of language, I have tried to write in a prose that is engaging for the scholarly reader but accessible for the nonspecialist as well. While it is inevitable in a project like this to use specialized vocabulary and complex argumentation that presupposes a certain disciplinary knowledge in one's reader, it is also true that original thoughts and analysis can be conveyed so as not to alienate readers from other fields of experience. As reading groups across the country and, in particular, the now defunct listserv CHICLE demonstrate, there are many potential readers beyond this discipline who are interested in literary criticism and analysis.[3] A book on readers would be ill conceived if it did not think of them as well.[4] As critics of Chicano/a literature, I believe that we have a moral obligation to write (always without sacrificing professional standards) so that potentially no Chicanos/as, regardless of their professional academic training or lack thereof, are excluded from the conversation.

As is to be expected of any research project spanning over a decade, this particular one resulted along the way in the publication in journals and as book chapters of some of its preliminary findings. Those publications, in turn, served as the basis for parts of the present book chapters. Whenever this happened, I have included endnotes to indicate those connections, even if most of the material incorporated from those essays has been reformulated and rewritten for inclusion in this book. I would like to express my gratitude to the original copyright holders for their permission to reuse some of those materials here.

CHAPTER 1

Life in Search of Readers: The Quinto Sol Generation and the Creation of a Chicano/a Readership

> In literature life is submitted into the labyrinth of finding form. . . . We can observe the Chicano's frenetic intent in getting into the labyrinth and searching for forms. We can sense that here is life in search of form.
> —Tomás Rivera[1]

> If El Grito is truly to function as a forum for contemporary Mexican-American thought, it must have the active participation of its Mexican-American readers.[2]

> In the past the reader was a minor character in the triangle of author-text-reader. More and more today the reader is becoming as important if not more important than the author.[3]
> —Gloria Anzaldúa

In this chapter I will analyze the gradual process by which an expanding audience was formed for Chicano/a literature from the nineteenth century until the recent past. My interest is in tracing, very briefly, the information that we have on audience formation belonging to the nineteenth century and early twentieth century and to then concentrate on major changes brought about by the Chicano/a Movement. I will argue that the literary establishment associated with the Chicano/a Movement represents the culmination of a set of aspirations to define an audience as both Chicano/a (in terms of identity) and national (in scope). I will also claim that Mexican American writers prior to the Movement had already concerned themselves with defining their audiences in either those terms that they found realistic (i.e., as a group they could reasonably attempt to reach) or in terms that were more the product of a desire to transcend pragmatic limitations (i.e., the audience as those they should attempt to reach). But since most of those writers could not rely on an organized system of publication and distribution, their labors (exceptions notwithstanding) are better defined as individual achievements than as a collective enterprise.[4]

Pre-Chicano/a Literature and Its Audiences

Prior to the 1960s, Mexican American literature was largely characterized by its reliance on local audiences and/or declamation and performance. That was not necessarily a deliberate choice made by its authors but rather, in large part, the result of socioeconomic and cultural conditions prevalent in the Southwest and California. Hispanic culture had survived in the area thanks to oral transmission from generation to generation as well as the printing of books and periodicals. Folkloric materials thus preserved include sayings, plays, and everything in between (riddles, jokes, folk tales, poetry, songs, legends, myths, etc.).[5] The desire to safeguard the tradition had prompted many to concentrate their cultural activity on precisely that kind of close contact with a familiar audience along historically defined rituals of interaction. This included poets and other writers who conceived their activity in terms of oral delivery to their audience, via community celebrations and other social occasions.

It is clear from books and manuscripts since the second half of the nineteenth century, however, that Mexican American intellectuals also felt the need to address what they perceived as a potential readership waiting to be tapped and, in some cases, formed. In trying to envision such an audience, some Mexican American authors wrote with their fellow Mexican Americans in mind, as we will see, while others were clearly conscious of the fact that their potential audience went beyond the immediate community and their own ethnic group. As early as 1885, for example, María Amparo Ruiz de Burton addressed her novel *The Squatter and the Don: A Novel Descriptive of Contemporary Occurrences in California* to an Anglo-American or even to what we could describe as a universal audience.[6] As a consequence, her text abounds in extensive intertextual allusions to well-known figures of the Western literary and essayistic traditions. In fact, whatever allusions to Hispanic culture appear in her text are carefully explained for the sake of her non-Hispanic readership.

In their efforts to reach their intended audiences, pioneer Mexican American authors such as Ruiz de Burton were keenly aware of extra-textual factors affecting the production and reception of literature. This is evident from Ruiz de Burton's letters to George Davidson. In them, she demonstrates an acute awareness of the need to control the editorial and the printing processes in order to ensure proper representation and agency if she is to succeed in communicating with her readership:

> I want to publish [*The Squatter*] this fall, in September. . . . Will you try to help me? Please do so. If I am able to pay for the stenotype plates I will make something; if not, all the profits will go to the pockets of the publishers and the book-sellers. (*Conflicts,* 505)

In spite of her many financial difficulties, also outlined in her letters to Davidson, Ruiz de Burton stresses the need to purchase the printing plates in order to control production and (one can assume) distribution and sales of the book. But despite her attempt to avoid the fate of many of her contemporary writers, whose voices were silenced or reduced to a footnote in somebody else's texts, her efforts had a limited effect, since her literary presence seems to have quickly faded away and her texts remained buried in special collections and archives until very recently.[7] Her attempt is, nonetheless, significant as a forerunner of contemporary efforts toward control of the means of cultural production.

Because of these same difficulties in accessing the proper channels of literary production and distribution, several other figures among the Mexican American writing elite remained equally isolated and ignored during this period. Eusebio Chacón, Felipe Maximiliano Chacón, Daniel Venegas, and others succeeded in printing their works, only to see them confined to limited distribution, which reduced the possibility of contact with large audiences as well as with other Mexican American authors. These writers' isolation from one another was so pronounced that at different times, many of them would claim to be the first American of Mexican descent to ever try his/her luck at literature, unaware of works that had been previously published by others.

Eusebio Chacón, for instance, prefaces his *El hijo de la tempestad. Tras la tormenta la calma* [*Son of the Storm. Calmness after the Storm*] (1892) with an introduction that is almost a disclaimer:

> A mi querido amigo Lic. D. Félix Baca éstas páginas dedico. Son creación genuina de mi propia fantasía y no robadas ni prestadas de gabachos ni extranjeros. Sobre el suelo Nuevo Mexicano me atrevo á cimentar la semilla de la literatura recreativa para que si después otros autores de más feliz ingenio que el mío siguen el camino que aquí les trazo, puedan volver hácia el pasado

la vista y señalarme como *el primero* que emprendió tan áspero camino. (n.p., original orthography maintained; my emphasis)[8]

From a national perspective, Chacón was clearly not the first Mexican American writer, at least not in a chronological sense. He was preceded not only by Ruiz de Burton but by several others—including the prominent Texan Lorenzo de Zavala—not to mention the authors of colonial texts that are now considered by most critics antecedents of contemporary Mexican American literature.[9] But Chacón was probably the first for his immediate audience, who had no easy access to books by other Mexican Americans from California or Texas.

The motif of "being the first one" became in fact a topos of great importance for Chicano/a literature until quite recently. So prevalent was this feeling of writing in a vacuum among authors who operated in isolation from one another that we find examples of it as recently as in the early stages of the Chicano/a literary movement. Perhaps the most well-known contemporary reference to this feeling of doing something no one else had done before is found in Ramón E. Ruiz's introduction to the second edition of José Antonio Villarreal's *Pocho* in 1970[10]:

> In the literature of the American Southwest, *Pocho* merits special distinction. Its author is *the first* man of Mexican parents to produce a novel about the millions of Mexicans who left their fatherland to settle in the United States. Not until 1970 did another Mexican-American duplicate this feat. (vii, my emphasis)

So much for Eusebio Chacón and the others I have mentioned earlier in this chapter. What is remarkable, though, is that even if Ruiz utilizes this topos to beg the reader's indulgence for the lack of social analysis in *Pocho* (as I will discuss in chapter 2), his comments indirectly reflect how much the previous literature by Mexican Americans remained invisible for readers in the 1970s.

To confirm that invisibility, one need only look at another major figure of that decade, New Mexican Rudolfo A. Anaya. As Anaya was giving the final touches to what would become the first Chicano/a bestseller, *Bless Me, Ultima*, his feelings about writing were no different than those expressed by Chacón or Ruiz (on behalf—we could say—of Villarreal). Reflecting on his experience, Anaya explains that he felt he was writing in a literary void; as he asserts: "I had no Chicano models to read and follow, no fellow writers to turn to for help" ("Rudolfo A. Anaya," 376).

This type of comment is a palpable demonstration that, as far as literature is concerned, chronology does not make tradition. Historical antecedents are not relevant cultural models until they become part of a succeeding generation's memory and are thus transformed into cultural capital. The vacuum that Anaya felt was not there because of the absence of texts but because of the absence of channels and institutions to disseminate and preserve those texts and to create a broader readership that would keep their memory alive. The lack of such an established audience at the national (or at least beyond the local) level condemned most early books to a short span of glory among those who were closest to the author. As opposed to oral cultural forms that circulate freely among individuals and groups, books and other texts are clearly dependent on a literary establishment that was not there for Chicanos/as before 1970. Material conditions among this group hampered the production and dissemination of print culture from the beginning but particularly after the United States' final takeover of the Southwest and California in 1848.

After the Treaty of Guadalupe-Hidalgo was signed in that year, socioeconomic conditions in the Southwest and California deteriorated for most Mexicans who decided to stay in those areas, including the former class of wealthy landowners.[11] Prior to the U.S.-Mexican War, the latter class was clearly literate and well-read, and books continued to be a part of well-to-do households even after the treaty, as analysis of some private libraries has shown.[12] This is also documented in such novels as Ruiz de Burton's *The Squatter and the Don*, where the rich protagonist Californio family is well versed in world history and literature. Even young Mercedes, the heroine of *The Squatter*, spends her free time reading French history rather than taking a siesta as she would probably have done in the more stereotypical literature written by outsiders about Californios and other Mexican Americans.[13] Likewise, Luciano, a character in Eusebio Chacón's *Tras la tormenta la calma*, is a voracious reader, so much so that he ends up confusing literature and reality in his pursuit of the beautiful Lola.[14]

Most Mexican Americans, however, lacked the leisure and the money for literary enjoyment. The endemic problems in an unfriendly school system further complicated the matter, since the formal education of Chicanos/as has historically been less than adequate.[15] Who, then, would read Mexican American literature? As Doris Meyer, A. Gabriel Meléndez, and others have demonstrated, the main vehicle to promote the printed word and, with it, literature among Mexican Americans from the nineteenth century to the mid–twentieth century was the newspaper, including daily periodicals, bulletins, weeklies, church magazines, and the like.

Since the publication of *El Misisipí* in 1808, Hispanic and later Chicano/a newspapers have been a constant fixture in most if not all communities where Chicanos/as have resided. With varying degrees of success and continuity, these periodicals conveyed information, aroused and polled the feelings of their readerships, and provided them with quick, inexpensive access to both universal and local literature.[16] Though mostly read in the localities where they were printed, some publications managed to reach beyond their immediate communities as well. Several of the most important newspapers, for instance, succeeded in selling subscriptions far from their home cities,[17] and editors frequently exchanged newspaper issues as well as texts and stories. Moreover, as Meléndez's research indicates, the role that La Prensa Asociada played in promoting and ensuring cross-regional communication represented a conscientious effort to transcend isolation and localism:

> In the decade prior to the formation of La Prensa Asociada, Spanish-language editors often reprinted items from one another. They also spent much time citing the works of fellow journalists ... but La Prensa Asociada had the immediate effect of enhancing the exchange of information among its membership. A network of *canjes* created by the association improved exchange among member editors and provided *Nuevomexicano* editors with a steady and inexhaustible source of texts. (66, original emphasis)

This system of exchanges was of extreme importance for readership formation, since it created a net of communications among authors and readers from different parts of the Hispanic American world.[18] An article from a Californian paper could be reprinted in New Mexico or Texas, while a poem by a New Mexican would perhaps find its way to a paper in northern California. Little by little, this process not only ensured a more fluid cultural communication between previously unfamiliar writers (and their readers) but also helped to surmount the regionalism that had marked the Southwest and California since long before the first half of the nineteenth century, which McWilliams, Acuña, and others have eloquently illustrated.[19] In fact, as Clark Colahan notes, regional isolation goes back to southwestern chroniclers, who "through viceroys' secrecy, lack of access to printing, and the spread of stories by word of mouth . . . were often unaware of what their predecessors had actually done and reported" (16–17).

Additionally, many of the major newspapers were associated with Hispanic presses in their respective cities, as was the case for San Antonio's *La Prensa,* a part of the larger Casa Editorial Lozano cultural emporium.[20] This had a twofold effect: first, the paper served the publisher by disseminating excerpts from those books that the press was printing and by running advertisements for them; second, the press would occasionally print in book form periodical works by an author who had made a reputation for himself/herself in the newspaper's pages, as was the case in California with Daniel Venegas, a successful playwright and journalist who saw his *Las aventuras de don Chipote o: Cuando los pericos mamen* (*The Adventures of Don Chipote or: When Parrots Breast-Feed*) published by *El Heraldo de México* in Los Angeles in 1928.[21]

The progressive creation of a national consciousness that journalistic interchanges initiated would eventually come to fruition in the 1960s with the Chicano/a Movement, a manifestation of the civil rights movement that united Mexican Americans from all over the country under a similar banner and a similar name, La Raza, casting away regionalistic terms prevalent until then.[22] In the intervening time, the gradual process of communication between Mexican Americans from different areas of the country was also aided by Mexican American participation in wars overseas, particularly World War II and the Korean War. A large number of Chicanos fought in those wars; for many, this represented the first time they had left their immediate community (Meier and Rivera, 161). While overseas, they came to know Chicanos from other parts of the country (as well as service-men from other ethnic groups) and built strong ties with them. This is a motif well illustrated in Chicano/a literature on the wars or the return home, including the works of Sergio Elizondo and Rolando Hinojosa. Wartime exposure to different ways of life and thinking, whether due to their relationships with other Chicanos or to those with non-Chicanos, caused many to have postwar difficulties reintegrating themselves into their communities and their ways of life. The erosion of traditional values that accompanied this maladjustment contributed to the acculturation that was to characterize the decades of the 1940s and 1950s. Further enhancing these changes was the GI Bill, which allowed many Chicanos/as to attend universities and other learning institutions for the first time in significant numbers. This was, no doubt, the beginning of a trend that would later result in the expansion of a Chicano/a middle class and, with it, a Chicano/a readership, as we will see in the next section.[23]

The Quinto Sol Generation[24] and
the Creation of a Chicano/a Readership

Even if the catalyst for the Chicano/a Movement was the United Farm Workers Organizing Committee's strike against grape growers in Delano, much of the strength of the Movement (particularly as it relates to reading and literature) came from the academic world. To be sure, many organizations involved in the Chicano Movement had no formal ties with academic institutions yet were operative in the transmission and creation of literature. One of the most influential was the Denver-based Crusade for Justice, whose leader—Rodolfo "Corky" Gonzales—was the author of one of the best-known Chicano/a poems, *I Am Joaquin/Yo Soy Joaquín.* But it was in the universities where the necessary institutional force was first gathered to support an emerging counterhegemonic literature such as the Chicano/a. Even El Teatro Campesino, originally founded to serve as the cultural arm of the UFWOC's strike (Huerta, *Chicano Theater,* 11–14), soon realized that the struggle had to go beyond the fields. As early as 1969, El Teatro Campesino began intensive tours of campuses across the United States and even of theater festivals in Europe, where their performances helped Europeans to discover Chicanos/as as a nation within the United States.

The initial impulse of the Chicano Movement was also effective in closing the gap between the world of printed literature and that of orality. Because of the many demonstrations, community gatherings, marches, and the like, poets and other writers found an audience that could be directly reached and whose feedback would in turn be felt immediately. Not surprisingly, many of the texts from this era rely on formulas and rhythms of the oral tradition, as Cordelia Candelaria has noted (41–42). Similarly, themes and language seek to address everyday concerns and speech patterns of Chicanos/as. The intent of much of the poetry, drama, and prose of this period is to get the reader/listener to be able to rejoice in the recognition of his/her own life and cultural experience as portrayed in the literary works. As Julián Olivares has noted in discussing Tomás Rivera's . . . *y no se lo tragó la tierra,* the aspiration of Rivera (and many other writers at this time, I would add) was to portray the experiences of a group of people who were not remembered or chronicled anywhere else in print and then to let the reader realize that yes, indeed, that was the way it was:

> We can perceive . . . [in Rivera's statements about his works]
> that Rivera had an ethical obligation to write of his people, to

record their collective experience, to document the existence of a people. In this regard, he chose to write of the people with whom he was most ideologically and socially tied: the migrant workers. As a result, his people can read of themselves, and those who are aware of this type of existence can say: "sí, así era" [yes, that's the way it was]. (in Rivera's *Tomás Rivera,* 45)[25]

But even in the case of Rivera, we can quickly verify how his works were being affected (for better or for worse) by the progressive institutionalization of Chicano/a literature and many of its writers from the 1970s on. In his social advancement from migrant worker to chancellor of the University of California, Riverside, Rivera exemplifies the gradual ascent of other Chicanos/as (although very few have been able to reach the type of position that Rivera obtained), as well as the almost inevitable association of Chicano/a writers with higher-education institutions (first) and later—particularly since the 1980s—also with other literary institutions (via fellowships, agents, creative-writing workshops, major presses, etc.).[26]

This climate, along with major developments in the sociopolitical struggle—the foundation of La Raza Unida Party, the Brown Berets, the Mexican American Youth Organization (MAYO), the Mexican American Student Confederation (MASC), United Mexican American Students (UMAS), Movimiento Estudiantil Chicano de Aztlán (MEChA), and other political and student organizations—made possible national interaction among Chicanos/as at a new level. The desire to create a national Chicano/a consciousness was visible in all aspects of the Chicano/a Movement. In the realm of literature, a telling indication is found in the launching in 1976 of the journal *El Grito del Sol,* which succeeded the influential *El Grito* after the split of Quinto Sol Press.[27] The goal of attaining national circulation resulted in the editors' offering a free lifetime subscription to *El Grito del Sol* to the first subscriber from each state of the United States. While much of the social struggle (and the literature directly associated with it) was still carried on at the local level, the intellectual world was clearly seeking to reach and serve a larger public. The issues dealt with in *El Grito* and *El Grito del Sol* were no longer restricted to a local readership; rather, they were intended to raise awareness at what we could call a pan-Chicano/a nationalistic level.[28]

This trend was also confirmed by the publication of the bilingual anthology *El espejo/The Mirror* in 1969, edited by Octavio I. Romano-V. For the first time in Chicano/a literary history, an anthology of Mexican

American writers from different parts of the United States (along with some from Mexico) reached beyond the local level to present a selection of what was then perceived as an emergent national literature. In fact, the search for a national culture and visibility became one of the major forces behind both the Chicano/a Movement and its editorial branch. In the realm of letters, it could be claimed that the zenith of this nationalistic drive was attained with the institution of the Quinto Sol annual literary prizes, which were publicized as national awards and granted in California to writers from Texas (Tomás Rivera and Rolando Hinojosa) and New Mexico (Rudolfo A. Anaya).[29] In fact, as suggested by Juan Bruce-Novoa, the Quinto Sol prizes (like much of the rest of Quinto Sol's sponsored publications) became the first and most powerful benchmark for assuring authors of a place in the Chicano/a canon in formation ("Canonical and NonCanonical Texts," 45). Rivera, Anaya, and Hinojosa are indeed some of the most recognizable names in Chicano/a literature and, without a doubt, three of the most influential writers to publish in the early 1970s.

The goals that Quinto Sol set forth in its editorials and advertisements clearly emphasized cultural unity and self-determination. These goals were concisely outlined in Quinto Sol publishers Octavio Romano and Herminio Rios's article "Quinto Sol and Chicano Publications" as a series of six points, from which I quote excerpts of those most relevant to the present discussion:

1. Since its inception in 1967, it has been the goal of Quinto Sol Publications to analyze the fallacious and educationally detrimental content of social science studies of Mexican Americans. (3)

4. It is the purpose of Quinto Sol to provide an autonomous publishing outlet for the wealth of talent that exists in Chicano communities throughout the nation. . . . Who can argue against the fact that Spaniards as well as Latin Americans have always enjoyed publishing outlets, a reading public in their own count[r]ies as well as in foreign countries, and that in the United States strong Departments of Spanish exist for the sole purpose of studying peninsular Spanish and Latin American works, and that in fact these same Spanish departments in the United States provide a vast and ready market for works from Latin America and Spain[?] All this is [in] painful contrast to Chicano literary efforts, which have had the doors of the publishing world sealed to them for the last 124 years, and that until the recent inception of Chicano Studies

departments their creative efforts went largely unnoticed. (4)

6. Finally, it is not the purpose of Quinto Sol Publications to loudly proclaim support for bilingual-bicultural education, and then proceed to publish only in English. (5)

And in a further caveat after those six points, Romano and Ríos remarked:

A final word. The production of Quinto Sol printed materials is an independent Chicano enterprise, from writing to editing to publication. They are not the property of some Board of Trustees of some college, but Chicano owned. (6)

These goals of rejecting stereotypes, providing an outlet for talent, establishing a successful relationship with other institutions (emergent Chicano/a Studies departments, in this case), promoting bilingualism, and controlling production later became the rallying cry for an expanding editorial enterprise that carried forward Quinto Sol's pioneering efforts. It is obvious from the above quote that the Quinto Sol editors were conscious of the fact that in order for a literature to survive beyond the purely regional or local limits, it must rely on some sort of institutional support. Without compromising the autonomy that they sought, Romano and Ríos hinted at the newly created Chicano Studies departments as the most likely establishments to sustain a constant demand for Chicano/a texts, much as the Spanish departments had done for Spanish and Latin American literature, as they also note. In this context, it is not surprising that publicity for Quinto Sol books was regularly supported by data about their use in schools and colleges throughout the country. Thus, for instance, on the same issue of *El Grito* quoted above, a promotional page reads:

Educators use QUINTO SOL BOOKS for contemporary literature in English, for minority literature courses, for ethnic studies, for social studies, for bi-lingual [*sic*] Spanish-English education, for history courses, for interdisciplinary courses, ESL, for courses in creative writing.... QUINTO SOL PUBLICATIONS receives requests for materials from more than 300 schools, community colleges, universities, and libraries each month— nationwide. QUINTO SOL PUBLICATIONS materials are eagerly sought by other national and international publishers for their own anthologies.... (n.p.)

The institutional use of books published by Quinto Sol (and soon afterward by many other small presses) guaranteed for the first time in Chicano/a literary history that successive groups of readers could get access to an expanding number of texts that started to shape and define the perception of Chicano/a literature.[30] In other words, educational institutions guaranteed to modern Chicano/a authors the continuous allegiance of groups of readers at the national level, something that nineteenth-century writers could not have counted on.[31] The success of writers in the past century was measured by exposure not to an institutional readership but to one that read for reasons that did not usually include professional training as readers.

As demand increased in the 1970s, the possibilities for publication and dissemination of texts by Chicanos/as increased as well. Following the lead of *El Grito,* in a historical moment that could be characterized as euphoric, countless other journals and presses were established. A partial list of the former includes *Tin Tan, Atisbos, Caracol, El Grito del Sol, Maize, La Palabra, Mango, El Tecolote, El Pocho Che, Tejidos, Xalmán,* and the highly successful *Revista Chicano-Riqueña* (later renamed as *The Americas Review*) and *The Bilingual Review/La Revista Bilingüe,* which is active to date. Among the latter, one could mention the Bilingual Review/Press, Arte Público Press, Pajarito Publications, M&A Editions, Penca, Trucha, Relámpago Books, and many others. As if to prove the assertion put forth by Romano and Ríos about the existence of Chicano/a talent in need of publishing space, a multitude of writers started publishing in these and other journals and presses around the country. Their agendas were mostly similar in that they advocated a literature that would not be separated from the popular. This may seem contradictory to my stress on the importance of the institutionalization process, but I would hasten to point out that what these editors were seeking was an elevation of the popular to the institutional level. Without co-opting its grassroots nature, editors and writers alike emphasized that popular literature was worthy of study at the university level.

In fact, as I noted earlier, most writers of this period attempted to write in a popular way; that is, they wanted to tell a story or a song as the common folk would. As Jean-Louis Bory has noted, in a different cultural context, "[t]he popular novel (popular in its aim) as it becomes popular (in terms of its success) soon becomes popular in its ideas and its form" (quoted in Eco, *The Role of the Reader,* 128). In the Chicano/a context, popularization resulted in the textual use of oral forms, as Candelaria and other critics have already underscored. The case of Tomás Rivera is once again exemplary in this sense, for Rivera explicitly comments on his self-conscious attempt not only to re-create the lives of those migrant workers he knew as a child but also to re-create them as the workers would have told those stories:

> In my work I emphasized the processes of *remembering, discovery and volition.* I will discuss remembering first, I refer to the method of narrating which the people used. That is to say, I recall what they remembered and the manner in which they told it. There was always a way of compressing and exciting the sensibilities with a minimum of words. (*Tomás Rivera, Complete Works*, 366, original emphasis)

In this attempt to reestablish the traditional way of telling a story, an oral culture that was perceived as endangered or vanishing is preserved in print for future generations of Chicano/a readers, as Bruce-Novoa has suggested ("Righting the Oral Tradition"). But the technique also serves a further purpose in that it attempts to create a popular poetics (in the sense defined by Bory) and a model for the reader's identification with the hero as someone who belongs to a world like that of the reader.[32]

This poetics, while grounded in the oral, nonetheless assumes a reader's familiarity with the more individualistic nature of reading. That is, the text often reenacts the atmosphere of an oral community, as Yolanda J. Broyles (in her "Hinojosa's *Klail City*") has astutely suggested, thus making the reader feel like another member of the community interacting with the characters as if they belonged to his/her own world. But at the same time, the transliteration from the oral to the written is based on a set of conventions and formulas that accentuate the gaps and other types of blanks characteristic of the written work and that for reception theoreticians, such as Wolfgang Iser, are said to constitute one of the main strategies to ensure the reader's participation.[33]

It is not surprising, then, that most of the literature of this period is also characterized by fragmentarism, the juxtaposition of apparently unrelated episodes, and open endings. This is so not only because oral narratives rely more on an associative mode of organizing facts (e.g., jumping from one idea to the next with no apparent causality); I will contend that it is also due to a certain anxiety on these writers' part in imagining their readers and the kind of strategies they can use to communicate with them. Precisely because the culture they have known has been predominantly of oral transmission, their foremost task seems to be that of constructing a mental image of their audience *as readers,* as Héctor Calderón has noted with respect to Rivera ("The Novel," 102). This is why, in my title, I am appropriating Tomás Rivera's influential definition of Chicano/a literature as life in search of form with a twist that shifts the emphasis from the authorial domain to that of the reader. Chicano/a literature, in my opinion, is first and foremost life in search of readers, since it depends on the actual creation and preservation of an audience to gain full existence. To further illustrate my point, I turn now to an analysis of three of the most well-known texts of this time: Tomás Rivera's . . . *y no se lo tragó la tierra,* Rolando Hinojosa's Klail City Death Trip Series, and Rudolfo A. Anaya's *Bless Me, Ultima.*[34]

Imagining an Audience: Tomás Rivera

An essay by Héctor Calderón ("The Novel and the Community of Readers") will serve as a starting point for my own discussion of Tomás Rivera, since Calderón has advanced several interesting insights on the issue of Rivera and his audience. Calderón starts by comparing the socioliterary context in which Rivera wrote with that in which Miguel de Cervantes created his works. For Calderón, both writers can be said to have inaugurated their national novelistic tradition, surrounded by a society of large numbers of nonreaders (100). In that context, Calderón rightly concludes:

> Much of the artistic success of *Tierra* . . . depended upon how well Rivera imagined his future Chicano audience, on his ability to judge what kind of rhetorical strategies were readers able to accept. (102)

And he then moves on to affirm: "Given the historical and social conditioning of Chicano culture, the possibility of a Chicano readership in the late sixties and early seventies was itself a revolutionary idea" (113). Calderón is right in this sense, and I would only add that imagining such a readership is precisely what distinguishes Rivera from previous Mexican American novelists such as Eusebio Chacón, who, on a different level, had also struggled with imagining his readership and the best strategies to connect with it. The difference in Rivera's case is that, due to the altered historical and social conditions in the late sixties and early seventies, he must (and he can) for the first time imagine his readership at a larger than local level, as a group with an ethnic and national identity that encompasses both the recent literary elite (to which Calderón refers) and the larger mass of population. That is, he is now able to imagine a

Chicano/a audience, whereas previous writers had sought either the universal ideal (Ruiz de Burton) or had restricted themselves to a particular group of local or regional readers (Eusebio Chacón).

Rivera's envisioning of this newer audience is, not surprisingly, dealt with in the novel on a more or less symbolic plane. Most of the novel concentrates on the daily labors of a group of Texas Mexican migrant workers. The emphasis is on the rural experience and on the collective, on creating a sense of community. Many characters remain nameless and many utterances remain anonymous, as if to accentuate the possibility of their being anyone and anyone's. These characters' existence is more definable in terms of their belonging to the group rather than in terms of their individual lives. In that sense, many of the symbols utilized in the novel are also related to the collective campesino experience that Rivera assumes in his characters as well as in his ideal readers.[35] Such is the case with *la tierra,* which evokes a set of connotations different from its English equivalent, "the land," as well as with the fact that the whole book takes place during a symbolic (rather than chronological) year, an idea put forward in the first chapter/story, "El año perdido" ("The Lost Year"), which immediately brings the reader to the cyclical time of farming.

Interestingly, though, as a structural device to hold together all of the book's episodes, Rivera introduces a boy as the main character. Although this boy remains nameless, he is clearly the focus of a parallel narrative line that is less concerned with the collective experience than with individual growing up, both physically and intellectually. To be true to the ambiguous spirit of *Tierra,* it is possible that, while reading the different stories, the reader will have doubts about whether or not the boy who appears in all of them is the same one throughout the book. These doubts are dispelled in the final chapter, "Debajo de la casa" ("Under the House"), when we realize that, since he is able to remember episodes from all of the chapters, he must be the same central character.

The story of this boy is one centered on language:

> Aquel año se le perdió. A veces trataba de recordar y ya para cuando creía que se estaba aclarando todo un poco se le perdían las palabras. . . . Trataba de acertar cuándo había empezado aquel tiempo que había llegado a llamar año. Se dio cuenta de que siempre pensaba que pensaba y de allí no podía salir. Luego se ponía a pensar en que nunca pensaba y era cuando se le volvía todo blanco y se quedaba dormido. Pero antes de dormirse veía y oía muchas cosas. . . . (7)[36]

Most critics have read this initial story as an indication of the boy's alienation, and they have interpreted his calling out to himself and the rest of the motifs as indicative of a searching process that will be initiated in the following section and that will culminate at the end of the book in the boy's awareness of who he is and of his societal identity.[37] However, I would suggest that the narrative line opened up here is one that deals with language not as an indication of consciousness or lack of it but as a linguistic exploration that will transform the speechless boy into an adult writer. Thus, I would agree with Bruce-Novoa ("Portraits of the Chicano Artist") that the boy's personal journey is the story of a novelist in formation, but I would also add that it is at the same time a story about audience imagining and formation, bringing to a metaliterary level Calderón's hypotheses about Rivera as author.

In this sense, I believe that the boy's lack of words in the passage quoted earlier is indicative of the changed cultural context in which he lives rather than of personal alienation. It could very well represent a generational difference and signal that the boy no longer operates in the collective, oral world of his elders but in the individual, silent world of mental ideation and (at least implicitly) writing/reading. Lauro Flores has been the critic to get closest to this idea in "Discourse of Silence," where he explores silence in *Tierra,* particularly as it refers to the boy's inability to communicate with the other characters. Flores's comments on the final episode of the book, when the boy (perceived as an old man by those who find him) is discovered under a house by other children, are worth quoting:

> Very noticeable and highly significant indeed is the fact that the only interaction the character is able to sustain with other human beings is by means of his imagination. His only real contact with concrete people, which takes place despite his resistance, becomes frustrated and, aside from its violent nature, only contributes further to his alienation. Silence, although briefly interrupted, triumphs in the end and thus comes to close the circle of subjectivity that structurally and thematically rules the novel. (101)

Flores chooses to interpret silence in relation to issues of identity and alienation, and he ends by concluding that the characters' silence reflects the lack of political consciousness of pre–Chicano/a Movement workers. On the other hand, I believe that silence, particularly along the lines that Flores traces for us, can be interpreted as an indication of the generational and cultural shift to which I alluded before. Thus, Flores's extremely useful analysis leaves one only to desire (at least for my purposes) the expansion of his argument to account for the fact that perhaps the boy does not want or need to (or simply cannot) communicate with the other characters orally. If we read *Tierra* as a novel symbolically written by the child when he has already become an adult, the adult writer would be remembering those episodes (as he is indeed in the final chapter, "Debajo de la casa" ["Under the House"]) but not telling them to the other characters in the book, many of whom we may suppose dead at the time of the narration. Rather, he would have to be telling them to his adulthood imagined readers. The boy remains silent, but that does not mean that the adult narrator he would become does not communicate; he does so in the ultimate silent way: by writing for his contemporary readers.

Although I am not trying to read this novel necessarily as an autobiographical novel, the fact that Rivera has revealed his intentions on writing *Tierra* could be helpful for developing a clearer picture of my argument. In this picture, Rivera would be the adult telling the story to readers in the 1970s, while the events actually took place between 1945 and 1955, when he was a youngster. In writing *Tierra* several decades later, he is no longer telling stories using the oral poetics that is cogent for the adult characters in the book but in a newer written form that *imitates* the oral but relies on a completely different mode of interaction with recipients.

Thus, for me, the epiphany of the book comes at the very end, just after the boy/adult discovers the secret of narration and remembering as a process of uniting episodes and closing the gaps between/within them (which is also a poetics of reading, as we will see):

> Se fue sonriente por la calle llena de pozos que conducía a su casa. Se sintió contento de pronto porque . . . se dio cuenta de que en realidad no había perdido nada. Había encontrado. Encontrar y reencontrar y juntar. Relacionar esto con esto, eso con aquello, todo con todo. Eso era. Eso era todo. (75)[38]

The defining moment comes immediately afterward:

> Luego cuando llegó a la casa se fue al árbol que estaba en el solar. Se subió. En el horizonte encontró una palma y se imaginó que ahí estaba alguien trepado viéndolo a él. Y hasta levantó el brazo y lo movió para atrás y para adelante para que viera que él sabía que estaba allí. (117)[39]

With these words, the final words of the book, we have come to the ultimate articulation of the poetics of silence, when the spoken word has been substituted by the visual sign, speaking by writing, listening by reading. It is obvious that the only one who can see the protagonist on that tree is the reader; that is, the person on the palm tree who the main character imagines.[40] We as readers are the ones who see him "writing" in the air, moving his arm to signal, to affirm our private, soundless communication. Reading is not listening but seeing, and writing is, like drawing, a visual art.[41] If Rivera indeed needed to imagine his audience, it is clear that he did so in this paragraph, when he decided not to emphasize the fading away of the oral heritage but rather the birthing of a "new" written tradition.

Rivera makes the collective the subject of his book, but he is clearly aware that reading is more frequently an individual than a communal activity, the common practice of reading aloud to a group notwithstanding. This is further confirmed by the way reader interaction is secured throughout *Tierra*. By using a fragmentary narrative, Rivera maximizes discontinuity. His style is elliptical rather than redundant, as would often be the case for oral narratives. The numerous loose ends that his stories generate are there as a challenge for the reader to pick up. They are, in fact, the main strategy that Rivera employs to bring the reader into the novel as an active participant (as do other contemporary novelists), what Iser has called "blanks" in his *Act of Reading* (182–203). By the time the reader arrives at the final chapter, "Debajo de la casa," s/ he is already aware of the fact that "encontrar y reencontrar y juntar. Relacionar esto con esto, eso con aquello, todo con todo" (to discover and rediscover and piece things together. This to this, that to that, all with all. That was it. That was everything) is indeed the only way to come up with a particular picture of the world of the characters (and, perhaps, of his/her own world). For John C. Akers, this means that

> fragmentation does not signal chaos or disintegration in Chicano literature; to the contrary, its development is a reflection of a consciously chosen path to bring readers to a deeper experience of the unique cultural identity of the Chicano. ("Fragmentation," 124)

Indeed, the question is not one of order and chaos but one of experiencing, of creating a shared reality by reading. Reading, then, becomes an inventive meaningful act that establishes the connection between the world of the text and that of the reader. It is by being read that the book takes significance, not simply by its physical existence as a printed volume. The exaltation of this joy of literature as communication was made clear by Rivera himself in one of his most famous essays, "Chicano Literature: Fiesta of the Living":

> To me there is no greater joy than reading a creative work by a Chicano. I like to see my students come to feel this bond and to savor moments of immortality, of the total experience. (*Complete Works,* 340)

It is interesting that Rivera, the celebrated writer, chose to emphasize in this important essay his joy as a reader. This is possibly so because, in his own search for readers, Rivera needed only to look inside and discover himself as one: it is by exploring his own exhilaration as a reader that he can envision the audience he wanted for his books. And part of that exhilaration had to do with picturing himself (as a child) as a member of a group of readers—or, more accurately for the times and the particular situation, an audience—for Bartolo's poetry:

> At twelve, I looked for books by my people, by my immediate people, and found very few. . . . When I found Bartolo, our town's itinerant poet, and when on a visit to the Mexican side of the border, I also heard of him . . . I was engulfed with *alegría* [joy]. It was an exaltation brought on by the sudden sensation that my own life had relationships, . . . that the people I lived with had connections beyond those at the conscious level. (*Complete Works,* 339, original emphasis)[42]

As an adult, Rivera's coming to terms with his own Chicanismo is also brought about by his experience as a reader, as he acknowledges in an interview with Bruce-Novoa:

> Then, one day I was wandering through the library and I came across *With His Pistol in His Hand* by Américo Paredes, and I was fascinated. I didn't even know Paredes existed, though we were only thirty miles away, pero no había comunicación alguna porque no había movimiento ni nada de eso. Saqué el libro ése. Lo que me atrajo fue el apellido *Paredes.* [. . . but there was no communication at all, because there wasn't a Movement or

anything like that. I checked out that book. What attracted me was the name *Paredes*.] I was hungry to find something by a Chicano or Mexican American. It fascinated me because, one, it proved it was possible for a Chicano to publish; two, it was about a Chicano.... Now that, also, was in 1958, and it was then I began to think, write, and reflect a hell of a lot more on those people I had known in 1945 to '55 (*Chicano Authors*, 150, emphasis and bracketed translation in the original)

While the citation is interesting in its recalling the problematics of the writer's isolation and lack of exposure beyond the immediate local (or professional, perhaps, in this case) level ("Ni siquiera sabía que Paredes existía, aunque estábamos a 50 kilómetros de distancia"), I am quoting it to accentuate how reading is the essence of Rivera's literary vision, how his literature is, first of all, (remembered) life in search of readers. Even his desire to become a writer is triggered by his experience as a reader and his aspiration to reproduce that experience with other readers. As his allusion to the Chicano/a Movement suggests, the main difference between his predecessors and himself was that he was able to rely on a series of promotional and distributional channels that would make his name recognizable and his works accessible to a larger number of Chicano/a readers.

As we will see, once this point in the history of Chicano/a literature was reached, there was no turning back.

Hinojosa and the Reader-Oriented Novel

Following the lead of his friend Tomás Rivera, in the early to mid-1970s Hinojosa started publishing his major works, a couple of experimental novels that soon evolved into a multivolume work titled Klail City Death Trip Series. Like Rivera, Hinojosa was interested in chronicling the experiences of his fellow Texas Mexicans and their history, a history left out of traditional works on the area and its populations or else deformed by stereotypes and prejudices in works such as Walter Prescott Webb's *The Texas Rangers*. Hinojosa's main thrust, therefore, is that of a historical novelist, but his works demonstrate his awareness that history is a narrative construct, as Hayden White has suggested (*Tropics*, 81–100), which is why Hinojosa resorts to nontraditional means to write his chronicle of the Rio Grande Valley, the main setting of his narrative.

Hinojosa's metahistorical novel differs from the previous historiography and literature about the area in two fundamental ways.[43]

First, the notion of the historian as ultimate authority is undermined: instead of the traditional authorial figure that we find, for instance, in Webb's books, what we encounter in Hinojosa's books is a group of characters who, in their capacity as witnesses or as interviewers of other witnesses, start collecting materials and stories that they then put together to form the chronicle. This, in itself, is indicative of a group of new historiographic strategies utilized in the series, which range from hinting at what kind of documents are suitable to construct a newer history to a metacommentary on the kind of people who should be mentioned in the historical text or consulted prior to its writing.

Second, since the authorial figure is all but absent, Hinojosa's text clearly emphasizes the need for continuous reader interaction in the final configuration of the (hi)story. In a more sophisticated way than that employed by Rivera, Hinojosa's multivolume Klail City Death Trip Series is virtually a reader's novel, as I have suggested elsewhere (*Rolando Hinojosa*). In what follows, then, I will explore how it is that the series reveals this novel attitude toward reader participation, as well as the way an ideal readership is envisioned.

As mentioned previously, the fourteen books published by Hinojosa to date are grouped under the title Klail City Death Trip Series.[44] Some of these volumes are Hinojosa's own rendering into English of books previously published by him in Spanish. The new versions go well beyond a mere translation, since Hinojosa alters the order in which narrative materials are presented, he includes or suppresses fragments, and he modifies the discourse to adjust it to the different audience to which he is telling the story.

All books are connected to one another as they deal with the population of the imaginary Belken County, which Hinojosa situates in southern Texas. In that sense, Hinojosa's work reads very much as an *intrahistoria,* in the sense given to the term by Miguel de Unamuno; that is, a history of the common folk in their daily endeavors. The historical reach of the series goes back to 1749 (the year Jose de Escandón's expedition reaches present-day Texas—then Nuevo Santander) and continues until almost the present.

Hinojosa uses several character narrators to tell his story (in addition to a third-person extradiegetic narrator): the three most important are the cousins Jehú Malacara and Rafa Buenrostro and a friend of theirs, P. Galindo. Their narration is, normally, retrospective. They start telling their stories in the 1970s by remembering anecdotes and events from the past or by retelling what other characters have told them. Through these narrators, Hinojosa's readers learn about the social transformation of life in the Valley, as well as about the narrators' own successes and failures in life. The name the three of them use to refer to their work, *cronicón*,[45] leaves no doubt about the historical importance they confer upon it nor about the somewhat irreverent attitude with which they approach the historiographic process.

Throughout the series, in addition to the voices of these narrators, the reader encounters those of countless other characters. With their presence and their incessant conversations, Hinojosa seeks to capture the essence of communitarian oral culture, to the point that J. D. Saldívar refers to the series as "a virtual textbook of ethnopoetic and folkloric techniques" ("Rolando Hinojosa's," 52). However, Hinojosa does so with a clear conscience about the need to twist and bend that oral world to fit it into the type of strategical interaction that readers expect to encounter in a printed text.[46] If, as Wolfgang Iser has suggested, a literary text provides its readers with the basis to construct the communicative situation (64), it is evident that Hinojosa wants to re-create in his early novels the communicative situation typical of traditional oral cultures; that is, a participative relationship between orator (the singer or the storyteller) and audience. But in the way he does it, Hinojosa acknowledges that his audience is now a *readership,* and he exploits in his text many of the strategies associated with print culture and reading; thus the constant references in KCDTS to previous books by the author or by other authors, as well as the many literary strategies that call attention to themselves as such. In fact, it could be argued that orality appears at the beginning of the series on the same level as many of the literary genres employed from those early novels on; that is, as one of the many stylistic possibilities at hand for engaging the reader in a reconstruction of (fictional) reality. As I will explore immediately, this is a calculated resource for increasing reader participation in the construction of the literary work.

As a large-scale historiographic project, KCDTS is not unlike previous all-encompassing literary chronicles, including the works of Honoré de Balzac, the Spanish realist Benito Pérez Galdós (on whose works Hinojosa wrote his doctoral dissertation), and more recent examples of family sagas or totalizing novels such as Gabriel García Márquez's *Cien años de soledad* and the novels of William Faulkner, among others. But KCDTS differs from them in the absence of the central narrator found in almost all of those precedents, in its generic experimentation, and in the capital role it reserves for the reader. Virtually all of the elements in KCDTS are at the service of readership interaction and readership formation, as we will see by considering a couple of examples.

The first one I want to explore in certain detail is Hinojosa's use of multiple literary genres throughout the Klail City Death Trip Series. Along with his noted reliance on forms from the oral traditions (including folk tales, corridos, and riddles), Hinojosa experiments with *costumbrismo* (the Hispanic version of the novel of manners), epistolary forms, narrative poetry, biography, the picaresque, the anthropological interview, the monologue, detective fiction, the journal, and many other literary genres, not to mention narrative modalities that seem to have been inspired by popular television series (the successful *Dallas,* for instance, which is somewhat recognizable behind Hinojosa's depiction— both in style and content—of the Klail, Blanchard, and Cooke families).[47] Many of these genres were popular in past eras and so their inclusion in the series may seem outdated, as the controversy over Hinojosa's use of costumbrismo reveals.[48] As I have demonstrated elsewhere, however, Hinojosa's use of this and other genres is conditioned by his alteration of at least one of the genre's main features, which results in a process I called "coherent deformation," borrowing the term from M. Merleau-Ponty (*Rolando Hinojosa,* 94 ff.). What the coherent deformation of a particular genre achieves is to call attention to itself as a literary mode of representation (in line, in this case, with Hinojosa's metahistorical intention) and, in so doing, to force the reader to recognize both the convention and the violation of that convention as an invitation to (re)construct reality from a literary point of view. In the case of costumbrismo, for instance, Hinojosa's lack of authorial commentary (so typical of his Hispanic predecessors, such as Larra and Mesonero Romanos and popular volumes such as *Los mexicanos pintados por sí mismos*) entices the reader to supply the missing ingredient by coming up with his/her own evaluation of the situation at hand. This process, in turn, radically reconfigures the genre by inserting as a major player the reader, who, in traditional examples of the genre, had never performed such an important role.

A second effect of the proliferation of genres throughout the Klail City Death Trip Series results from the fact that each genre is forced to enter into a metaliterary dialogue with all others, thus exposing their respective biases and limitations in the construction of a particular reality. This, once again, is a process that can only take place in the reader's mind, as happens when the text exposes its audience to the same episode narrated not only in different books but also through the lens of diverse literary genres. Narrative poetry and the journal, for instance, are used to re-create Rafa Buenrostro's experiences in the Korean War. A violent incident in the cantina "Aquí me quedo" is likewise told through monologues, interviews, and legal and journalistic documents that in many ways cancel each other out or, in Derridean terms, put each other "under erasure," since one perspective never invalidates the others entirely.[49]

In connection with this continual interplay and mutual "cancelation" of genres, a second major strategy that Hinojosa employs to demand the reader's involvement could be described as syntagmatic indetermination. The text of a Hinojosa novel is often interrupted before a resolution is found, or else it is constructed in such a way that the reader must jump from page to page to establish connections between episodes that would otherwise seem awkwardly juxtaposed. This is evident for any reader trying to make sense of the death of Rafa Buenrostro's father, Don Jesús "El Quieto," since dispersed and contradictory versions of the incidents are found in both *Estampas del Valle* (128 and 171) and *Klail City y sus alrededores* (27, 29–30, and 53). The different versions are the product of different narrators who rely, in turn, on the recollections of different characters. The mention of this incident in *Estampas* (128), furthermore, is so tangential that only after reading *Klail City* can the reader understand that Javier Leguizamón's murder in that chapter is in revenge for the previous killing of Don Jesús. The resulting indetermination requires the reader to connect the dispersed fragments, to interpret and evaluate them in order to come up with his/her own interpretation, and to be on the alert for further developments in future additions to the KCDTS, since it should be obvious to the reader at this point that Hinojosa's narrative world is not only under continuous expansion but also under permanent rewriting and self-referencing.

Another example of how the Klail City Death Trip Series devotes itself to readership expansion and formation is also related to the process of rewriting and re-creating textual material. The translation into English of works previously published in Spanish is, I believe, Hinojosa's most radical statement on Chicano/a literature as life in search of readers. As I will discuss at greater length in chapter 4, the changes to which Hinojosa subjects his original versions are not purely linguistic or semantic but an entire cultural rearrangement of the text and its context to fit the needs of a different segment of his audience. After all, the works that Hinojosa rewrote were already translated into English by other people, which made them accessible to non-Spanish-speaking readers. However, as we will see in chapter 4, Hinojosa's aim is not linguistic accessibility but cultural significance. In this sense, Hinojosa's reasons for rewriting his own works seem to evolve from his realization that accommodating all readerships in a single text (even if printed with an accompanying translation) may prove impossible.[50] The originality of Hinojosa's approach rests in his realization that different repertoires (in the sense given by Iser to the term, 68 ff.)[51] are needed in order to communicate with different audiences. The changes in the repertoire, in turn, also modify some of the main strategies used in the original work, including literary genres. But in the case of Hinojosa, as we will see, the rewriting of the text for a new audience goes well beyond the use or recalling of a different literary genre. The whole set of social norms that Iser believes to form part of the repertoire is also altered when Hinojosa envisions a different, transcultural readership.

The First Chicano/a Bestseller: Rudolfo A. Anaya's *Bless Me, Ultima*

In their quest for an audience, Rivera and Hinojosa successfully blended themes and referents familiar to Chicano/a culture with modern and postmodern literary techniques. Rudolfo A. Anaya, on the other hand, followed a different approach in *Bless Me, Ultima*. Anaya wrote much less experimental prose, and he grounded his narrative in legends and myths that, while clearly inspired by Chicano/a folklore, would nonetheless be accessible to readers from different cultures (not to mention the fact that he wrote in English, while the other two wrote most of their 1970s texts in Spanish).[52] Anaya's novel is also fairly lineal, with a basic respect of chronology and a clearly defined plot. These differences alone could be indicative of the difference in popularity enjoyed by all three texts (Rivera's *Tierra*, Hinojosa's KCDTS, and Anaya's *Ultima*). But there are also differences in Anaya's perception of the role of the reader that, I believe, account for the fact that *Ultima* had sold over 300,000 copies (according to Quinto Sol, its original publisher) even before its release by a major East Coast press in 1994.

Not surprisingly, many more critics have dealt with issues of readership and success in this case than in any of the others. For some, like Daniel Testa, *Ultima*'s success is due to the book being

> a good action novel, a work in which intense and dramatic happenings make up a considerable part. . . . The technique and calculated effects of certain scenes seem deliberately to have been drawn from popular literature and movies that reflect a legendary "wild" west, replete with stock situations and characters. (71)

Others, however, find different reasons, ranging from the intended audience to the context of production and everything in between. Thus, at the opposite end of Testa's position is that of Horst Tonn, for whom the novel succeeds because it appeals to Chicano/a readers concerned about identity issues:

> One explanation for the success of *Bless Me, Ultima* may be the fact that the novel responds to a pressing need for adaptation in the vision of the collective identity. . . . Apart from curiosity about [the novel's] particular environment, what may appeal to a broader audience is the probing and truly exploratory character of the text. *Bless Me, Ultima* does not present a finished version of adapted identity, but rather prefigures the process of identity formation itself. (5)

The fact that the novel is about growing up would help both this presentation of the process of identity formation and the success of the novel, as Tonn admits (2).

Héctor Calderón, on the other hand, attributes the novel's success to its insertion within a previous artistic context. Calderón ("Rudolfo Anaya," 66–67), quoting a then unpublished manuscript by Genaro M. Padilla, believes that the novel inserts itself into the context of "an aesthetic discourse of myth and romance" that Anglo-American writers and artists who came to reside in New Mexico created and that "deeply inscribed itself upon the popular consciousness and provided one of the few forms through which Hispanos could compose their lives for public view" (66–67).[53] In this sense, what might seem a rather local story set in an isolated area of rural New Mexico is actually channeled (even as a resisting text) through that popular discourse to which Padilla refers and made immediately accessible to the most remote readers.

Also suggesting a larger than Chicano/a readership is French critic Jean Cazemajou, who ventures the following interpretation about Anaya's success with non-Chicano/a audiences:

> [S]ince the starting point of his creative process is "a sense of place," something is needed to prevent the distant reader from feeling out of place in Anaya's universe with its rich Aztec and Pueblo heritage. The first instrument that he uses is the power of *myths*. (256, original emphasis)

Mythical structures certainly help to organize the narrative material and to present it to what Cazemajou terms "distant readers." Even if the reader is not familiar with particular Aztec or Pueblo myths (or with legends that Anaya himself invents), s/he will most likely be familiar with other similarly structured mythical narrations in his/her own culture.

In this same vein, Roberto Cantú suggests that the novel was actually written with an ethnically unidentified (rather than a Chicano/a) audience in mind, since *Ultima* was first submitted to East Coast presses prior to being sent to Quinto Sol (57). To a certain extent, Anaya himself has confirmed this suggestion when he acknowledges that his wife, an Anglo-American from Kansas, "somehow represents our eventual readership" ("Rudolfo A. Anaya," 375). But then, a few pages later in this same autobiographical statement, he seems to relativize his prior assertion when he talks about literary response among Chicano/a readers:

> *Bless Me, Ultima* has touched a chord of recognition in the Mexican-American community. Teachers and professors were reading it, but most rewarding of all, the working people were reading it. . . . Most of the Chicanos who had lived the small town, rural experience easily identified with it. Everybody had stories of *curanderas* they had known in their communities. The novel was unique for its time; it had gone to the Mexican-American people as the source of literary nourishment. It became a mirror in which to reflect on the stable world of the past, a measure by which to view the future. (380, original emphasis)

The quote reinforces my point about the mimetic drive of the literature written during this period, already discussed in relation to *Tierra*. The idea of the novel as a mirror for memory satisfies both the need to see one's own experience in print and the desire to participate in a retelling of well-known stories. Having said that, I would caution that the work of historians and other social scientists has shown that the Chicano/a population has been overwhelmingly urban for most of the twentieth century. Therefore, it is not far-fetched to infer that many readers of *Ultima* may not have had a firsthand experience or recollection of the small town, rural experience Anaya depicts, although they very well may have had a vicarious one, via stories heard from their elders, for instance. This possibility is worth entertaining for my purposes since it would prove those readers to be familiar not with the experience itself *but with the telling of the experience.* Their previous exposure to this type of story would make them, then, particularly receptive to a novelistic version of it, since they would recognize that experience as the subject of oral narratives with which they were already acquainted. It would be easy for these readers to adapt their experience as listeners to the reading process.[54]

Anaya's construction of his readership as twofold and his avowed preference for the nonacademic reader are likewise indicative of the type of book that he has written. Put another way, *Ultima* is a bestseller because it is written as a bestseller. The reader's activity is kept to a minimum since the narrator and/or the characters do most of the interpreting for him/her, as we will see. To this, add the mythic-symbolic substratum to which I previously referred, a lineal plot with a certain dose of suspense, the frequent intervention of the seemingly magic or supernatural, the theme of growing up, and a heavy dose of nostalgia, and the result is a combination of some of the most powerful ingredients of the bestseller.

In elaborating on these features of *Ultima*, I am not trying to pass a particular judgment on the value of the book, although I do believe (along with Anaya, although perhaps for different reasons) that it works better for the popular than for the academic reader. Most academic readers have been trained to enjoy a text's difficulty and literariness and, in this sense, *Ultima* may let them down because of Anaya's (or rather, his narrator, Antonio's) insistence on explaining and interpreting everything for his audience. For the nonacademic reader, on the other hand, those challenges that open the book to indeterminacy of the kind found in Hinojosa's novels are usually not as enjoyable, while closure and interpretation of the kind found in *Ultima* indeed are.

Closure and resolution are at the center of this book in a more integrated way than we found in Rivera's *Tierra*. *Ultima*'s main character and narrator, Antonio Mares y Luna, is torn by several choices that others expect him to make while he is growing up. Some of these choices include opting for the vaquero culture of his father or the farmer culture of his mother, deciding between Catholicism and pagan religions, and learning from school and learning from nature. While this pattern of opposites builds up tension in the book, the reader is carefully led to accept the final conclusion that they are not really that antithetical after all but rather are subject to a possible synthesis. Synthesis is, indeed, the main lesson that Antonio learns while growing up and, one could argue, it is also the epitome of Anaya's poetics. This need for a *coincidentia oppositorum* is explored in several key passages of the book, lest the reader miss the point.

Already around the middle of the book, when Antonio is introduced to the legend of the golden carp and wonders about the possibility of the flooding of his town as a punishment for the townsfolk's sinning, he seeks advice from Ultima, the curandera. But Ultima gently rebuffs him, insisting: "I cannot tell you what to believe. Your father and your mother can tell you, because you are their blood, but I cannot. As you grow into manhood you must find your own truths" (119). Two pages later, revelation comes to Antonio during a dream: "The waters are one, Antonio" (121). The interconnectedness of things, which was also at the root of the final epiphany of *Tierra*'s protagonist, is then developed for the rest of the book. By the end of the novel, the message is more clearly articulated in what becomes not only the resolution of all conflicts in the book but also an *ars poetica* for Anaya:

> "Take the llano and the river valley, the moon and the sea, God and the golden carp—and make something new," I said to myself. "*That is what Ultima meant* by building strength from life." (247, my emphasis)

It is this type of continuous commentary by the narrator or by other characters that regulates our reading of the novel without letting us stray too far from the explicit evaluation. This strategy is not applied only to the final consequential message; rather, it is employed at every moment of the narrative in order to facilitate the reader's comprehension as much as possible. Consider, for example, this paragraph from the beginning of the book. In it, Antonio's mother and her children are discussing Ultima's coming to live with them. By the end of their conversation, their mother says:

> "Now run and sweep the room at the end of the hall. Eugene's room—" I heard her voice choke. She breathed a prayer and crossed her forehead. The flour left white stains on her, the four points of the cross. (8)

At this point, the reader may be captivated by the poetic sadness of the paragraph, wondering what is wrong with Eugene, whether he is alive, dead, or in danger. The reader may also be mentally running over everything s/he has read already to find some clues for interpreting this passage, or s/he may be anticipating new narrative developments. S/he may even want to reread the preceding few pages to see if s/he missed something the first time. But this thrill that for many readers has become associated with filling in the textual gaps, mentally ideating what is to come, or actively participating in any other way is quickly taken away from him/her as Antonio states: "I knew it was because my three brothers were at war that she was sad, and Eugene was the youngest" (8). In a different type of novel, this could have come later or could have been conveyed obliquely to the reader so that s/he would have been able to delight in discovering the fact by him/herself. But the bestseller nature of *Ultima* requires that the reader learn to relax and be told what is going on.

Some critics would, of course, disagree with my analysis. For Horst Tonn, for instance, there is a subtext with which the reader may interact at a different level. He develops this claim while discussing how nostalgia can be one of the key factors in making *Ultima* a success:

> No doubt, the elements of nostalgia in the text may well contribute to the reader's enjoyment. A vision that emanates serenity, peace, and wholeness will not fail to exert its attraction, regardless of whether that perfect state stems from verifiable fact or idealization. The reader, however, should not be absorbed by this. There is another level of significance in which the ramifications of historical nostalgia are explored and found wanting. (9)

This subtext is perhaps the same as the one to which Ramón Saldívar has alluded when analyzing the novel in his *Chicano Narrative,* in which we find references to the killing of Comanches, the Alamogordo nuclear test, and the effect of the war on veterans:

> The popular and critical success of [Anaya's] narrative, making it the most widely read of Chicano works by both Mexican American and Anglo audiences, emphasizes the difficulty of maintaining history and the extent to which we all desire to turn away from it. (126)

By the same token, it may be that what many readers desire is to turn away from active reading: they may want just to sit back, relax, and be told a good story in which they will not have to be active partners in any sense other than that of fulfilling their willingness to become the book's audience. It is in this sense that I proposed that *Ultima* was written as the successful bestseller it has become, without implying that the novel does not have deeper or different reading possibilities. It is also in this sense that Anaya is right in rejoicing in the popular success of his novel, since popular reading habits are closer to those required for engaging with *Ultima* than they are to those required for making sense of *Tierra* or the Klail City Death Trip Series. As I will consider in the next chapter, "turning away from it all" was already associated with reading in what many considered for long "the first" Chicano/a novel, José Antonio Villarreal's *Pocho.*

CHAPTER 2

Characters as Readers and as Writers:
A Metaliterary Reflection on the Reading Process

> *I read everything that I had access to. It was very difficult in those years [of my childhood] to find reading material until I began using the town library. I had no direction whatsoever and the only specific direction my reading took was fiction.*
> —José Antonio Villarreal[1]

> *As a student of American literature, I have long been struck by the degree to which American texts are self-reflexive. Our "classics" are filled with scenes of readers and readings.*
> —Judith Fetterley[2]

Many Chicano/a novels from the 1970s on (and even some earlier texts) have concerned themselves with characters who become writers. This, in turn, has attracted considerable critical attention as scholars have analyzed the significance of the *künstlerroman* as a genre in Chicano/a literature.[3] Undoubtedly, these characters struggle in their fictional worlds with many of the same issues that their real-life creators had to deal with when conceiving their novels. Thus, these novels function somewhat as narrative mirrors for the act of creation, its difficulties and its joys, as they produce a most significant metaliterary discourse. But, we could ask, what about the act of reception, its difficulties and its joys? How does Chicano/a metaliterary discourse address issues of readership and reception?

Although this aspect has sparked considerably less thought among critics, there are many Chicano/a texts that have made their characters readers, some of them voracious readers. The motif is present since, at least, the nineteenth century.[4] I already mentioned the case of the characters in María Amparo Ruiz de Burton's *The Squatter and the Don*, where reading plays an essential role in creating the literary image of a cultured elite that transcends ethnic barriers. We even have an echo of Don Quijote in Luciano, a character in Eusebio Chacón's *Tras la tormenta, la calma,* whose readings of romantic literature guide him in his own amorous pursuits, much like chivalric novels guided the Spanish *hidalgo.* But if Burton's Mercedes Alamar and Chacón's Luciano (a student at St. Michael's College) are still literate representatives of a privileged sector of U.S. Hispanic society, contemporary Chicano/a literature introduces a significant variant in the profile of the Chicano/a audience: that of the working-class and the middle-class reader.[5]

What interests me the most about these characters as readers, at least in a study like this, is the information that they give us about their creator's views on reading as an essential part of the literary process. This, in turn, is affected by factors of class, gender, and ethnic self-perception, among others. The social and metaliterary information that we can gain from analyzing these characters will contribute to the general argument that I am developing in this study about Chicano/a literature being on a constant search for readers. Needless to say, individual texts will present differences in their views about reading, so a cohesive, monolithic view on the part of Chicano/a authors about literature and reading should not be expected from such an analysis, nor would I try to construct such a view. Rather, I will deal with the tensions implicit in writing for a largely unknown, yet imagined audience, most often one that belongs to the same cultural and ethnic group as the writer. Although I plan to draw on examples from several other Chicano/a texts, the rest of this chapter will concentrate on analyzing José Antonio Villarreal's *Pocho* (1959) and Miguel Méndez's *Peregrinos de Aztlán* (1974), the two Chicano/a texts that have constructed the most comprehensive metaliterary discourses on reading to date. As I analyze reading in these novels, I will also pay attention to how they have been read at different times.

In the Beginning Was Pocho: Reading (in) "The First" Chicano/a Novel

The first text that I want to explore in this chapter is Villarreal's *Pocho,* in which we find perhaps the most detailed exploration of reading in all of Chicano/a literature. While most critics have read *Pocho* as a novel about the development of a writer,[6] I have chosen to read it as the chronicle of a reader in formation. That is, I will problematize what several critics have taken for granted, namely, that Richard Rubio—the protagonist—is the fictional author of the narrative, and concentrate on an indisputable aspect of Richard's fictional life: the fact that he is an insatiable reader.

In reading *Pocho* and in discussing reading in *Pocho,* I will be addressing not only how reading shapes the world for the book's characters but also how empirical readings of *Pocho* by some of the most influential scholars of Chicano/a literature are illustrative of the pitfalls involved in the writing of traditional literary histories that concentrate on authorial and textual data while neglecting readership and reception.

Since the early 1970s, it became a matter of literary routine to consider *Pocho* the first Chicano/a novel. While textual rediscovery of earlier texts and the reinterpretation of other texts written and/or published earlier than *Pocho* have shaken the tenability of that assertion, many still claim that *Pocho* is the first contemporary Chicano/a novel. This in itself is interesting, since the way *Pocho* has been read almost contradicts the poetics of reading that the novel contains, as we will see. I already mentioned in chapter 1 how the claim of inaugural role for *Pocho* was not done without a little embarrassment on the critics' part. Thus remember the quote from Ramón E. Ruiz's introduction to the 1970 reprint, in which he spoke of Villarreal as

> the *first* man of Mexican parents to produce a novel about the millions of Mexicans who left their fatherland to settle in the United States. Not until 1970 did another Mexican-American duplicate that *feat.* (vii, my emphasis)

In spite of the epic tone and vocabulary that Ruiz employs, his discomfort with the novel he prefaces is evident when he tries to adjust *Pocho*'s intriguing ending, in which Richard decides to join the navy during World War II, and the book's scarce explicit social commentary to his own (Ruiz's) militant times:

> The ambivalence that colors Villarreal's handling of his theme and conclusion reflects the ambiguities and *ideological confusions* inherent in Mexican-American thinking of the time—a point that the reader of *Pocho* must keep firmly in mind lest he *misunderstand and misinterpret* its major premise. (viii, my emphasis)

Ruiz's analysis is not surprising coming from a historian who may be tempted to read literary texts as documents and to attribute to them a given, more or less fixed meaning. But if we discard the notion that texts are predominantly documents or testimonials of their times and engage in a reader-oriented analysis of *Pocho,* we will soon realize that the whole point of *Pocho* may precisely be the absence of a fixed meaning.[7] *Pocho* deals with individual identity in formation and individual ideation/ interpretation of reality. As such, the novel constructs the character of Richard Rubio as one of the most unpredictable Chicano/a characters, in the sense that he, as Ramón Saldívar has noted, usually opts for not opting (62). In clear contrast with Antonio Mares, Anaya's protagonist in *Bless Me, Ultima,* he does not find synthesis or resolution to the conflicts to which he is exposed; he simply observes them and moves on, trying to "read" what the world and the people are like. Similarly, his ideas fluctuate so much and become so entangled that he incessantly discards the old ones for new rearrangements of his thoughts, thus producing unstable meanings and values, subject to further and constant modifications.

Even the literary genre employed in this novel is used with a twist that undermines some of its typical features, not unlike the effect that I explored earlier while discussing Hinojosa's Klail City Death Trip Series. Whereas other *bildungsromane* are told from the perspective of a mature reflective character looking back on his or her childhood and adolescence experiences, *Pocho* ends abruptly without any clear indication of what the life of Richard as an adult is like (or even if he survives World War II, for that matter). That is, at the end of the book he remains an adolescent with literary aspirations. It is only through a rhetorical leap of faith that one can interpret Richard's future. That is, I believe, what Ramón Saldívar has done in proposing the following interpretation:

> [T]hat Richard Rubio may turn to the politics of change is suggested by the fact that the book that he has always hoped to write *is* written, as semiautobiographical fiction, in the form of the novel *Pocho.* (67)

However, this reading (a 1980s "correction" of Ramón Ruiz's ideological dilemma) may well be wishful thinking on the part of Saldívar, since there is no textual indication that would prove his assertion. To be sure, there is no indication that would deny it, either, but that is precisely my point: that *Pocho,* as Richard, opts for not opting, for leaving it to the reader's imagination, be that Saldívar's or anybody else's. As a consequence, and to ascertain whether *Pocho* would accept any possible reading or if, on the contrary, it guides the potential reader toward a preferred one,[8] I believe it is extremely relevant to look at what the book says about reading. After all, if there could always be doubt as to whether or not Richard becomes a writer, there is none whatsoever that early on in his life he becomes a reader, and an avid one at that.

Reading appears foregrounded in *Pocho* in a minimum of three ways. First, we could speak of a certain "reading" or, at least, reception of the oral tradition; then there is reading in the most traditional sense (that is, as an interaction with written texts); and finally there is a "reading" (once again in a more semiotic than purely literary sense) of the mass media, particularly the movies. I will proceed by analyzing these "readings" in the order that I have just outlined.

As a receiver or "reader" of the oral tradition, Richard strikes our interest because of his failure to really participate and empathize with the "texts" to which he listens. It is as if, somehow, he misses the point over and over. By this I do not mean that he does not understand the meaning of the stories he is told but rather that he is unable to interpret and to appreciate the conditions and the contexts in which those compositions are told or sung and those to which they refer. Richard cannot sense the pathos associated with the oral tradition. Instead, he perceives it as something magical, an understandable reaction from someone who is an outsider to a particular cultural form. Consider, for instance, the following passage, in which Richard listens to his mother singing:

> He walked into the house and heard his mother singing in the kitchen. In a clear, fine voice, she sang ballads of the old days in her country, and the child was always caught in their magic. He was totally unaware that his *imaginary remembrances,* being free of pathos, were far more beautiful than the real ones. (34, my emphasis)

In addition to the idea that Richard is no longer able to participate in the cultural world of his parents (which introduces several key topics of the book and of much of Chicano/a literature from this era—among them acculturation, the generational split, and the fading away of the oral tradition), this quote is already suggesting one of the most pervasive notions that *Pocho* conveys about literature: namely, that it is not like reality but somehow better and more beautiful, a subject to which we will return when discussing history and fiction at the end of this chapter.

The previous quote seems to suggest, furthermore, that the reader (the listener, in this case) plays an active role as cocreator in the literary/ cultural process. That is, Richard's ideations, or "imaginary remembrances," as the text calls them, are different and somehow more beautiful than those actually sung by his mother. This is also a recurring motif throughout the novel, as we are told over and over about Richard's ability to weave a parallel fantasy that he juxtaposes alongside the stories he hears or reads, as in the following excerpt:

> With his father, Richard sat around campfires or in strange kitchens, with wood stoves burning strongly and the ever-present odor of a pot of pink beans boiling, freshly cooked tortillas filling the close, warm room, and listened to the tales of that strange country which seemed to him a land so distant, and the stories also seemed of long, long ago. It was then, listening and weaving a parallel fantasy in his mind, that he felt an enjoyment so great that he knew he could not possibly savor it all. (43)

As in the previous quote, the distance between Richard and his parents is expressed in relation to culture through the motif of the strange land and the old days. It is this distance that proves to be insurmountable for Richard, since we see him not (re)integrating himself into the cultural world associated with the stories but rather creating newer stories in his head. These stories, we may assume, are also free of the pathos associated with the original ones. Aisthesis and poiesis (rather than catharsis) define Richard's mental activities, since he compensates for what he misses of the original contexts through sheer enjoyment and mental creativity.[9] This, it may be argued, reveals a side of Richard that brings him closer to the profile of the writer he might one day become; at the same time, as metaliterary discourse, it advocates the kind of active reading I have delineated earlier and thus carefully prepares the reader to supply with her/his own "weaving" ability what the text is refusing to offer; among other things, a conclusive ending.

At this point, my reader could point out that Richard's inability to empathize with the oral tradition is presented as a negative trait of his character, which would endanger my interpretation of the previous passage as an element of the theory of reading I believe to be contained in *Pocho*. The oral tradition, after all, passed from parents to their children, from generation to generation, has been a most important means for the preservation of Mexican American culture. That interpretation, however, would be conditioned by the reader's own background and cultural baggage (with which Villarreal may be intentionally playing here) since the novel, as I will explore later, has still a far more radical commentary on the value of the oral tradition in store, one that presents it as inadequate or of limited value for Richard's generation. Thus, in this facet of Richard as a "reader" of the oral tradition, we see his inability to perform his role of listener in a conventional way. What *Pocho* dramatizes (or, perhaps, even celebrates) is the rupture with that tradition once the social conditions that kept it alive are radically changed. In that sense, the novel seems to suggest, it would be of no use to ask Richard to participate in a form of communal culture when the notion of community has been so drastically altered. His life experiences have prepared him for becoming a reader and, more importantly, as we will see next, for the enjoyment of reading as a leisurely, solitary, nonutilitarian activity.

As a reader of written texts, Richard is much more at ease than he is with oral stories and narrative songs. The conflict with his parents remains nonetheless visible at this level, since they expect his reading to be the means to achieve an improvement in their family position, whereas Richard sees it merely as an enjoyable activity. He reads for the sake of reading, not in order to become a learned man, as he clearly states in the following conversation with his mother:

> "But all this reading, my son," she asked. "All this studying—surely it is for something? If you could go to the university, it would be to learn how you could make more money than you would make in the fields or the cannery. So you can change our way of living somewhat, and people could see what a good son we had, and it would make us all something to respect. . . ."
>
> "Ah, Mamá! Try to understand me. I want to learn, and that is all. I do not want to be something—I *am*. I do not care about making a lot of money and about what people think and about the family in the way you speak." (64, original emphasis)[10]

And then, a few paragraphs later, he gives us the key to what he feels as he reads (and maybe, once again, a hint at the implied author's views on reading):

> "Mamá, do you know what happens to me when I read? All those hours that I sit, as you sometimes say, 'ruining my eyes'? If I do ruin them, it would be worth it, for I do not need eyes where I go then. I travel, Mamá. I travel all over the world, and sometimes out of this whole universe, and I go back in time and again forward. . . . I am always thinking of you and my father except when I read.

Nothing is important to me then, and I even forget that I am going to die sometime." (64)

As was the case for his reception of the oral forms of his parents' tradition, Richard's reading removes him from history and reality. In reading, he creates his own personal world where, one could assume, challenges to his personal identity are canceled out and where he can proudly assert "I am" in an almost Promethean fashion. Reading also unties him from family and collectivity. While some (along the same lines already traced by Ruiz) could dismiss Richard's attitude as simply escapist, it could be argued that his theory of reading—and the same could be said about Ruiz's, for that matter—is also a theory of identity and a questioning of what reality is or the way it is defined. Thus, when confronted by his mother about his less than realistic attitude, Richard simply replies: "But that is exactly what I mean, Mamá. Everything does not necessarily have to be real" (65).

What we are seeing dramatized in these scenes is a change in paradigm that entails significant alterations in worldviews and in the role of traditions. Once the models of learning operative in the world of the (largely) oral tradition have been subverted, Richard feels that his parents cannot teach him anything; even his parents seem to agree with that notion:

> "Look, little son," [Richard's] mother said. "Many times I do not answer you when you ask me things, and other times I simply talk about something else. Sometimes this is because you ask things that you and I should not be talking about, but most of the times it is because I am ashamed that I do not know what you ask. You see, we are simple people, your father and I. . . . And I am deeply ashamed that we are going to fail in a great responsibility—we cannot guide you, *we cannot select your reading for you*, we cannot even talk to you in your own language. (61–62, my emphasis)

A similar attitude is later expressed by his father: "Forgive me that I cannot help you. I feel your problem, but I am not an educated one" (131).

Since his teachers do not seem to be able to guide him either (103), Richard's solution involves indiscriminate reading of the kind described in chapter 6 of *Pocho*, where we follow Richard as he reads all the books in his school library, a few Spanish books lent to him by a friend of his father, newspapers, and some other books acquired through diverse means.

While this incessant exploration of new texts increases Richard's intellectual expertise, he soon begins to have doubts about whether he should be reading about things or actually experiencing them. His doubts in this area stem from his days at the library. As the narrator puts it: "He was disturbed by the thought that now, while he was young and strong in body, his wanderings should be physical. Imagination would do only when he became old and incapable of experiencing actual adventure" (102–3). In this slight change of attitude toward reading, his father's urging him to experience things for himself seems to play an important role: "Only when riding out in the country lanes was Richard forbidden to read. Twice his father threw his books out the window of the car. 'Look!' he would say. 'Look at the world around you, burro!'" (103).

But that is precisely what Richard does: he just looks at things and "reads" into them, always from the perspective of the detached interpreter. When he observes the pachucos and the newly arrived Mexicans, "[t]he newcomers became the object of his explorations. He was avidly hungry to learn the ways of these people" (151). When he runs out of books, he constructs the whole world as a book for him to read, not unlike Sor Juana Inés de la Cruz centuries earlier. The ensuing feeling of living only vicariously leaves him puzzled for a while, but his ultimate resolution of the conflict reveals how for him literature has become a way of living and the way to understand reality.

The issue of experiencing life for oneself or learning about it through books resurfaces once again when Richard feels the pressure of his peers to experience sex. The narrator's report is ironic, as we shall see, letting us glimpse one more time how Richard's mind is absolutely dominated by books: "And because Richard remembered reading somewhere that a writer should try to live a full life in order to write about it, . . . he finally had the courage to do it" (113–14). He does decide to experience things for himself . . . but only because he has read somewhere that that is what he is supposed to do if he wants to become a writer."

A third sense in which *Pocho* thematizes reading entails the way Richard and other characters "read" the mass media, particularly cinema. The first reference to films in the text is actually made by Richard, still a naive child who has not learned to "read" in a critical way. When discussing with his father why he prefers white horses, Richard states: "Everybody knows that a white horse is the best horse there is" (97), to which his father, still in command in terms of his empirical knowledge on the subject (he was a horseman in Mexico), replies with skepticism: "That shows how much you know. That is only in the moving pictures, but if you knew anything about horses, you would know that a good horse is not chosen for his color" (97).

Juan Rubio remains skeptical about movies and their manipulation of reality for the rest of the book. In this sense, he provides an immediate contrast with his son, Richard, since Juan trusts only what he knows from experience, not what texts say about reality. Thus, when he learns that a movie theater will show a film about Benito Juárez, he decides: "There is a picture about Benito Juárez in Mountain View. I must go see how the films distort history" (126).[12] While the film is later confirmed to have been less than good for the characters, a second feature in the program achieves a different kind of critical success for at least one character—Richard's mother, Consuelo:

> The second feature, however, had been very good. A tragedy, and she had cried and cried. Everyone in the theater cried, a mark that it was a good story, and even her husband had had an itching in his eyes, for she had noticed he rubbed them. She was still a little lachrymose and sentimental. Her body felt relaxed, like after a good laxative. (126)

The cathartic effects of the tragic film for Consuelo are evident. Not only does it affect her immediately, but it also makes her think about her recent behavior toward her own family. After watching a movie that we can assume relies on the values of traditional Mexican culture, she starts feeling guilty about her own drive to bring about changes in her household: "But tonight she felt deep shame for the way she had been acting, because she had been to Mexican movies and had seen Mexican wives and, for an hour or two, lived with them, so that she was wholly Mexican and knew she had been difficult" (127).[13] Carlos Monsiváis's comments on the cultural role of melodramas may serve to illustrate Consuelo's feelings, even if this Mexican cultural critic does not consider the migratory experience (an even more unsettling traveling than the one from rural to urban areas he discusses) in his analysis:

> Los melodramas facilitan a sus espectadores ese viaje de las tradiciones rurales a las urbanas, y de regreso. En la década de 1940 se inicia la explosión demográfica que poblará con abundancia incontenible la América Latina, y en el estallido de las costumbres el melodrama se responsabiliza por el resguardo de lo tradicional. Todo cambia a tu alrededor, oh, público, sería el mensaje, pero si ves estas películas seguirás obteniendo con rapidez la experiencia catártica. (78)[14]

The cathartic experience that Monsiváis describes entails a longing for a return to tradition that, in the world of *Pocho,* seems no longer possible. In fact, as we saw in the analysis of Richard as a reader of written texts, what *Pocho* is chronicling is the shift of cultural paradigms, first from the oral tradition of his parents (closely associated with a rural experience), to what Walter J. Ong has called "secondary orality" to differentiate the technological oral/aural (television, film, radio, and other similar media) from the traditional oral culture, which entails a set of norms and values, as well as an agonistic participative atmosphere that secondary orality no longer possesses,[15] and then to a world in which writing and reading are invested with the fullest authority and individual concerns substitute for the concerns of the group. That does not mean that the shift in paradigms is complete or that it is achieved without mixed feelings by the characters. Thus, it is not surprising that when Richard feels that his family is breaking apart, he tries to resort to a kind of surrogate communal cultural experience to try and hold it together, at least for a brief moment. The citation is long but worth quoting:

> That night, for the first time in months, they had dinner together in the old way. After dinner, his father sat on the rocker in the living room, listening to the Mexican station from Piedras Negras on short wave. When the kitchen was picked up, the girls sat around restlessly in the living room, and Richard knew they wanted to listen to something else, so he said to his father, "Let us go into the kitchen. I have a new novel in the Spanish I will read to you."
>
> In the kitchen, around the table, his mother also sat down, and said, "It is a long time, little son, that you do not read to us."
>
> How blind she must be, he thought. Aloud he said, "It is called `Crime and Punishment,' and it is about the Rusos in another time." He read rapidly and they listened attentively, interrupting him only now and then with a surprised "Oh!" or "That is so true!" After two hours, he could not read fast enough for himself, and he wished that he could read all night to them, because it was a certainty that he would not get another opportunity to read to them like this. They would never get to know the book, and he knew they were to miss something great. He knew also that they would never be this close together again. (147)

Notice that the scene is constructed as the climax in the change of paradigms to which I referred above. While it looks like a typical family gathering and could have been a typical night of storytelling in the traditional way, the circumstances have been carefully reversed in order to portray this major cultural change. The scene opens with the radio, a reference that brings us into the world of "secondary orality," thus destroying the potential for a return to the old ways of primal orality. But a second, even more important cultural inversion in this scene involves the fact that the elders are listening to and learning from one of their youngest, as opposed to the traditional convention of elders telling stories or teaching the young ones in other ways.[16] Finally, it is ironic that the book selected for this reading is Dostoyevsky's *Crime and Punishment,* not only because of the book's story line, which includes family disintegration, but also because, as Richard puts it, "it is about the Rusos in another time," thus transposing into this family reading experience the previous situation in which he felt stories from Mexico to be those of a strange country and a remote time. Needless to say, Richard is right in sensing that the family will soon split: cultural changes, including major attitude changes in the women of the family, do away with family unity, as each member seems to pursue his/her own way of coping with their new environment.

As the preceding discussion shows, reading and reception serve for Villarreal the purpose of foregrounding cultural and value changes in the Mexican American population. In this sense *Pocho*—as Wolfgang Iser suggests is intrinsic to literary texts—reformulates the predominant thought system of its time so as to make that system appear in a different light, therefore making the reader question his/her assumptions and his/her own values (74–75). Traditional Mexican culture, represented throughout the book by Juan Rubio, takes on a new meaning in *Pocho* as his wife and daughters start to take a belligerent approach to the servitude expected from them at home.[17] Likewise, religion is explored in *Pocho* as something that many Mexicans shun or abandon altogether as they relocate in the United States and they need to make adjustments of a pragmatic nature.[18] Even the much cherished idea that education is the best tool for minorities to advance up the social scale is reformulated by Richard, as we saw in his arguments with his mother: reading and learning are not a means for him, but an end in themselves.

An even more radical reevaluation of norms is brought to the fore by Richard's comments on the army and on homosexuality. While military life had been exalted in almost epic tones during the film about Benito Juárez (even if its epic tone had been decried by Consuelo as one of Mexico's worst afflictions), Richard's comments about the U.S. Army and, particularly, about changes in attitude toward the military by the general population reflect a deep awareness of the manipulation of reality by mainstream discursive powers. The time is 1940, and Santa Clara is full of soldiers. The approaching U.S. intervention in World War II and the preceding military buildup following the Conscription Act transform collective appreciation by the population of San Jose and Santa Clara: "But now everybody loved a soldier, and he wondered how this had come about" (149), particularly since Richard still recalls a time when soldiers camped outside his town "and the worst thing one's sister could do was associate with a soldier. Soldiers were common, were drunkards, thieves, and rapers of girls, or something, to the people of Santa Clara" (148). No doubt, this change in attitude shapes his eventual decision to join the navy, despite the fact that he is bitter about the forced internment of Japanese Americans and about army hindrances for people of Mexican descent.

Likewise, Richard's observations on homosexuals may very well contradict readers' expectations on this almost taboo issue for traditional Mexican culture (especially when the novel was first published):

> They just happen to be like that, that's all. Like a guy with only one leg, or a deaf-and-dumb guy, or a guy with the con. They can't help it, but they make the most of their life. And, another thing—they like being that way, and they never fool with me, because they know I'm straight, and I respect them for that. Those two guys live together, and they really love each other. You ought to see them, how nice they talk to each other and the way they take care of one another. Hell, even married people don't act that good. (177–78)

Although homosexuality is still associated with disease and disability in Richard's mind, it is clear that the homosexual couple has made him rethink what sharing a life together means. In the context of his parents' failed marriage, the gay couple's behavior takes on an added significance as a novel formula that works, something unthinkable from the point of view of traditional Mexican culture or any other Judeo-Christian culture, for that matter, as demonstrated by his Italian American friend Ricky's reply to Richard: "I guess you're right, in a way, but, just the same, if they're fruit, they're fruit, and that just isn't right" (178).

Moving on to the second point I want to address in this analysis of *Pocho*, I will now explore why contemporary Chicano/a literary history has insisted on reading *Pocho* as a foundational starting point. It is evident that *Pocho*'s founding role cannot be justified for chronological reasons.

Even if one were to disregard recently recovered texts, such as those by
Ruiz de Burton, Venegas, and Chacón, if chronology were indeed the
guiding principle behind Chicano/a literary history, critics would have
used as their starting point Fray Angélico Chávez's *La Conquistadora* or
Fabiola Cabeza de Baca's *We Fed Them Cactus,* both from 1954 and both
known to Chicano/a critics since, at least, the early 1970s.[19]

Clearly, the positing of *Pocho* as the beginning of contemporary
Chicano/a literary history is due to hermeneutical and not to
chronological reasons, since Villarreal's novel furnished critics such as
Ramón E. Ruiz with the necessary contrast with later novels written
during the Chicano/a Movement; hence recall Ruiz's apologetic prologue,
which is also an implicit comparison with Tomás Rivera. As such, this
strategy was effective in *Pocho*'s 1970 reprint in order to mark the radical
ideological and even aesthetic novelty of the Quinto Sol Generation,
thus helping to set the tone for an appreciation of post-1960 Chicano/a
literature as revolutionary in form and intention.

Even when *Pocho* is reread and vindicated almost two decades later
by Ramón Saldívar in his *Chicano Narrative* (1990), Villarreal's first novel
is still granted a foundational role, as this is needed to support Saldívar's
thesis on the ties of Chicano/a literature to history since "the beginning":

> [I]t is not accidental that here, at the "beginning" of the
> Chicano novel, we find the events of fiction firmly rooted in the
> events of history. The novel, more so than any other literary genre,
> insists on this tie to the real. (60, quotation marks in the original)

But the same could be said of Chávez's *La Conquistadora,* a historical
novel, and even Cabeza de Baca's *We Fed Them Cactus,* a memoir (not to
mention Ruiz de Burton's *The Squatter and the Don,* significantly subtitled
A Novel Descriptive of Contemporary Occurrences in California). Moreover,
although I agree with Saldívar that *Pocho* is firmly rooted in history and I
acknowledge Saldívar's use of "beginning" in quotation marks, I cannot
help but notice how Richard—who, for Saldívar, is the figurative author
of the text—consistently dehistoricizes reality when he reads.

In order to look at the issue from a different angle, then, I propose
that Chicano/a literary history be considered not as the mere
chronological sequence of known works but as a process of changes in
critical and popular reception; that is, that we look not only at the works
themselves but also at their interaction with contemporary and successive
readers. In so shifting our perspective, I would like to recall Hans R.

Jauss's caveat against establishing (or attempting to establish) very precise beginnings when writing a literary history (*Toward an Aesthetic,* 54).[20] From Jauss's point of view, the quest for a beginning is relatively irrelevant, since the focus of the literary historian should shift from chronology to the reasons for continuous interest (or lack of it) in a particular text. According to Jauss, this would involve the text's ability to respond to newer questions and a changed horizon of expectations in succeeding generations (*Toward,* 184–85). In the case of *Pocho,* for instance, one could even ask which date of publication is more meaningful, 1959—when it was first published but virtually ignored by the public—or 1970, when it became a Chicano/a classic thanks to a process of critical rereading and reevaluation.

It is in this sense, I believe, that *Pocho'*s place in Chicano/a literary history needs to be reevaluated. *Pocho* is not just (or primarily) a novel published in 1959 but a novel read in 1970 (by Ruiz, among others), in 1990 (by Saldívar, among others), and in 2002 (by myself, among others). This clearly suggests that *Pocho* is much more than its text: it is also the succession of readings that have shaped it into a culturally relevant discursive object for Chicanos/as and non-Chicanos/as alike. One would then need to explore the reasons for the continual critical interest in *Pocho,* perhaps noticing how many of the concerns it addresses, even if it does so from a 1950s point of view, are still valid and hotly debated today. These issues include, among others, the social role of Chicana women and women's liberation, societal perceptions or misconceptions on homosexuality, and the idea that identity is not an immutable given but something that the individual creates in a process of both embracing and rejecting his/her own culture. In this sense, the ambiguous open ending of the novel is a most successful device that challenges the reader to question his/her own prejudices and to try to come up with an answer to the final question that the text leaves unanswered: why?

It is in this foregrounding of the reader's role that *Pocho* contributes an important dimension to Chicano/a literature. *Pocho* thematizes the fact that the literary work is not solely the product of its author but the result of its interaction with its readers as well. In so doing, Villarreal's *opera prima* forcefully exemplifies Chicano/a literature's incessant quest for readers. No wonder critics have paid back with such devoted attention.

Peregrinos de Aztlán: In Search of the
Forgotten Chicano/a Literary History

As I have explored elsewhere, *Peregrinos de Aztlán* is a novel obsessed with literary history and rich in metaliterary discourse.[21] Despite its immediate commitment to depicting some of the most pressing ills affecting Chicanos/as in the 1970s, the novel is much more than a social protest work. In fact, an entire narrative line concentrates on metaliterary issues, which allows Méndez's reader to enter into a dialogue with the text about literary history and the act of reading, as well as about other issues of interest in Chicano/a cultural life.

This metaliterary narrative begins in a "Preface," signed by "The Author" and addressed to the reader, in which questions about the text's potential audiences are first posed. "The Author" is clearly a textual figure reminiscent of what Wayne C. Booth termed "implied author," and he should not be confused with the real Miguel Méndez.[22] In the "Preface," then, "The Author" explains his literary aim:

> Hice un plan y una estructura previa, lector, para escribir algo que commoviera sensibilidades exquisitas, con el anhelo agregado de alcanzar una sonrisa de aprobación de parte de alguno de los muchos académicos de la lengua, de tantísimos como los hay dados a la tarea de espulgar el vocabulario. Te confieso que falló mi intento preconcebido, no por mi voluntad, sino por una extraña rebelión de las palabras. (21)[23]

This ironic prologue starts, as suggested by this quote, by delimiting the ideal reader, who is not an academic but rather someone who would share in "el dolor, el sentimiento y la cólera de los oprimidos" (21).[24] The rebellious words, the prologue goes on to tell, end up as winners in this linguistic struggle and thus dictate the tone for the rest of the novel. If, as Tomás Rivera postulated, Chicano/a literature is "life in search of form," Méndez seems to be stressing here the need to find an adequate language to perform that action (something to which Rivera alluded as well, as we saw).[25] For Méndez, the issue seems to be one of vindicating the speech of the downtrodden as worthy of literary treatment. This is further stressed when "The Author" adds: "Me reí de veras viendo que las voces de los desgraciados pugnaban por subir a los sagrados escenarios de la literatura con las caras sucias y sus trajes de villanos, rotos y desfondillados" (21).[26] For the rest of the novel, the language of the oppressed will be the real protagonist, interrupted at times by an ironic, grandiloquent narrator or else by poetic digressions in which the sublime and the grotesque struggle for textual space. Spanish and English alternate with Caló, as *Peregrinos's* borderlands nature dictates that its discourse reflect the linguistic patterns of the border.

A second aspect of interest in the prologue has to do with literary history and its construction. "The Author" claims that the manuscript of *Peregrinos* was completed in 1968, even if its first printing date was not until 1974 (22). What this means, of course, is that the writing of this novel predates the editorial boom of the early 1970s under the auspices of Quinto Sol.[27] This, in turn, implies that the editorial outlets that resulted from that boom had not been available to Méndez when he was writing the novel. Therefore, his novelistic alter ego, "The Author," is forced to imagine his readers rather than tailoring his text to the tastes of a preexisting readership, and hence his inclusion of the prologue.

In any case, the "Preface" is by no means the only component of that metaliterary discourse to which I alluded above. Rather, it is the first installment in a series of narrative fragments that thematize the role of the reader and confirm that (even if the "Preface" was an addition to the 1974 printing and not part of the 1968 manuscript) metaliterary reflection is an intrinsic component of the novel and not an afterthought. Thus, along with "The Author," we find inside the novel a plethora of characters who are writers and/or readers. These characters serve Méndez to engage in a much more extensive reflection on the reading process and on literary history than a simple prologue might have allowed.

Surprisingly, though, critics have been little inclined to deal with Méndez's characters as writers or as readers. Critical interest has dealt with social issues (Gutiérrez-Revuelta, "Peregrinos"), intertextuality (J. S. Alarcón and Rojas), archetypes and myths (L. Cárdenas and Segade), structural aspects (Brito's "El lenguaje" and Bornstein de Somoza), and, last but not least, with the transition from an endangered oral culture to a written tradition in the making, whose purpose would be to document orality before it disappeared (Bruce-Novoa in "Miguel Méndez" and "Righting").[28] According to this last interpretation, the most relevant for my own analysis, Méndez assumes the role of the "voice of silence"; that is, a narrative voice that allows the voiceless to speak. At the same time, Bruce-Novoa argues, the textual difficulties that other critics have noted in *Peregrinos* are something akin to trials that the reader has to endure to demonstrate that s/he is worthy of receiving the cultural inheritance from the fading oral tradition ("Miguel Méndez," 208). In passing, Bruce-Novoa also notes that in this handing down of the oral tradition to his readers, Méndez avoids the fate he reserves for two of his own character-writers: oblivion ("Miguel Méndez," 209).

In "Righting the Oral Tradition," Bruce-Novoa reiterates his views on the role of the reader in *Peregrinos* while expanding his analysis by considering this novel alongside Méndez's book of poems titled *Los criaderos humanos (épica de los desamparados) y Sahuaros* (1975). The following quote is of relevance for Bruce-Novoa's views on metaliterary questions in Méndez's works:

> [W]hereas the previous works ["Tata Casehua" and *Peregrinos*] concentrated on the reader's role, and only implicitly on that of the writer's function in the process of converting the oral tradition into a written text, this book [*Los criaderos*] explicitly names the central character and first person narrator as a poet. And since the book offers a line of thought and a technique completely consistent with the prose, *Los criaderos* can be read as an *ars poetica*. (80, original emphasis)

I would argue, however, that even if reading was a foremost concern of Méndez's in *Peregrinos*, writing and writers were certainly not of tangential importance in that book. Rather, I believe that the novel is a deep reflection both on the reading and the writing process, as the "Preface" and the existence of reading and writing characters demonstrate. The main difficulty, though, is in constructing this metaliterary narrative line, since the text is deliberately confusing in identifying its characters. As far as possible writers are concerned, there may be as many as six within the pages of *Peregrinos*. However, due to the limited information we have about some of them, that figure might be lower, since two or more of those characters could actually be the same. With that reservation in mind, here is the list of possible writer characters within the text, from those who can most clearly be identified as such to the most ambiguous cases: (1) "The Author" of the "Preface" already discussed; (2) Lorenzo Linares; (3) El Vate (the Bard); (4) a nameless character, of possible autobiographical nature, characterized as follows:

> [E]ra el otro chicano un sujeto alto y gordo, encanecido prematuramente, en su mestizaje triunfaba sublevado el legendario yaqui, encajaba en el estereotipo de la ignorancia y desde allí se burlaba de los avestruces emplumados de pavos reales, escribía libros que no leía nadie ... (126–27)[29]

(5) the narrator of an italicized fragment that begins on page 133,[30] who reveals himself to be a pimp and a frustrated poet; and (6) Loreto Maldonado, in whose shack documents and "un puñado de papeles amarillentos" (172) (["a handful of yellowing papers," 165]) are found upon his death; these papers might be Loreto's memoirs or other writings, but they could also be old letters or some other nonliterary materials, of course. I have excluded from this list other characters, such as reporters and technical writers (in charge of forensic reports and the like), who do not engage in any form of creative writing within the novel's pages.

The last three characters in my list of six pose the greatest challenge in terms of identification not only as writers but as different from one another. As mentioned, it is impossible to determine whether or not Loreto is a writer; to further complicate the matter, Méndez's reader lacks sufficient information to sort the other characters out. Thus we are left to ponder—at the very least—the following questions: is El Vate the writer of books that nobody read and/or the pimp-poet? Is Loreto the writer of books that nobody read (both are of Yaqui origin) and hence the yellowing papers? Are the pimp-poet and the writer of books that nobody read the same character but not El Vate or Loreto? Are they all different characters?

As I suggested earlier, this confusion is probably an artistic device to accentuate borderland imprecision. But most importantly, the textual existence of up to six character-authors in *Peregrinos* allows us to rephrase Bruce-Novoa's thesis on the novel as a testimony of the passing of the oral tradition. Read from the perspective that I am outlining, *Peregrinos* reveals itself to be first and foremost a novel about the lost or unknown *written* tradition of Chicano letters. If, as Bruce-Novoa claims, the oral tradition is endangered by the lack of intergenerational communication ("Miguel Méndez," 206), it is also true that pre–Chicano/a Movement literature was likewise affected by the lack of an appropriate literary establishment and of a wide readership, as I suggested in the previous chapter and as I will explore in greater detail in chapter 5. In this sense, *Peregrinos* explores literary history (rather than the oral tradition) from a 1968/1974 point of view in which textual recovery was not yet a part of Chicano/a letters but in which Méndez knows that there are and there have been writers before him who struggled (often in vain) to see their works in print.

Miguel Méndez himself, in an interview transcribed by Rodríguez del Pino, acknowledges that he had written other texts prior to *Peregrinos:*

A los dieciocho años Méndez escribe su primera novela [1948].

> Esta obra, nos dice el autor, "era una novelita de 120 a 150 páginas
> a la que nunca le puse nombre y que todavía la tengo sin publicar."
> La necesidad de publicar no le interesaba por el momento porque
> pensaba que sus historias sobre la gente que había conocido no le
> interesarían a nadie. (40)[31]

This situation, Rodríguez del Pino acknowledges, did not change until
the Chicano/a Movement: "Méndez presintió, en ese nuevo movimiento
que postulaba la emancipación del pueblo chicano para preservar su
herencia cultural, la brecha que esperaba para dar luz a su creación
artística" (40).[32] This confirms my hypothesis that the character who
writes books that nobody read in *Peregrinos* is (at least in part) a
fictionalized echo of the real author, as Rodríguez del Pino also suggests
(45–46). Above and beyond autobiographism, this fact is important for
my reading since it serves to introduce the topic of the unknown or
unread Chicano/a writer as well as an even more important subject, dealt
with in detail in the pages of the novel: the acknowledgment that literature
is communication and that a text depends on searching for and "finding"
its readers to fulfill its potential.

Not surprisingly, then, within the novel the author of books that
nobody read posits the same kind of literary questions that "The Author"
ventures forth in the prologue. The former, to continue with the
biographical analogy I just outlined, reminds us of Miguel Méndez in
1948, while the latter would be closer to Méndez in 1974. The distance
between the two is not only temporal but is also one of literary impact
and even confidence, as the 1974 "Author" is clearly bold in approaching
his readers: "Lee este libro, lector, si te place la prosa que me dicta el
hablar común de los oprimidos; de lo contrario, si te ofende, no lo leas,
que yo me siento por bien pagado con haberlo escrito desde mi condición
de mexicano indio, espalda mojada y chicano" (22).[33] The final word in
this quote is crucial in understanding that Méndez is not suggesting that
he does not care if we read the book or not. His insistence throughout
the novel on the importance of the act of reading should be enough to
dispel that notion. In identifying himself as a Chicano, "The Author"
situates himself within a sociopolitical movement that is also literary; in
other words, Méndez is not saying, "I don't care if you don't read my
books," but rather, "If you are offended by Chicano/a speech, I don't want
you to read this book." His comment is not meant to undermine the
importance of reading for the literary process but to delineate a
readership that, as of 1974, already identified itself as Chicano/a.

Not far from the author of books that nobody read is the poet-pimp of pages 133 through 137, to the extent that it is impossible to ascertain whether they are two different characters or the same one. The common element in both is a sense of frustration. On pages 133 through 137, the pimp narrates an encounter in a brothel with his former mentor, a teacher who "había dispuesto, con el fervor de un San Isidro, la buena simiente en las mentes tiernas, un estímulo que no crecería, que se volvería lejano, empequeñecido, pero que subsistiría como una planta sedienta" (134).[34] After a flashback remembrance of his childhood, which prompts the teacher to praise poetry's ability to transcend immediate reality, the pimp confronts his teacher: "¡[M]ientes! No hay poesía ni poetas, todo es mascarada para no ver la tragedia humana; sólo los holgazanes que ignoran el dolor y el crimen, aduladores del poder, le cantan a las flores" (135).[35] Immediately after this literary manifesto, the fragment closes with a naturalist description of the miseries of the border town, a poetical response to the poets "who sing of flowers."

Both the author of books that nobody read and the pimp-poet exemplify an unresolved artistic crisis: the latter decries poetry because he finds no beauty to sing; the former likewise condemns academic art ("se burlaba de los avestruces emplumados de pavos reales" [126–27]),[36] most likely for similar reasons. In any case, neither of them resolves his own crisis, as they fail to produce a literature that would convey to its audience the brutal nature of life on the border, a task that would be reserved for "The Author" a few years later.

More developed as characters, and further removed from the implied and the real author, are two other writers: Lorenzo Linares and El Vate, both of them poets. They first appear as they cross the Sonoran Desert on foot. Lorenzo's sensitivity, fueled by the nightly beauty of the desert, explodes in a profusion of images and metaphors in a series of narrative digressions. In one of his poetical raptures, for instance, he cries to the moon: "¡Guiña luz viva, radiante yerta! Azogue en los ilusos, disco de aullidos, escamas, anillos, cabellos de arena. ¡Gira, perjura, gira! Sinfonía de símbolos, ¡gira en tu inmenso féretro!" (65).[37] Inebriated by the surrounding beauty, he almost dies in this episode, a subtle warning against the dangers of singing to nature in times of dire necessity and, as such, a forewarning of what the pimp-poet is to discuss later.

El Vate, on the other hand, is described as a more somber character: "[S]iempre estaba velado por una tristeza que le venía de muy hondo" (67).[38] As such, he acts as a contrast to Lorenzo. But where that tension between the two is of interest for our discussion is in the realm of literature, where El Vate, in a discussion with his friends, gives us one of the main clues for interpreting the metaliterary subtext in the novel: something we could describe as the connection between the author of books that nobody read and the pimp-poet on the one hand and "The Author" of the "Preface" on the other. El Vate comments the following on the poets' inclination to sing of the moon: "Ahora entiendo por qué el poeta ama a la luna; porque la luna es como la poesía, brillan ambas con luces ajenas. Mientras no haya quien lea los versos, estarán muertos" (67).[39] El Vate's implicit poetics here is one of communication. As such, it affirms the need to take the literary work beyond the bitter solipsism represented by the pimp-poet and the author of books that nobody read and into a creative dialogue with the reader.

Despite his literary clairvoyance, El Vate succumbs to drinking (which brings him closer as a character to the pimp-poet), and his mind, according to the text, becomes "una estrella errante que arrastraba una cauda de palabras huérfanas" (84).[40] His ending is an almost fatidic defeat, not unlike that of the former comedian El Cometa, with whom El Vate is implicitly compared here. In El Vate's case, his literary theory does not translate into practice, and toward the end of the novel he ends up so disoriented and confused that he kills himself.

El Vate's literary production appears in several passages throughout the novel, and it consists of the following: a text on the desert crossing (86–88/72–74),[41] a description of a dream in which Chicanos/as and wetbacks establish a homeland in the desert (95–96/82–83),[42] and an elegy to his friend Lorenzo Linares, which is found among his papers after he commits suicide (144–46/136–38). These three narrative fragments complement one another. The first gives us an almost apocalyptic, epic description of the sparse vegetation that manages to survive in the desert. The second concentrates on human beings who, as stubbornly as the desert vegetation, impose their will on the desert to find and found their promised land, the Republic of Despised Mexicans. This fragment also contains the fundamentals of a Promethean poetics in which the artist appears as a god who creates in the void:

> En el desierto, virgen de la voluntad del creativo, se colaron entre las polvaredas mis voces pronunciadas. . . . A toda invocación sólo respondía la nada con sus campanarios muertos. Y fui dios escribiendo páginas en el viento, para que volaran mis palabras. . . . ahora sé que Él crea la vida y que yo invento el lenguaje con el que se habla. Sin embargo me pierdo en la maraña de los vocabularios,

los vocablos que aún no nacen del pensamiento duelen en su entraña. (95)[43]

This affirmation of the creative power of the word is succeeded (in the third fragment) by the acknowledgment that literature cannot exist without a reader, an idea that is hinted at in the last lines of the above quote. Lorenzo, the poet who felt like a god (as did his friend El Vate):

> Quiso florecer el desierto con poemas, avanzó extasiado a plantarlo de metáforas verdes y fuentes con surtidores de letras policromadas.... En la página borrada de la creación oyó los gritos que sepulta el silencio.... ¡Maldito desierto!, te has bebido el idioma y los alientos de mi pueblo antaño señorío Nahuatlaca. (145–46)[44]

The three fragments together seem to suggest that the literary work without a reader is destined to disappear, as did Lorenzo, El Vate, and the power of the Nahuatlaca people. These three interconnected sections, therefore, synthesize the novel's entire metaliterary discourse by exploring the crucial issue of whether the work is created by an almighty godlike author or by a reader who consumes and makes the text his/her own. The desert is a metaphor for the blank page on which the demiurge poet can imprint his/her writing as s/he wishes. But continuing with the metaphor, Méndez's text is explicit in its condemnation of solipsistic writing: "Aquí [en el desierto] las voces caminan lejos porque naiden las detiene," says a character named Ramagacha on page 65, but two pages later El Vate warns us: "Mientras no haya quien lea los versos, estarán muertos" (67).[45] Without an audience, writers remain in the presocial moment of language, in that individualistic realm that is more an echo of thought than proper communication. That is why the language El Vate wants to create is destined to fail, because El Vate forgets that language is social, the product of sociohistorical interactions. Without a reader who shares and re-creates the writer's language the literary text is dead, Méndez implies.

Given this interest that Méndez demonstrates for literary reception, it is not surprising to find several sections of *Peregrinos* entirely devoted to reading. The "Preface," as we saw, already rejects those readers with a taste for the exquisite while demonstrating preference for a reader who would empathize with the plight of the downtrodden. I also outlined Bruce-Novoa's theory, according to which "Méndez's texts are rituals consisting of ethnic testing, proved by understanding, sympathy, and sheer endurance, followed by sacred revelation to the survivors of the test" ("Righting," 79). Whether or not *Peregrinos* amounts to an initiatory rite, it is evident that the text's linguistic and structural difficulties call for a careful, experienced reader. My own troubles identifying writer-characters should suffice as an example. In this sense, *Peregrinos* counters contemporary attempts by other Chicano/a writers to produce fairly accessible texts firmly rooted in the oral tradition. Méndez's first published novel is a celebration of writing and reading as passionate, consuming activities. As we will see immediately, this high concept of reading results, within the novel, in a sustained condemnation of light and escapist reading, which is achieved through the introduction of several more or less naive characters.

Among these readers unable to penetrate a text's substance is Lencho García y del Valle, of whom the narrator says: "[S]e había formado un lenguaje a base de frases presuntuosas ya hechas, no eran sus clichés extractos de la gran literatura, sino frases repetidas por generaciones de políticos y periodistas lambiscones, ciegos de imaginación" (88).[46] We also find Mr. MacCane, a landowner who employs the Pérez family and who "[a] la hora de cenar con toda la familia a la mesa, . . . leía la Biblia con voz enérgica y apuntando con el índice, por el que parecían salir llamas" (151).[47] His histrionic antics seem ludicrous as we are able to tell how disparate his readings and his actions are.

But the critique of escapist reading is centered in the world of comic books as representative of a hegemonic ersatz popular culture: popular in appearance and appeal, but ideologically designed to alienate its readers. With a heavy dose of authorial irony, El Buen Chuco is used to introduce the topic as he complains about his life to a friend in the Happy Day bar: "¿Sabes qué?, ora como que apaño güergüenza, siempre camellando como un pinchi animal, ése, usté que ha leyido tantos 'comics', ¿qué somos slaves, nosotros la raza?" (37).[48] The bittersweet humorous effect achieved in the previous quote by attributing authority to someone who has read many comic books becomes tragic near the end of the novel as we enter the fragments narrating the death of Frankie Pérez. Whether Frankie knows about superheroes solely from comic books or from television as well is not entirely clear, but I think it is safe to assume that he must have been exposed to both media. In reading either or both, Frankie is as naive as the young Richard Rubio watching movies in *Pocho*. Therefore, once he finds himself in danger while fighting in Vietnam,

> invocaba a los ídolos legendarios que habitan en el corazón de
> sus coterráneos. Superman destruyendo aviones en el aire a puros

escupitajos. . . . Batman con su genio y su fuerza dominando a los tontos asiáticos. . . . Y si estos seres ultrapotentes no dominaban al injusto enemigo, ¡ah!, ahí estaba el grande, el sublime, el invencible y además exquisitamente bello, ¡El Gran Cowboy! (154)[49]

The introduction of the Great Cowboy allows Méndez to situate his critique within a double-edged context (similar to that presented by El Teatro Campesino in "Vietnam Campesino" in 1970), in which fighting the Vietnamese is equated with the violent repression against Mexicans throughout the U.S. Southwest and California. Unlike El Teatro Campesino, though, by focusing on literature and reading, Méndez is also able to direct his critique against an entire tradition of both popular and scholarly literature glorifying the cowboy at the expense of the Mexican American.[50] Frankie's death in combat puts a violent end to his immature reader fantasies while serving as an implicit warning against escapist reading, to which *Peregrinos* juxtaposes an engaged (both in the political and in the literary sense) kind of reading.

The self-referential, metaliterary discourse that I have analyzed so far (centered around characters who are readers and/or writers) has yet another feature of interest for readers since the 1990s, inasmuch as it anticipates one of the most relevant cultural phenomena of our decade: the recovery and reprinting of forgotten or long lost books by Chicano/a authors, an effort that began in the late 1960s but has only blossomed recently with the concerted effort of scholars and presses intent on reprinting and distributing nineteenth-century and early twentieth-century texts.[51] As such, this movement entails reclaiming an unknown or forgotten written tradition that, in turn, confirms that literary activity among Chicanos/as did not start in or around 1959 but rather that it has been a continuous endeavor throughout the ages. The fact that this tradition has remained obscure until recently does not denote its absence but the way literary history has been constructed in the past, with a total disregard for counterhegemonic and alternative writings.

In that sense, one of the final paragraphs in *Peregrinos* can be read as a warning and a denunciation of practices that attempt to relegate Chicano/a literary tradition to institutional oblivion while depriving many Chicanos/as of the opportunity to benefit from a formal education, thus reducing the potential number of Chicano/a readers:

Así la historia, de pronto, como en un mal sueño nos dejó varados en la isla del olvido, presos. No sólo eso, han quedado encadenados los genes que guardan la cultura, esencia de nuestra historia, vedando las arterias que como ríos traen el ímpetu de la sangre que anima la voz y el alma de nuestro pueblo. Ni dignidad ni letras para los esclavos, dijeron los dominadores, solamente la ignominia, la burla y la muerte; si acaso, la trágica baba de la demagogia, falsa moneda de los perversos. (183–84)[52]

Against that demagoguery and to counter the effects of institutional oblivion, the recovery of older texts sequestered in archives and private libraries (those cultural chained-up genes to which Méndez seems to refer in the above quote) becomes of utmost necessity as a way to reclaim the Chicano/a cultural past and literary history: "Cuando la amnesia empezaba a plantar tinieblas en nuestra memoria, fuimos a nuestros antiguos lagos, buscando en el fondo los rostros que habíamos perdido" (184).[53] This is, precisely, what some of the writer-reader characters in *Peregrinos* accomplish. The metaliterary discourse in Méndez's novel underlines the need to keep the writing tradition alive, perpetuating the chain of readers generation after generation to avoid what the novel calls "páginas borradas" ("erased pages"), those moments in time when we lose track of the existence of writers and literary works that, marginalized by the literary establishment, fade away for the lack of readers who would keep them alive. Thus, in commenting (as a reader) upon Lorenzo's work, El Vate rescues it from oblivion and offers it to us (through "The Author," who is the one who "rescues" and reads El Vate's works) in a historiographic and literary exercise of extreme importance, namely that of reconstructing Chicano/a literary history. Méndez's characters, as writers and as readers, are surely pilgrims as he calls them but not only in a historical and geographical sense, for they are also literary pilgrims: they are those writers that literary history forgot but who paved the way for the boom of the Chicano/a movement. Starting in the past two decades, Chicano/a literary historians have realized at last the importance of these forgotten writers, and they are working toward recovering and reinterpreting their works.

(En)gendering the Reader:
Chicana Literature and Its Implied Audience

> *Básicamente, lo que quiero decir es que para mí el ser mujer es tener la lectura.*
> —Lucha Corpi[1]

> *We Chicana writers are singled out for being closer to our audiences than to our subjects. Our audiences are our subjects.*
> —Bernice Zamora[2]

Chicana literature is by no means a new phenomenon. As a matter of fact, the oldest-known literary text published by a Mexican American is María Amparo Ruiz de Burton's *Who Would Have Thought It?* (1872). But it was not until the 1930s and 1940s that Mexican American women started publishing in significant numbers, although many earlier manuscripts are being recovered as I write. Two well-known writers of the 1930 to 1950 period are Josephina Niggli and María Cristina Mena-Chambers, who started carving a name for themselves as the authors of books centered on life in Mexico and addressed to an ethnically undifferentiated audience, although the care they exert in explaining Mexican culture certainly suggests that they wrote with a non–Mexican/Mexican American audience in mind. Indeed, as Leal and Martín-Rodríguez have noted in Mena-Chambers's case: "Her purpose seems to have been to acquaint the young Anglo-American reader with Mexican culture" (565).

A similar purpose has been suggested in the case of several New Mexico women writers who, in the words of Rebolledo, "were conscious of their heritage and cultural identity, and . . . they wanted to communicate their sense that this culture and identity was somehow slipping away, that it was being assimilated through history and cultural domination" (*Women Singing,* 29). These writers, Rebolledo goes on to argue, wrote their books as an act of resistance against that domination and to set the record straight in the face of distorted interpretations set forth by Anglo-American writers settling in New Mexico.[3] Their ideal reader, then, was also Anglo-American, but in this case, their choice of a target readership resulted from a more ideologically charged set of circumstances than that motivating Niggli and Mena-Chambers. As a consequence, their access to printing outlets was also far more limited and problematic. Cleofas Jaramillo, for instance, reminisced as follows on the troubles she experienced in getting her books printed:

> I tried sending my manuscript to some of our Western universities. After holding it for several months, they would return it, saying that they did not have the funds with which to publish it. One professor said he was writing a book. Would I permit him to use two or three of my stories in his book? I then understood. All they wanted was to read my manuscript and get ideas from it, so I decided to have it published by a small private press here in my city. (168)

Jaramillo's story is not atypical, and it recalls similar difficulties faced by Chicana/o writers since the mid–nineteenth century. Her story is also representative of the usurpation of authority that until recently has threatened the survival of many texts and documents from the early stages of Chicano/a literature. Jaramillo's professor is not unlike H. H. Bancroft, who assembled and collected many memoirs and other texts by Californios, only to relegate the originals to his archives while freely borrowing from them for his own texts.[4] Jaramillo's ordeal signals, then, a need to reterritorialize her work in order to maintain control and intellectual ownership, not unlike what Ruiz de Burton did by privately printing *The Squatter and the Don* several decades earlier. In a sense, though, this reterritorialization goes against Jaramillo's attempt to "set the record straight," for while Anglo-American accounts of New Mexican culture benefited from wide, national exposure in magazines such as *Holland Magazine*,[5] Jaramillo was forced to address a local audience, thus reducing the impact of her culturalist statement. In this light, Genaro M. Padilla is correct in pointing out the importance of the cultural context in which Jaramillo and other *Nuevomexicana* authors wrote:

> Jaramillo's reconstruction of such filiations takes place at a time and a place–Santa Fe in the 1930s—when the reconstruction of the history and culture and lore of the Southwest was being enacted by nonnative fabulists whose vision of the land and its

people produced a just-so story of the Southwest, steeped in romance and fantasy that glossed over strained intercultural relations because it occluded the social history of the region. Writing to preserve her culture during this period, Jaramillo's work discloses the stresses and contradictions of articulating resistance in a language, idiom, and sociodiscursive configuration determined by the cultural Other. (*My History,* 198)

But, I would add, the cultural Other was also responsible for controlling most of the channels theoretically available to Jaramillo and others for their discursive enterprise. That is, the cultural context was being distorted by nonnatives' accounts, but nonnatives were also in control of the publishing and distribution channels that gave access to the larger audiences that Jaramillo wanted to reach. Jaramillo's case was no longer that of someone like Eusebio Chacón, who wanted to address (in Spanish) his fellow Nuevomexicanos. Rather, Jaramillo attempted to appropriate the Other's language[6] in order to speak to that foreign Other. Still, the Other (read: Western university presses) refused her the right to do so while attempting to appropriate and misrepresent her voice and her stories.

It was not until the mid-1980s that Chicana writers were able to tap into the wider readerships that Jaramillo and others could only desire. For even within the Chicano/a Movement of the previous two decades, Chicana writers experienced difficulties in publishing and receiving the kind of critical attention that male authors had enjoyed since the late 1960s. Poets had certainly gained attention a little earlier (Bernice Zamora, Carmen Tafolla, Lucha Corpi, and Angela de Hoyos, for instance, were among the recognizable names during the 1970s and early 1980s), but the limited readerships associated with poetry precluded their success in addressing a larger number of people. The few prose writers who published during that period, such as Berta Ornelas (*Come Down from the Mound,* 1975) and Isabella Ríos (*Victuum,* 1976), did not make a visible impact. Only Estela Portillo-Trambley had received noticeable critical appreciation for her *Rain of Scorpions* (1975) and her earlier play *The Day of the Swallows,* but in many respects, she remained an isolated pioneer for the boom in Chicana narrative that would dominate the following two decades.[7]

A most decisive aspect contributing to the critical and popular success enjoyed by Chicana writers of prose since the mid-1980s was the continual growth of feminism within the Chicano/a Movement and, in particular, the eventual disenchantment with Euro-Anglo feminism and the subsequent shift toward a "third" feminism or feminism of color. From the beginning, the question for Chicana cultural agents was one of reclaiming a space of their own. Sonia A. López, for instance, reminds us of the internal subordination inherent in the student organizations of the Chicano/a Movement:

> In the organizing of conferences, symposiums, meetings, *and publication of newspapers or magazines,* Chicanas usually provided their invisible labors by being the cooks, secretaries and janitors. ... But as Chicanas became more politically aware, they began to question assigned roles on the basis of sexuality in the Mexican culture and in the Movement. (23, my emphasis)

The repercussions of this subordination for the field of Chicana literature were obvious for critics and authors alike. Much as the Quinto Sol publishers had complained about the lack of appropriate cultural channels for Chicanos, writers such as Norma Cantú denounced the silence that Chicano critics were imposing on female writers, even within organizations such as the (then) National Association for Chicano Studies[8]:

> Women are perceived as followers, not leaders. ... But denying our existence in this arena—by excluding Chicana writers from courses in Chicano literature, for example, we perpetuate the stereotypes, and this exclusion thereby invalidates our work. ... By not reading Chicana literature, by not supporting our work in any academic or professional area, our organization ... follows the pattern of other professional organizations that by exclusion invalidate the work of certain groups. (10)[9]

Inevitably, Chicana writers' demand for recognition and the lack of support that Cantú referred to resulted in the need to build cultural and publishing alliances that sometimes went beyond the immediate cultural group. As suggested by Eliana Ortega and Nancy Saporta Sternbach, Chicana literary discourse thus situated itself within the context of both contemporary Chicano/a literature and "the discourse of U.S. women writers, most especially Black writers, which provided a female context" (18).[10] Cooperation with other minority women, in turn, became a challenge to mainstream feminism and intracultural sexism in the respective authors' communities, and it took its most visible shape in the form of collaborative publishing venues (Kitchen Table Press,

Spinsters/Aunt Lute, and Third Woman Press, for instance) and collective anthologies such as *This Bridge Called My Back: Writings by Radical Women of Color* (1981) and the more recent *Making Face, Making Soul/ Haciendo Caras: Creative and Critical Perspectives by Women of Color* (1990). It also influenced the target audience for some Chicana writers, as suggested in the following quote from Gloria Anzaldúa's "Speaking in Tongues: A Letter to 3rd World Women Writers":

> I sit here naked in the sun, typewriter against my knee trying to visualize you. Black woman huddles over a desk in the fifth floor of some New York tenement. Sitting on a porch in South Texas, a Chicana fanning away mosquitos and the hot air, trying to arouse the smoldering embers of writing. Indian woman walking to school or work lamenting the lack of time to weave writing into your life. Asian American, lesbian, single mother, tugged in all directions by children, lover or ex-husband, and the writing. (165)

Anzaldúa's envisioning of her audience, inserted as it is in a third world feminist publication, is careful to construct an imagined community of working-class, minority women. While her situation is not immediately applicable to other Chicana writers, I would like to claim that most of them have had to deal in their work with the same task of delineating an ideal audience by exploring either the interconnection and/or the tensions between the parameters that Anzaldúa invokes; that is, gender, class, race, ethnicity, sexuality, culture, and geographic location, as well as others that she does not account for in the previous quote but that are nonetheless important for the rest of her work and for that of most other Chicana writers, such as language and linguistic preference.

As a consequence, and as I will explore throughout this chapter, the development of contemporary Chicana literature was significantly marked by the double task of both engendering and gendering its audience, as my title for this chapter suggests. That is, contemporary Chicana authors needed first and foremost to find and define an audience, and in many cases, they felt the need to do so by bringing previously neglected issues of gender into the literary arena.[11] These two tasks are not necessarily independent of each other, and I will not try to separate them in my analysis. What I will do next is to explore different ways some of the most read Chicana texts have set about interacting with their audience(s).[12]

A House of One's Own: Chicana Narrative and the Feminine Space

In taking positions vis-à-vis Chicano and mainstream feminist discourses, contemporary Chicana narratives have been the site of continuous cultural and literary struggle. Chicanas, as suggested above, have problematized since early on Chicano cultural nationalism's relegation of women to secondary roles and spaces. Exceptions notwithstanding, the cultural enterprise of re-creating Chicano/a life, past and present, produced a plethora of texts in which women were either absent or relegated to subordinate and submissive roles, either defined by their family relation to male protagonists (mother, sister) or by their role in making the male hero stray from a devoted family life (seductress, prostitute).[13] Chicana characters were thus most likely to be found within the house or at church (in the first case) or in brothels and cantinas (in the second). Only the fields and the streets provided a third kind of space for Chicana characters as, indeed, they were also portrayed working alongside the male characters and moving around barrio streets and plazas.[14]

Chicana authors have been interested in expanding the spaces in which female characters have appeared, and often this has implied writing the author and/or her readers into the texts as well, either explicitly or implicitly, in order to create a novel literary space for women. For instance, in one of her best-known poems, "Afirmación culinaria" ("Culinary Affirmation"), Miriam Bornstein introduces the figure of the Chicana as writer in opposition to the more traditional role of housewife and cook:

> se me han quemado los frijoles
> por vivir
> en un no sé qué mundo de versos
> por querer decirle a alguien
> que no soy una leyenda
> por pensar y sentir
> un mundo que existe
> sí existe
> en el aire
> agua
> fuego tierra
> y unas cuantas líneas de un poema.
> —*(Martín-Rodríguez, La voz urgente, 215)*[15]

Bornstein's reference to "un no sé qué mundo de versos" is quite effective in its ambiguity for, although the text seems to suggest that the poetic persona is the one writing the verses, those lines could equally be read as the image of a female reader "lost in a text," to use Victor Nell's well-known phrase.[16] The poem's indeterminacy maximizes the poetic effect by thus presenting us with not just one but two atypical images of the Chicana (the writer and the reader) while at the same time engaging in a fundamental redefinition of the domestic space: to the restrictive world of the ethnically marked kitchen, the poet opposes the cosmological world of poetry, which she situates in connection with the four primal elements ("aire, agua, fuego, tierra").[17] According to the text, both the female writer and the reader can find in that poetic world an alternative to the drudgery of domesticity and to the "legends" that others have formed about them.

Like Bornstein, many other Chicana writers embarked upon a radical remapping of the feminine space in literature by presenting female characters in unusual spaces and by reinscribing traditionally feminine spaces such as the kitchen and the house. Nowhere is this rewriting of domesticity more evident than in Sandra Cisneros's 1984 bestseller *The House on Mango Street*, a text in which old repressive metaphors and symbols of the domestic subordination of many Chicanas are reformulated into liberatory spaces of feminine literary communication.

As I have suggested elsewhere ("The Book on Mango Street"), Cisneros's title needs to be read both literally and metaphorically. In the first sense, the title makes reference to the house that the protagonist's family inhabits on Mango Street. Metaphorically, it also refers to the book as a "house" that the characters inhabit; for, indeed, Cisneros's novel is organized in a way that is suggestive of a house's floor plan. This may hold the key for understanding the ultimate futility of the disagreement over the particular genre to which *Mango Street* belongs; critics have debated whether the text is a novel or a short-story collection.[18] The either/or way the question is normally posed obscures the fact that the book intends to be both, as Cisneros herself has acknowledged: "I wanted to write a collection which could be read at any random point without having any knowledge of what came before or after. Or, that could be read in a series to tell one big story" ("Do You Know Me?," 78). As such, the stories in the book function (metaphorically) much like the rooms in a house: they provide independent space when taken in isolation from one another, yet they are interdependent to properly constitute a house. While Cisneros gives many of her characters a "room of their own" by making them the subject and/or protagonist of at least one individual vignette, she insists on reclaiming an entire "house of her own" for

Esperanza, the narrator and protagonist of the book as a whole. Moreover, critics have tried to determine whether or not this book is a novel by looking at structural and formal characteristics pertaining to the realm of literary production while ignoring all along the emphasis on reading and reception that Cisneros's quoted comment reveals. Notice that, from an authorial point of view, Cisneros avoids the generic question to emphasize instead the two different ways her text could be read. Cisneros's declaration of intentions is thus an invitation to get lost in her book and in her house, because they are one and the same: the question of whether to stay in a particular room or to occupy the entire house, so to speak, is entirely left up to the reader.[19]

The metaphorical reading of the house as a book is further enhanced by several textual passages in which Esperanza describes her habitational/literary desires in terms that equate or compare one with the other. In the story "A House of My Own," for instance, she depicts her desired house as "a house quiet as snow, a space for myself to go, clean as paper before the poem" (108). This statement is both illustrative and deceiving, coming as it does toward the end of the book (in the penultimate story). On the one hand, this passage underscores the fact that ultimately the house in question is a paper house. But at the same time, if the blank paper can be interpreted as encompassing the narrator's desire for a space of her own, the fact that the statement is printed on a no-longer-blank paper reveals a much more complex dynamic affecting the narrator's aspirations since, in order to communicate her wishes, Esperanza needs to write on the paper (and by extension, to metaphorically occupy the house). In other words, by the time we read about her wishes, they have already been fulfilled, since the book has already been written, thus becoming the "house" the narrator longed for all along. This is why, in the previously mentioned "The Book on Mango Street," I described Cisneros's book as an illocutionary speech act (253), appropriating J. L. Austin's term. For Austin, this type of utterance performs an act *in* saying something rather than the act *of* saying something (99). In telling the stories of the women in her neighborhood, Esperanza (and, of course, Cisneros) opens up a new kind of narrative space for Chicanas and Latinas, thus building the figurative house that is not the house on Mango Street nor a man's house, nor a daddy's, but truly a house of her/their own.[20]

This new, created house/book is a feminine space where Esperanza's narratorial voice coexists with those of the other characters in a nonhierarchical way, as demonstrated by the fact that the discourse of the characters is not separated from hers by commas, italics, or any other devices.[21] Thus, Esperanza manages to bring together her own spatial/ literary needs and those of the other characters—some of whom, like Minerva, are also writers—by bridging the gap between her present house (on Mango Street) and the ideal house of her own in the last story:

> I write it down and Mango says goodbye sometimes. . . . One day I will pack my bags of books and paper. One day I will say goodbye to Mango. . . . Friends and neighbors will say, What happened to that Esperanza? . . . They will not know that I have gone away to come back. For the ones I left behind. For the ones who cannot out. (110)

This coming back for the ones left behind underscores the book's explicit commitment to include the voices of the voiceless, of the trapped women like Rafaela, of the abused girls like Sallie, and of the other subordinate females who populate the book.[22] Thus "written down" on the page, these characters—excluded heretofore from traditional narrative spaces—are the inhabitants of Cisneros house/book, much like the downtrodden and their language were the rebellious protagonists of Méndez's *Peregrinos,* as we saw in chapter 2. Cisneros further underscores this point in the story "Bums in the Attic," in which Esperanza daydreams about owning a house on a hill like the ones with the gardens her father tends. But this is no simplistic wishful fulfillment of the American dream[23]; rather, Esperanza emphatically asserts:

> One day I'll own my own house, but I won't forget who I am or where I came from. Passing bums will ask, Can I come in? I'll offer them the attic, ask them to stay, because I know how it is to be without a house. (87)

This quote, and the whole story, can be read as a clever double take on the literary history of representation/exclusion of women. On the one hand, Cisneros debunks the figure of "the madwoman in the attic" by portraying her character as a homeowner in control of both the physical (the house) and the textual spaces (the book).[24] On the other, she insists on providing a space in her house (her book) for those who were absent from traditional narrative spaces, the metaphorical bums of earlier patriarchal fiction. Now the reader can hear those voices by entering Esperanza's house, which is to say by reading Cisneros's book, and the latter takes on a life of its own every time it's read and interpreted, as Cisneros herself has acknowledged:

> [I]n many ways, the book is no longer a part of me, a child I birthed who grew up and who I hardly recognize.... If *The House on Mango Street* has brought me anything, I'm grateful for the luxury now of writing and knowing someone out there is listening. ("Do You Know Me?," 79)[25]

Having established this general context of reference for exploring gender and reading in *The House of Mango Street*, I would like to turn now to a detailed exploration of how Cisneros constructs a set of norms and strategies (what Iser calls "repertoire")[26] that, without denying access to her book or enjoyment to male readers, privileges the female ones as her implied audience.

Gendering the Reader: Constructing a Feminized Repertoire in *The House on Mango Street*

In their study of *Mango Street*, Erlinda Gonzales-Berry and Tey Diana Rebolledo provide a provocative and insightful reading of Cisneros's text in comparison to Tomás Rivera's *. . . y no se lo tragó la tierra*. Their analysis is of interest for my purposes because it engages in issues of repertoire construction while providing a contrast between female and male Chicano narratives. Gonzales-Berry and Rebolledo first set out to explore the many formal and generic characteristics shared by both Rivera's and Cisneros's texts, pointing out that they are both collections of stories that can be read together or separately, their being bildungsromane, and their narrators' desire to tell their personal and collective histories. Then Gonzales-Berry and Rebolledo explore the differences between the two texts by looking first at significant variations in how literary tradition has marked the bildungsroman genre. Following Annis Pratt, Gonzales-Berry and Rebolledo point out how the male bildungsroman normally culminates in the hero's successfully completing certain rites of passages, while the traditional female bildungsroman is aimed at giving young girls "tests in submission" and at preparing older girls for marriage (110). Or, to put it in Pratt's own words, traditional bildungsromane for girls were a contradiction in terms, "a genre that pursues the opposite of its generic intent—it provides models for 'growing down' rather than for 'growing up'" (14). Cisneros, however, does not conform to this particular generic feature as Esperanza "breaks with the traditional female bildungsroman to portray her heroine as a true hero" (Gonzales-Berry and Rebolledo, 118) and as she "refuses to accept gender determined limitations" (Gonzales-Berry and Rebolledo, 118).[27]

A second difference of importance, and the one I want to concentrate on here, revolves around the intertexts at play in the works by Rivera and Cisneros. As noted by Gonzales-Berry and Rebolledo,

> [b]oth Cisneros and Rivera utilize the rich oral tradition of stories told and incorporate it into their narratives; they simply choose different facets of that oral tradition. Rivera uses Catholic belief and mythology as well as folk beliefs, folk tales, tall tales and gossip.... Cisneros incorporates children's games and rhythms as well as the female-to-female tradition into her narrative. (117)

This last point, I believe, is exemplary of one of the most salient characteristics of many contemporary Chicana narratives: the desire to insert themselves into the female-to-female tradition to which Gonzales-Berry and Rebolledo allude. This does not mean that their texts are restricted to a female readership only; rather, it is an indication of the revaluing of the feminine experience as a particular lexicon from which to start literary communication and from which to invite a reader's response.[28] At the same time, the existence of such an oral intertext should not detract from the fact that *Mango Street* is also a text in which many other written texts are invoked in a more or less obvious way, as we will see in more detail below.[29]

Thus, the feminization of the repertoire occurs both at the level of the characters (a predominantly oral world, although several characters are writers) and at a metanarrative level in which the reader actualizes more or less obvious points of connection with other books by/about women (Virginia Woolf, Gilbert and Gubar's *The Madwoman in the Attic*, etc.). Together with skipping-rope rhymes and other children songs, the feminization of the folkloric repertoire of *Mango Street* includes references to "fairy tales such as Rapunzel, Sleeping Beauty, Little Red Riding Hood, and imprisoned fairy princesses" (Gonzales-Berry and Rebolledo, 118). These references function as a commentary on the ideological role of traditional narratives in assigning women a subordinate role. Yet while those stories are sadly applicable to the world of *Mango Street* (and we find a Rapunzel in the locked-up Rafaela, a wide-awake Sleeping Beauty in Marin "waiting for a car to stop, a star to fall, someone to change her life" [27], and several Little Red Riding Hoods in the girls who try on the high heels in the story "The Family of Little Feet"),[30] the progressive maturing of Esperanza and her budding literary vocation contain the seeds of a contestatory discourse of femininity. This is seen as early as in the story "My Name" (the fourth in the book),[31] in which Esperanza compares herself to her grandmother while confessing: "I have inherited her name, but I don't want to inherit her place by the window" (11), thus rejecting her grandmother's fate as a woman imprisoned at home. As Renato Rosaldo has suggested in comparing Esperanza with one of the most famous corrido heroes, the self-baptizing that concludes the story amounts to a novel understanding of identity:

> In contrast to Gregorio Cortez, she does not stand in one place, looking straight ahead, and shout, "Yo soy Esperanza." . . . As she concludes the tale, Esperanza yet again turns things topsy-turvy by baptizing her invisible, real self: Zeze the X. Nothing stands still, especially not her name. (163)

Esperanza's new discourse is, Rosaldo suggests, one that necessitates a continuous redefinition of referents, much as Esperanza's identity keeps changing throughout the book. The contestatory discourse of Esperanza then continues in several other stories from the book. These include "Beautiful and Cruel," in which the semiotics of film serve for Esperanza as a means to declare her "own quiet war" (89) on the roles that domestic life reserves for girls, and those chapters that deal (even partially) with reading and writing, such as "Born Bad," "Edna's Ruthie," and "Minerva Writes Poems," culminating in the final two stories, "A House of My Own" and "Mango Says Goodbye Sometimes." But beyond referential developments in the plot, the fact that the book is—among other things—about telling stories is also a major help for the reader in reconstructing this process of awareness, most explicitly explored in the final story, "Mango Says Goodbye Sometimes." In it, we find two contrasting styles of storytelling side by side. The first is explored in the second paragraph:

> I make a story for my life, for each step my brown shoe takes. I say, "And so she trudged up the wooden stairs, her sad brown shoes taking her to the house she never liked." (109)

Any reader will recognize here the overcharged style of the fairy tale, with some more or less evident echoes of the story of Cinderella. The fact that the style is at odds with that of the rest of the book sets this narrative modality as unfit for the story Esperanza really wants to tell. This is further emphasized by the use of quotation marks, which is inconsistent with the practice of introducing reported speech without punctuation marks in the rest of the book.[32]

The second narrative modality, however, proves truer to the spirit of the book, as exemplified in the following two paragraphs of "Mango Says Goodbye Sometimes":

> I like to tell stories. I am going to tell you a story about a girl who didn't want to belong.
> We didn't always live on Mango Street. Before that we lived on Loomis on the third floor, and before that we lived on Keeler. (109)

The story Esperanza tells in this second paragraph is, in fact, a story already told, since the beginning of the second paragraph I quoted reproduces verbatim the first lines of the book.[33] As I have suggested elsewhere, this act of sending the reader back to the beginning of the book serves to clarify that Esperanza prefers a story firmly grounded in reality to that of the glamorized fairy tales ("The Book on Mango Street," 251). Implicitly, it also serves to underscore the fact that a new kind of narrative is needed if one is to contest the status quo and the ideology contained in the alienating stories of female objectification. This is most clearly seen in the fact that the glamorizing story ("And so she trudged up the wooden stairs . . .") is told in the objectifying third person while the preferred modality ("We didn't always live on Mango Street") is told in the first person (whether singular or plural, as in this instance), which immediately stresses the role of Esperanza as both subject and object of the narration. It is precisely in the process of gaining subjectivity and agency that Esperanza escapes the fate of her grandmother as well as that of her mother (who "could have been somebody" [90]) and thus the circularity of the story: in writing herself and her community down, Esperanza reverses the fate of her silenced, locked-in female ancestors; therefore, to the end of the process of maturation as a character and as a writer corresponds the beginning of the act of narration.

A second way *The House on Mango Street* feminizes the repertoire involves a revisionist reading of Gaston Bachelard's *The Poetics of Space*. Cisneros acknowledges reading the text while at the Iowa Writers' Workshop, and she recalls the sense of alienation that reading and the subsequent discussion on the symbolism of the house provoked in her ("Ghosts and Voices," 73). Following that lead, Julián Olivares has analyzed *Mango Street* via Bachelard, exposing the French critic's interpretation of the symbolism of home through a "house conceived in terms of male-centered ideology" ("Sandra Cisneros," 160). As Olivares proposes, the construction of the house as a sign of stability and protection is of little use for a Chicana feminist writing from a gendered perspective. In particular, Olivares's reading of Bachelard's dialectics of inside and outside (or what R. Saldívar has called "the mutually overdetermining spheres of the private and the social" in *Chicano Narrative,* 182) is of relevance since, according to Olivares, Cisneros "inverts Bachelard's pronouncement on the poetics of space; for Cisneros the inside, the *here,* can be confinement and a source of anguish and alienation" ("Sandra Cisneros," 161, original emphasis) rather than the integration that Bachelard postulates. That is to say, Cisneros fleshes out Bachelard's symbolic house in order to expose its closet skeletons. Women, as noted by Olivares, are trapped in the patriarchal house of Bachelard between the "tortilla star" with which Alicia rises to prepare her father's lunch and the linoleum roses on the floor of Sally's married prison house ("Sandra Cisneros," 165).

Esperanza's wish for a house of her own, in this light, should be interpreted once again as a double take on social and literary discourses. As the former, Esperanza's house is the house on "man: go!" street ("Not a man's house. Not a daddy's," as on page 108), a liberatory space for women in which they would be subjects rather than objects, agents in control of their lives and their stories instead of the victims of a daddy's violence, a husband's jealousy, or a narrative erasure. As the latter, Esperanza's house-as-book is a literary response to Bachelard and to other explicit and implicit narratives of patriarchal domination, a resisting reading that reinscribes Chicanas as narrative voices in control of their lives and their stories.[34]

It is in this sense, I believe, that the very useful analysis by Gonzales-Berry and Rebolledo could also be expanded beyond the comparative to interpret *Mango Street* as a privileged instance of Chicana narrative "reading" the Chicano canon as well. Interpreted in this light, Cisneros's work is a response (beyond Rivera's novel) to an entire body of 1960s and 1970s literature that failed to provide female readers with that kind of take on the female-to-female tradition that Mango Street strives to construct.[35] Thus, paraphrasing Olivares's comments on Rivera's audience (in "The Search for Being"),[36] I would describe this response as if Cisneros, the reader, would say, "No, así no era" ("No, that's not the way it was") upon failing to see her history and that of other Chicanas reflected in earlier texts by Chicano writers.

In fact, and although the quote does not seem to refer to Rivera,[37] Cisneros has been quite eloquent in this respect when describing her reasons for writing *Mango Street:*

> I wrote it as a reaction against those people who want to make our barrios look like Sesame Street, or some place warm and beautiful. Poor neighborhoods lose their charm after dark, they really do. . . . I was writing about it in the most real sense that I knew, as a person walking those neighborhoods with a vagina. I saw it a lot differently than all those "chingones" that are writing all those bullshit pieces about their barrios. (Interview with P. E. Rodríguez Aranda, 69)

Cisneros's dissenting voice ("no, así no era") is a clearly gendered one, and it is one that insists on writing the body into the text.[38] Her "poetics of space" is marked by the vagina that, objectified, makes her a potential rape target (as is Esperanza in *Mango Street*'s story "Red Clowns") but that can also become a subjective source of self-definition and expression, as in the poem "Down There," from *Loose Woman.*[39] In this long poem, after ironizing on "the miscellany of maleness" (81) for over sixty lines, the poetic persona emphatically asserts:

Yes,
I want to talk at length about Menstruation. Or my period. (82)

The clever disposition of these three lines transforms them into the deconstructive center of the poem. The first line, the only one-syllable line in the text, initiates a major change in rhythm, thus suggesting as well a change in topic, from the "miscellany of maleness" to the "poem of womanhood" (84) that is to follow. In fact, these three lines can be read almost by themselves as an artful haiku in the seventeen-syllable Japanese tradition,[40] and the grouping of the first two or the last two lines together even invites a bisected haikulike reading: "Yes, / I want to talk at length about Men-" (which is what the poem has done to that point; hence the hyphen as a closure sign), and "I want to talk at length about Men-/struation. Or my period" (which is what the poem will do after that point; hence the hyphen working properly as a connector and the final pun on "period" as a false closure sign).

Anyone who has ever taught this poem in class or used it in any kind
of public forum knows that what follows in the poem are perhaps the
fifty-five most difficult lines for male readers to endure (even if the poem
has a male addressee), to the point that even the poetic persona asks at
one point, "Still with me?" (84). In those fifty-five lines, the poetic I
indulges in a detailed description of her period, including details about
texture, color, smell, and many other fine points that have made many
of my male students visibly uncomfortable during class discussion.

Regardless of this expected reaction from male readers (hence the "Still
with me?" line), the poem sails forth in its radical feminization of its
repertoire.[41] It is during that course that the poetic persona transforms a
descriptive-evaluative account of menstruation into a veritable *ars poetica*:

In fact,
I'd like to dab my fingers
in my inkwell
and write a poem across the wall.
"A Poem of Womanhood"
Now wouldn't that be something? (84)

In an artful linguistic twist, Cisneros guides us from the euphemism
in the title ("Down There"), through the chauvinistic term "cunt" invoked
in the reference to "a *Playboy* poem" in line 81 of the poem (82),[42] to a
gynocentric celebration of the vagina that culminates in the metaphoric
equation vagina equals inkwell. In doing so, I believe that Cisneros is
also playing with both the Freudian concept of "penis envy" and the
Lacanian discussion on girls' introduction to language (as a patriarchal
system based on phallic/nonphallic oppositions) by substituting the penis
(and the pen) for the fingers her poetic subject dabs in her own vagina
in order to write her poem of womanhood. Notice, in this regard, the
poetic effectiveness of the contrast between the gentleness of the dabbing
fingers and the implicit aggression in the image of the tampax-pulling
teeth in the image from (Updike's) *Playboy* poem.[43] In contrasting these
two images, Cisneros brings us back to the polemics of her quote from
the interview with P. E. Rodríguez Aranda. Objectified (a cunt, as in
Updike's poem), the vagina and the woman are at risk of sexual
aggression. Perceived as a subject, the vagina and the woman are the
source of inspiration and the origin of writing.

In a poem where words are chosen this carefully, it is important to
note how the verb "dab" in the preceding quote is the mirrorlike inversion

of the adjective *"bad"* used (italicized) in the first lines to describe the male addressee's evaluation of his own poem: "Your poem thinks it's *bad /* Because it farts in the bath" (79). The childish attitude of the male poet is further underscored by the prosaism of the second line and the almost ridiculous rhyming of "bath" and "bad," which culminate a series of onomatopoeic alliterations. But more importantly, the "bad/dab" mirrorlike opposition functions to undermine yet another stereotypical view of women's writing that, traditionally, has seen it as characterized by a discursive excess of adjectives. The poem "Down There" strikes back by assigning the passiveness traditionally associated with superfluous adjectivation to male writing while reclaiming the dynamism of the verb for the female creation. The struggle synthesized in the opposition of these two referents is, of course, carried out in detail throughout the poem to the point that Rebolledo (in her brief commentary on this poem) has described it as "a contestatory poem to all the male poems that exult masculine sexuality" (*Women Singing,* 198). I think that Rebolledo is only partially right on this, for the contestatory impulses in "Down There" go beyond poems exulting masculine sexuality to also challenge the entire chauvinistic frame of mind that another Chicana author, Evangelina Vigil, has succinctly but brilliantly characterized in the title of her poem "para los que piensan con la verga (with due apologies to those who do not),"[44] and—most importantly—to write the body as the ultimate source of gendered communication between Chicanas.

"Down There" can be read as the foremost example of how Chicana authors have written the body into their texts while at the same time engaging in a critical reading of patriarchal discourses, be they Chicano or not.[45] It represents an effective deconstruction of Lacanian views on gender and discourse, for the poet not only appropriates and reclaims language and discourse but does so precisely by subverting the phallic/ nonphallic oppositions and feminizing the repertoire. This, in turn, places her texts in the distinctive double position I have analyzed so far: first, as texts that "read" and reformulate tradition, and second, as texts that seek to (en)gender their readers. With this double position in mind, the rest of this chapter will now be devoted to analyzing the works of other Chicana authors who continue to expand this double positionality.

Diosa y hembra:[46] Feminizing Mythology and the Metaphysical
Another strategic move undertaken by Chicana writers in order to both critically read tradition and create a feminized narrative space involves revisiting and realigning cultural iconography, in particular that associated

with the ancestral past. During much of the 1970s, many Chicano writers embraced a cultural nationalist agenda that attempted to promote unity and ethnic pride by invoking ancient myths, religions, and beliefs. Poet Alurista, one of the leading forces behind this cultural revival, proclaimed the need to find a "unifying metaphor" that would unite Chicanos/as nationwide.[47] The metaphor he is credited with having popularized is that of Aztlán, the mythical home of the Aztecs, from which they started south to eventually found Tenochtitlan, the Aztec capital.[48] The story of Aztlán called for a return to the northern lands of origin, which Alurista and others interpreted as the true beginning of a Chicano/a nation.

Because the chosen metaphor was one that associated Chicanos/as with the Aztecs, many of the Aztec deities were regularly evoked in texts from this era. In particular, Quetzalcoatl (mostly as a symbol of wisdom) and Huitzilopochtli (a symbol of both strength and fighting) became standard literary currency in poems, stories, and plays.[49] Interestingly, most of the deities appearing in texts from this period were male ones, a surprising aspect considering the abundance of female deities in the Aztec pantheon. Furthermore, in the occasional texts where female deities appeared, they were mostly cast in unfavorable ways, either as subordinate or as negative characters. The latter is the case for the many allusions to Cihuacoatl (often referred to as her legendary counterpart, La Llorona) as an ominous force. The former is the case with Coatlicue (Mother Earth) as, for example, in Luis Valdez's play *Bernabé*. In this play, Coatlicue (La Tierra) appears chaperoned by a pachuco character (La Luna) as they wait for Tonatiuh (the Sun) to come out and bless Coatlicue's union with Bernabé, the village idiot transformed at the end of the play into "a child of the sun" by means of a ritual sacrifice (Huerta, *Chicano Theater*, 195).[50] In discussing this play's ties with Mayan and Aztec beliefs, Jorge Huerta's comments on the connections between *Bernabé* and the Aztec story of the birth of Huitzilopochtli are of relevance:

> *Bernabé* is in reality Valdez's myth. In the Aztec pantheon, Coatlicue, the earth goddess/virgin mother, gives birth to Huitzilopochtli, the sun. The moon, Coyolxauhqui, is the sun's sister. Valdez's dramatization of the sun as father and the earth and moon as children thus differs from the Aztec legends. In changing the sexes and relationships of this cosmic triumvirate, the playwright creates his own *mito,* based on his interpretation of the hero/quest myth. (*Chicano Theater,* 198)

The playwright's changing of the sexes observed by Huerta, which could also be described as a combination of both goddesses (Coatlicue and Coyolxauhqui) into the character La Tierra, has the immediate double effect of limiting feminine roles (from two to one) and also of casting the one female character left into a very traditional, domestic role. Coatlicue's immediate subordination to La Luna (a male character here, who acts as her brother and chaperon), her ultimate dependence on Tonatiuh (as his daughter), as well as her additional attributes as mother and whore[51] do nothing to depart from traditional stereotypical roles of women defined solely or mostly by their relations to men; as such, this character is not an element with which many women viewers and readers could relate.[52]

Given this kind of appropriations/manipulations of pre-Hispanic mythology by Valdez and other Chicano authors, it comes as no surprise that Chicana writers began to show an interest in feminizing the Chicano/a literary pantheon and in reinterpreting other feminine images and icons such as Malintzin/Doña Marina/Malinche and the Virgen de Guadalupe. Chicanas have written extensively on the former, seeking to disassociate her figure from the label of traitor to her race (a sort of Mexican Eve). That revisionist discourse had a most powerful burst into the Chicano/a intellectual arena with Adelaida del Castillo's "Malintzin Tenépal," in which she sets out to rebuff what she calls Octavio Paz's "ego-testicle worldview" (145) on nationality and history by analyzing how Doña Marina "embodies effective, decisive action" by acting "not as a goddess in some mythology, but as an actual force in the making of history" (125).[53] Likewise, the latter has been appropriated by Chicanas (and Chicanos) in a different set of contexts, but where her iconography has been most drastically altered and renegotiated is in the artistic works of Esther Hernández and Yolanda M. López, who have created nontraditional depictions of the Virgin (Hernández) and striking artistic combinations by mixing elements of traditional guadalupana art with portraits of herself and her family members (López).

In this intellectual and artistic context, the reappropriation of the female side of ancient Amerindian mythology was foremost accomplished in 1987, with the publication of Gloria Anzaldúa's *Borderlands/La frontera: The New Mestiza,* which thoroughly articulates the need for this new dimension of the (feminized) repertoire. In this very ambitious and successful text, Anzaldúa sets out to analyze the Chicana/o experience in social, historical, linguistic, mythological, literary, and metaphysical terms. While her provocative and groundbreaking understanding of the border and the borderlands is, by far, the element that has received the most critical attention, my interest is in exploring how Anzaldúa's reconstruction of the feminine side of pre-Hispanic religions "reads" Chicano/a Movement indigenist and cultural nationalistic literature while proposing an alternative female-to-female cultural text.

Even as Anzaldúa does not restrict her religious/mythological investigation to the feminine side of the Aztec pantheon,[54] two sections of *Borderlands* concentrate on Tonantzin ("Entering into the Serpent," chapter 3) and on Coatlicue ("La herencia de Coatlicue/The Coatlicue State," chapter 4). In the first of these two chapters, Anzaldúa explores the connection between the much revered Virgen de Guadalupe and her indigenous antecedents: Coatlalopeuh, Coatlicue, and Tonantsi (Tonantzin). A most important aspect of Anzaldúa's analysis involves her critique of Aztec patriarchy:

> The male-dominated Azteca-Mexica culture drove the powerful female deities underground by giving them monstrous attributes and by substituting male deities in their place. . . . They divided her who had been complete. . . . *Coatlicue,* the Serpent goddess, and her more sinister aspects, *Tlazolteotl* and *Cihuacoatl* were darkened and disempowered. (27)

Paving the way for later, significant critical analyses such as Daniel C. Alarcón's "The Aztec Palimpsest," Anzaldúa's text stresses the need to account early on in Chicano/a history for gender and internal differences. At the same time, Anzaldúa's critique of the Aztec patriarchal system exposes some of the questions that Cultural Nationalism's romanticization of the past had left unaddressed.[55] Thus, Anzaldúa suggests that the patriarchal trend and the splitting of the female goddesses initiated by the Nahuas was further prolonged during colonial times by reinforcing the opposition between the figure of the virgin, Guadalupe, and the whore, Tlazolteotl/Coatlicue (28), a cultural paradigm that—as we saw—has been kept alive well into the Chicano/a period.

But what is most interesting about Anzaldúa's recuperation of the feminine pre-Hispanic pantheon is that she uses it as a rhetorical discourse aimed at creating a pan-ethnic sisterhood in which communication is based not on the restrictive norms learned in school or in society at large (including institutionalized religion and academia) but on communion with nature and with the inner self. The last part of

"Entering into the Serpent" is devoted to exploring the psychic experiences that Anzaldúa and other Latina and Native American women she names experience, something she calls "la facultad" ("the capacity"), a sort of sixth sense. While she has alienated some women readers—including former fellow editor Cherríe Moraga—with her exploration of what she terms "deeper realities" (38),[56] these two chapters of Anzaldúa's *Borderlands* are effective in stressing the need for women authors and readers to rely on alternative sets of norms and communicative strategies: "The work of *mestiza* consciousness is to break down the subject-object duality which keeps her a prisoner and to show in the flesh and through images in her own work how duality is transcended" (80). Both duality and the overcoming of duality are exemplified by Coatlicue, whom Anzaldúa develops in "La herencia" into an internal force that solves the mind/body opposition as well as the I/us separation:

> I see the heat of anger or rebellion or hope split open that rock, releasing la *Coatlicue.* And someone in me takes matters into our own hands, and eventually, takes dominion over serpents—over my own body, my sexual activity, my soul, my mind, my weaknesses and strengths. Mine. Ours. Not the heterosexual white man's or the colored man's or the state's or the culture's or the religion's or the parent's—just ours, mine. (51)[57]

While Moraga is right in pointing out a certain difficulty in following Anzaldúa's style and images, I believe that the difficulty is both intentional and necessary in describing the kind of inner-world metaphysical experiences invoked here and throughout the book. In this, Anzaldúa's style is not unlike that of other metaphysical and even mystic poets. In fact, so many of the pieces in Spanish in *Borderlands* contain clear echoes of the foremost Spanish mystic poets (Santa Teresa de Avila and San Juan de la Cruz in particular) that the book almost demands such an intertextual reading.[58] A case in point is the poem "En mi corazón se incuba" ("In my heart incubates"), from which Moraga takes the title for her review of the book. The last stanza of the poem reads as follows:

> En este oscuro monte de nopal
> Algo secretamente amado
> Se oculta en mi vientre
> Y en mi corazón se incuba
> Un amor que no es de este mundo. (144)[59]

The scenery (darkness, a mountain), the slight hesitation (something secretly loved, a love that is not from this world), the oppositions (mountain/womb), and the vocabulary itself of this poem (in which we also read about "la huella del amor" ([love's trace/footprint]) are all reminiscent of mystic poetry, as are many other poems in the book, such as "Antigua,[60] mi diosa," in which the poetic persona speaks of herself as "[a]cantilada por tus ojos vulnerada voy" (188). A literal translation of that line would be difficult, as Anzaldúa uses a rather unusual term here. The verb "acantilar," from which "acantilada" would be a regular adjective, is listed as a maritime term by the Real Academia de la Lengua Española's *Diccionario de la lengua española*. As such, it is given two meanings, the first of which could loosely be translated as "shipwrecked," as it refers to a bad nautical maneuver by which a ship would end up stranded on a steep bank. The second meaning of "acantilar" refers to the process of creating a cliff out of a body of water by dredging it. Interestingly, both meanings would be poetically coherent within the context of this poem (even if there are no other maritime references), for Anzaldúa gives us a wandering poetic subject (not unlike the wandering ships of many folkloric and literary stories),[61] stranded in New York during the winter[62] and feeling very much emptied out as if by a dredge.[63] Suggestive as these lines of readings are, the movement indicated by the verbal form "voy" ("I go") is at odds with the interpretation of "acantilada" as "stranded," but mystic and metaphysical poetry is, almost by definition, paradoxical. The poetic persona, therefore, may feel both dredged out and replenished, may wander around and be stranded all at the same time, as the rest of the poem demonstrates.

In fact, there are many other points of connection with Spanish mysticism in this poem: the word "vulnerada" (repeated twice) is a favorite word for "wounded" or "harmed" in mystic poetry; the expressions "tus dedos cantando como espadas" (188) ("your fingers singing as swords do"), "Me entraste por todas las rendijas / con tu luz llenaste el hueco de mi cuerpo" (188) ("You entered me through all my crevices / you filled the hollow of my body with your light"), "Me consumaste enterita" (188) ("you completed me entirely"), "nada me satisface" (188) ("nothing satisfies me"), "mi incendiada piel urge el saberte" ("my burning skin is anxious to know you"), and the syntactically convoluted line "no te puedo darme no" ("I cannot give me to you no") are all footprints of mystical discourse, particularly in combination with the pervasive eroticism that may (or may not) be read literally.[64]

This poem, of course, does not embark on this literary and spiritual journey without securing a connection with the essayistic part of the book, in particular with that which intends to accomplish the restoration of the pre-Hispanic feminine pantheon. After all, as noted, Antigua stands for Coatlicue. Therefore, even within the lines that I commented on in relation to Spanish mysticism, Aztec mythology is at play, and so the reader recognizes in the "acantilada" poetic persona a reminder of Cihuacoatl, La Llorona, who wanders around the edges of rivers and other bodies of water looking for her dead children.[65] In fact, the word "cantil" (meaning edge of a cliff), from which "acantilada" derives, also refers to a kind of snake in the Mexican region of Chiapas.[66] Coatlicue, therefore, is present at each level of the poem, and Anzaldúa's mixture of erotic and metaphysic themes is ultimately at the service of expressing the desired union with the goddess, what the essayistic part of *Borderlands* calls "the Coatlicue state" in her chapter 4.

Interpreted from this intertextual perspective, the metaphysical in Anzaldúa's *Borderlands* may be less a case of New Age obfuscation, as Moraga wanted, than yet another example of how Chicana writers have reread literary and cultural traditions in order to create and discard lines of filiation or affiliation. This is further confirmed by the inclusion in *Borderlands* of a six-page poem on Santa Teresa de Avila, titled "Holy Relics." The poem chronicles the death, burial, and several exhumations of the uncorrupted body of the saint of Avila. More importantly, this long poem is a detailed account of the process by which several friars and other churchmen gradually dismember St. Teresa's body. Symbolically and, of course, literally this process can be read as a commentary on violence against women. This reading is reinforced by the last lines of the poem (before the final repetition of the refrain): "Above the high altar at Alba, / the fifth and final resting place, / lie the remains of a woman" (159). By thus ending the poem with the words "a woman," Teresa of Avila becomes not only herself but any other woman subject to patriarchal violence of one kind or another. Moreover, only at this point does the refrain that is repeated three other times during the poem acquire full meaning and poignancy:

> We are the holy relics,
> the scattered bones of a saint,
> the best loved bones of Spain.
> We seek each other. (159)

Santa Teresa is a woman, any woman, and all other women that came after her, the poem seems to suggest, are nothing but her fragments in a continual search for one another (building feminine alliances) and for redressing historical processes of violence against women.

But while the poem itself and the mystical subtext I outlined earlier clearly favor this feminist-religious interpretation, another line of reading opens up when we connect the story of Santa Teresa with that of Coyolxauhqui, the daughter of Coatlicue, dismembered by her brother Huitzilopochtli upon his birth. It is upon making these kinds of connections that Anzaldúa's reader realizes that the fragmentarism and hybridism that characterizes the text (a mixture of essays, poetry, personal narratives, and stories) is also an invitation to "seek each other" to unite the disjointed and to reconcile oppositions: this is precisely what she terms "the Coatlicue state," because Coatlicue is both the contradictory and the fusion of opposites, the (ir)resolution of a mobile new identity not unlike that which Rosaldo sees in Esperanza's renaming herself in *Mango Street*. Coatlicue is the border and the borderlands, the new mestiza.

A final note on Anzaldúa's process of reclaiming a feminine mythology, literary tradition, and cultural history: she does so not only on mystical/metaphysical terms but also by writing the body. Both the mystical and the mythological inclinations in her text converge in a discourse about the female body: the former by recalling the story of the dismemberment of St. Teresa in full detail; as for the latter, the following quote from the chapter "Entering into the Serpent" should suffice: "Forty years it's taken me to enter into the Serpent, to acknowledge that I have a body, that I am a body and to assimilate the animal body, the animal soul" (26). Discovering Coatlicue and recovering the mystic poetry of Santa Teresa are thus two roads in the path to feminine self-affirmation. But these are not the abstract ways of cultural nationalism: this is flesh and blood affirmation, a feminist insistence on writing the body that pervades Chicana literature and that we could further confirm by analyzing Ana Castillo's *The Mixquiahuala Letters*.

On the Monte Albán and Other Periods:
The Mixquiahuala Letters **and the Female Reader**
Ana Castillo's *The Mixquiahuala Letters*, published just one year before *Borderlands*, is perhaps the most sophisticated attempt to bring together all aspects involved in the effort of creating a female-to-female Chicana literary tradition. As such, I will analyze it from four perspectives in order to explore the following: the ways Castillo contributes to the process of feminizing the repertoire for an implied feminine reader, the construction of a gendered narratee and its consequences for the literary process, the

way *Mixquiahuala* writes the body in connection with other works analyzed in this chapter, and *Mixquiahuala* as a response to previous literary works, both Chicano/a and non-Chicano/a. My analysis, however, will not separate these four perspectives from one another, as they are very closely interconnected. Rather, my unified discussion of the novel will occasionally branch out into one of the four perspectives as needed.

A personal anecdote might serve as entry into the world of *Mixquiahuala*. When this (Castillo's first) novel was published, I was a graduate student at the University of Houston, and I was in close contact with Arte Público Press, which was distributing the book, then just released by Bilingual Review/Press. The administrative assistant at Arte Público told me that most of the people who called to order this book asked either for "the letters" or for "Castillo's novel," often commenting on the fact that the title was most difficult to remember or to pronounce. Those (would-be) readers of Castillo held on to the generic identification of the title due to the evident difficulty of remembering its toponymic referent. This, in itself, is an attractive point of entry for my analysis, for it is clear that Castillo must have had substantial reasons for choosing such a "difficult" name to remember for her title and/or for (in doing so) stressing the importance of her chosen genre.

Within the book, Castillo's choice is indirectly explained as early as in the third letter.[67] In it, we learn that Teresa and Alicia (the author and the addressee of all forty letters, respectively) met during a summer course on Mexican culture and language at a Mexico City school with a "heavy Aztec name just a notch above fraudulent status" (24). The reader also learns that they stayed at the same boardinghouse and that they visited Mixquiahuala together as part of the cultural component of the course. Mixquiahuala, in letter Three, is described as

> a Pre-Conquest village of obscurity, neglectful of progress, electricity notwithstanding. Its landmark and only claim to fame were the Toltec ruins of Tula, monolithic statues in tribute to warriors and a benevolent god in self-exile who reappeared later on Mayan shores, and again, on the back of a four-legged beast to display his mortal fallibilities. (25)

In a couple of pages, Castillo gives us, condensed, a topographical and cultural history of pre-Hispanic Mexico with the references to Mexico City/Tenochtitlan, Mixquiahuala/Tula (the capital of the Toltecs), and the Mayan shores (which would reappear later in the book as the site of one of the many failed love stories). Of these peoples, the Aztecs and the Mayas are the most well known, as they were the two most prominent powers at the time of the arrival of the Spaniards. The Toltecs, an earlier civilization, are generally credited with providing a link between the Olmecs and the Mayas (first) and the Aztecs (at a later date). They are also the ones who introduced the figure of Quetzalcoatl, as Castillo notes, which was then passed on to both the Mayas (as Kukulcan) and the Aztecs (as Quetzalcoatl).

Quetzalcoatl's legend, to which Castillo alludes, is one of sibling rivalry and self-exile, and it may prove of interest for our analysis. Tricked by his brothers Tezcatlipoca and Huitzilopochtli, Quetzalcoatl got drunk and had sex with his sister Quetzalpapalotl. Upon sobering up, he realized his incestuous relations and fled to the East, where he incinerated himself, after which he was transformed into the morning star (Venus). But before his self-sacrifice, Quetzalcoatl had promised to return. Knowing this myth, the Aztec emperor Moctezuma is said to have interpreted that Hernán Cortés was the returning Quetzalcoatl (and hence Castillo's reference to him as mounting a four-legged beast, a horse).

This introduction of Mixquiahuala, seemingly in line with cultural nationalist practices of the previous decades, is nevertheless marked by its being preceded by an ironic commentary on the "heavy Aztec name" of the quasi-fraudulent school Alicia and Teresa attended, which is in itself a telling critique of the abuses to which cultural nationalism can be subjected when commodified for market-driven exoticism. But the irony cuts both ways, since Castillo's reader might be inclined at this point to think about the novel's difficult title as just another "heavy" indigenous name intended to cover up some kind of "fraud." The reader's curiosity is therefore piqued as s/he can only guess what Castillo's treatment of the pre-Hispanic past is going to be like. The issue is of particular importance for readers familiar with previous Chicano/a texts since for many of them, as we saw, the indigenous cultures of the Mesoamerican region had played a pivotal role in terms of the definition of a collective identity and of an identity politics.

Castillo's irony, here and elsewhere,[68] casts a definite shadow of doubt over such attempts at the rhetorical use of the past, as her choice of words ("heavy" and "fraud"), the location she chooses for this part of the story (Toltec ruins of Mixquiahuala), and the overall sardonic tone already explored by Norma Alarcón[69] are all combined to deconstruct previous discourses on ethnicity and on the search for Chicana/o roots in (ancient) Mexico.[70] Furthermore, the subtle way the story of Quetzalcoatl touches upon issues of sex and gender should not go unnoticed. In this sense, the story serves as a background warning for subsequent violence against the two female friends while in Mexico, as several inebriated and sober individuals attempt to rape or otherwise molest them.[71]

This critical—at times irreverent—reading of tradition (both pre-Hispanic and colonial) is constant throughout the book, and it is marked by a gendered perception not unlike that which prompted Sandra Cisneros to demystify barrio life from her perspective as a Chicana. Letter Three in *Mixquiahuala,* for instance, problematizes the much cherished Chicano/a topos of looking for one's roots and origin in Mexico for, as Teresa states about their trip to Mixquiahuala: "The experience, in short, took us back *at least* to the time of colonial repression of peons and women who hid behind shutters to catch a glimpse of the street with its brusque men" (25, my emphasis). "Mixquiahuala," then, stands as the signifier for a dystopian space of violence and repression against women and the working classes. For the reader familiar with earlier Chicano/a texts, Mixquiahuala is at the opposite end of the spectrum from Ron Arias's Tamazunchale (from his 1975 *The Road to Tamazunchale*). Tamazunchale, as we learn from Arias's protagonist, "*is* our home. Once we're there, we're free, we can be everything and everyone" (88, original emphasis). Castillo's Mixquiahuala, by contrast, seems to be the place where you cannot be what you are or what you want to be. At least if you are a woman.

The ensuing disappointment is what gives *Mixquiahuala* the overwhelming sardonic tone that Alarcón has noted. But since (contrary to *Mango Street*) this is not a story about growing up, the disenchantment and the irony welcome the reader almost from page one, rather than appearing as a rite of passage or revelation toward the end. In fact, nowhere are Castillo's demystifying powers more effective than in letter Two, where Teresa reminisces about her visit to the ruins of Monte Albán with Alicia while wishing the latter a happy, men-free thirtieth birthday:

> . . . In the musk halls
> of a sacrificial temple at the ruins of Monte Albán
> you changed your tampon
> before the eyes of gods, ghosts, and scorpions
> while i watched for mortals. (23)[72]

Continuing with her task of debunking many of the cherished motifs of Chicano literature, Castillo's appropriation of the indigenous sacred locus is cleverly effective here.[73] Because of her/his knowledge of the Chicano repertoire, a reader familiar with earlier Chicano texts cannot help but evoke certain mental images upon reading about the musk halls of a sacrificial temple. Powerful gods, ancestral rituals, sacredness, and blood are but several of the many images that the author seems to expect in her reader's mind.[74] After giving the reader time and pause (hence the breaking of the narration in verselike lines) to savor these familiar images, Castillo's narrator proceeds to invalidate the accustomed connections by transforming the divine into human and the masculine imagery of ritual sacrifice (as perpetuated in traditional stories and images) into a reclaiming of the female body: the only blood involved in this ritual is that impregnating Alicia's tampon and this, in itself, is a tongue-in-cheek negation of the reproductive, regenerative aspect of the offering of blood to the gods, as it signals not pregnancy and (re)birth but its opposite, menstruation. The accompanying gradation of (potential) witnesses to the ritual—gods, ghosts, scorpions, and the excluded mortals—is likewise a powerful rhetorical device (not unlike final-verse recollection in Baroque poetry), aimed at symbolically limiting the power of the masculine, as the series starts with "gods" (in lowercase, deprived of any agency and limited to a very passive role as spectators, but still divine), loses whatever corporeity "gods" may have in the reader's mind with the second term ("ghosts"), brings us down to the feminine-chthonic underworld (also explored in detail by Anzaldúa in *Borderlands*) with the inclusion of "scorpions,"[75] and finishes with the reference to "mortals," most properly understood here as a substitute for "men," since a female onlooker might not represent a major inconvenience for the two protagonists. This process of descending gradation thus brings us down from gods to men through ghosts and animals, and the process is repeated throughout the novel as we encounter other demystifying letters about gods (cf. letter Three), ghosts (letter Twenty-four), and men (in both letters Three and Twenty-four and in most of the other letters in the book).[76]

This constant satire of patriarchal motifs common in earlier Chicano stories is one of the many ways *Mixquiahuala* "reads" tradition while constructing an image of a female ideal reader for itself, a reader who will rejoice in the narrator's rebellious and humoristic criticism of tradition and social roles. But there are also explicit ways the ideal audience is so gendered, as the next section will explore.

Dear Reader: Narratees and Other Recipients in
The Mixquiahuala Letters

No other Chicana text has made metatextual discourse on reading as explicit as Castillo's *The Mixquiahuala Letters,* to the point that this part of my analysis might as well have been part of chapter 2. In fact, two separate levels in that discourse are worth exploring here. First, as we saw, Castillo's "prologue," offering several possible readings, works at the extradiegetic level to provide valuable information on the reading process. Internally, Teresa's letters to Alicia are very much shaped by their being addressed to a specific narratee, and they can be analyzed for the strategies that the narrator employs to communicate with that "reader" (Alicia). The two levels are interdependent, as I will illustrate below, and they combine to construct a totalizing commentary on literary communication.

What I am calling the "prologue" here is in fact a short note to the reader,[77] offered alongside three different orderings of the letters: "For the Conformist," "For the Cynic," and "For the Quixotic." The note itself reads as follows:

> Dear Reader:
> It is the author's duty to alert the reader that this is not a book to be read in the usual sequence. All letters are numbered to aid in following any one of the author's proposed options. (n.p.)

After delineating the three options, the note concludes: "For the reader committed to nothing but short fiction, all the letters read as separate entities. Good luck whichever journey you choose! A.C." (n.p.).

While most critics have been content with seeing Castillo's prologue as just a set of guidelines for the reader, I believe it is too restrictive to conceive of this piece as a sort of unidirectional directive from the almighty Author (in ultimate control of the game) to the reader. It is obvious to me that Castillo herself brackets her "Authority" by dedicating her book as follows: "In memory of the master of the game, Julio Cortázar" (n.p.). By thus prefacing her own version of "the game," Castillo is in fact problematizing the dividing line between "authors" and "readers" by acknowledging the influential role of her reading of Cortázar's *Rayuela* in her authoring *Mixquiahuala.*[78] It is as if Castillo had placed a set of mirrors in front of her readers in order to create literary reflections (or refractions) that complicate anyone's "reading" of any of the texts involved. In this sense, Castillo's reader, regardless of whether s/he has read Cortázar or not, is made aware from the beginning that s/he is reading a text that, in turn, "reads" another text. When Castillo's reader is familiar with Cortázar, an extra dimension of potential enjoyment or frustration is opened as s/he tries to figure out what kind of connection establishes itself between the two texts: is it plagiarism, adaptation, retelling, parody, criticism, revision, expansion, or something else?[79] In the case of the reader not familiar with *Rayuela*, enjoyment of the double effect is limited, as any one guess may sound as possible as the next, but the reader is still left to wonder about the possible relationship.

In this game of literary mirrors, Castillo's authorial intrusion into the world of *Mixquiahuala* (via the initials A. C., with which the note to the reader is signed) needs to be regarded as an ironic double positioning of her authorial persona (not entirely unlike what Méndez does in *Peregrinos,* as we saw in chapter 2), for if it is obvious that she is the author of the text we are about to read, it is equally evident that she wants to be perceived as Cortázar's reader as well. It may be, as Peter J. Rabinowitz suggests, that "we live in an age of artistic recycling" (241) in which authors borrow not only techniques, as in this case, but at times even characters and passages from previous authors, thus relativizing their own authority while strengthening the creative role of the reader.[80] But if that is indeed the case with *Mixquiahuala,* one might wonder what the reasons are behind Castillo's interest in recycling Cortázar's "hopscotch" method of reading.

I will propose two complementary hypotheses to answer that question. The first, which concerns generic evolution in cultural analysis, is that Castillo sees in the hopscotch model of reading the (only) twentieth-century postmodern alternative to both the ethnographic diary of the nineteenth- and twentieth-century explorer and to the eighteenth-century epistolary perspectivism of such venerable precedents as Montesquieu's *Lettres persannes* and José de Cadalso's *Cartas marruecas.* Both genres have concerned themselves with cultural analysis, and they are visible presences in *Mixquiahuala*'s literary repertoire, as we will see. My second hypothesis concerns literary theory, as it deals with the role of the reader, and thus I would suggest that Castillo's "recycling" is (or ends up being) an engaged, gendered commentary on Cortázar's well-known differentiation between an active "lector complice" (accomplice reader) and a passive "lector hembra" (female reader).[81]

In terms of generic precedents, the literary model inaugurated by Montesquieu in his *Lettres persannes* (and followed by Cadalso, among many others) proved to be a successful means of engaging the reader in a critical observation of society and culture. This model was largely dependent upon the exchange of letters by different characters, normally of different national and ethnic backgrounds so as to exacerbate the distance between their respective points of view. Through the eyes of the foreign character(s), national readers were exposed to novel ideas and original observations on their way of living. Castillo's novel, which contains a maximum of forty letters (depending on the reading one chooses) by a single character, could be understood to be a somewhat distant offspring of that tradition, inasmuch as most of Teresa's letters are written about her observations of Mexico as a foreigner and/or on the observations by foreign characters about her and her companion.

On the other hand, the absence of letters from any other correspondent seems to bring *Mixquiahuala* closer to the ethnographic journal, as Alvina Quintana has explored. For Quintana,

> Because Castillo's epistolary novel consists of letters that systematically observe, record and describe experiences that take place in the daily life of Mexican American culture—a process we have previously described as the fieldwork method—we can read it as a parody of modern ethnographic and travel writing. (79)

But even Quintana seems to admit that *Mixquiahuala* is much more than "the voice of [Castillo's] informant, Teresa" (80) and thus that the novel's marked heteroglossia demands a radical departure from the ethnographic journal model, even beyond the parodic. While Quintana attributes this effect to Castillo's becoming "an active participant in her own novel" (82), I believe that this effect is achieved, in more ways than one, by including the figure of Alicia as an apparently silent pen pal. I say apparently silent for, although the novel does not contain Alicia's letters to Teresa (thus giving the false impression that the latter is the only one to write), it should be clear to the reader that Alicia does indeed write to Teresa in their fictional world and that she does so frequently.[82] Many of Teresa's letters actually give us an impression not entirely unlike the famous passage of *Rayuela* in which a character is reading a novel by Benito Pérez Galdós and Galdós's text alternates line by line with that of Cortázar.[83] While Teresa does not reproduce the text of Alicia's letters, she does include so many elements from them that the reader is able to reconstruct much of what Alicia actually says almost as if s/he were reading over Teresa's shoulder. In this, *Mixquiahuala* is once again closer to the perspectivist formula first utilized by Montesquieu than to the journal, particularly since Alicia is in part a cultural other for Teresa (Alicia is part Spanish, part Anglo) and a foreigner while in Mexico.

Castillo, then, grounds *Mixquiahuala* in the tradition of the "letters" genre, but with two important points of departure from the original model: the first is the assumption of the nonsequential reading of the type proposed by Cortázar, and the second is the substitution of multiple letter writers for a single narrator whose voice is deeply marked by dialogism and heteroglossia.[84] Teresa is, of course, her own voice, but she is also that of many other characters (most notably Alicia) whom we can perceive through her. The effect that Montesquieu or Cadalso accomplished by allowing their characters to reply to each other's missives is achieved in *Mixquiahuala* by weaving Alicia's voice and responses into Teresa's own discourse. This, in turn, explains the somewhat awkward effect noted by several critics of having Teresa tell Alicia what she already knows (and even what she herself has said).[85] Norma Alarcón, on the other hand, considers the effect disturbing but effective, inasmuch as it allows Castillo to explore cross-cultural influences. After quoting a passage on "mental nepantlism" (i.e., being torn between ways) from Anzaldúa's "La conciencia de la mestiza" (in *Borderlands*, 77–91), Alarcón explains this effect as follows:

> Indeed, this may explain the rationale behind addressing the letters to Alicia, who was Tere's traveling companion and ought to have known what they experienced. Nevertheless, the technique enables Tere to bring out, through Alicia, the Anglo-American cultural influence. ("The Sardonic," 98)[86]

I believe Alarcón is right in explaining the technique as one that belongs to the perspectivist tradition. But I would add a second reason behind the use of Alicia as an addressee: the fact that in doing so Castillo postulates, perhaps for the first time in such an explicit way, a female reader figure for a Chicana text. If, as Judith Fetterley has reminded us, "women's reading of women's novels is not a culturally validated activity" in our society ("Reading about Reading," 151), then the incorporation of Alicia as reader into the textual world of *Mixquiahuala* is a foremost strategy of empowerment and a foundation for beginning to answer Patrocinio P. Schweickart's (echoing E. Showalter) axiomatic question, "What does it mean for a woman, reading as a woman, to read literature written by a woman writing as a woman?" (51).[87] Only in this case, the question should probably be rephrased to read: "What does it mean for a woman, reading as a woman, to read literature written by a Chicana writing as a Chicana?" since Teresa's discourse is as much an internal process of soul-searching on mental nepantlism as it is a reaching out cross-culturally to explain Chicana subjectivity and culture (and hence the importance of having a non-Chicana narratee). The use of a female reader figure works to cement a liberatory female-to-female tradition that moves beyond patriarchal narratives of the past; the use of a non-Chicana female reader figure, at the same time, works to minimize the risk of a simple cathartic consumption of the text in which the actual reader would passively identify with the characters' problems, as Cortázar's "lark reader" would do.[88] And this is where the other point of departure from the "letters" genre (i.e., the nonchronological or even sequential reading) comes into play.

By not including the dates on which the letters are supposedly written, Castillo opens up her text for such possible dis-ordered readings as the ones she herself suggests for the Quixotic and the other types of readers. But as Robert Y. Valentine has noted on this technique in discussing Cortázar's *Rayuela*, "With the pretense of seeking reader participation, Cortázar actually creates a complex system of controls over the reader's involvement in the author's fictional world" (212), an affirmation also supported by Lucille Kerr, for whom the existence of prescribed reading orders "eventually undermines or subverts the freedom which the Table first appears to offer" (31). The same cautionary approach should be used in discussing "A. C.'s" suggestions to the *Mixquiahuala* reader.[89] In fact, as N. Alarcón has noted,

> the apparently unconventional suggested readings actually lead to resolutions that are more conventional than the handful of letters attributed to Tere. . . . If, as readers, we play along with the suggested charts, we are forced to come into terms with the notion that Tere is very much trapped by a variety of ideological nexus that she, and we, need to question and disrupt. ("The Sardonic," 105)[90]

But besides the fact that the different readings give us diverse information on Alicia, an aspect that should not be overlooked is that in choosing any one of the three proposed reorderings of the letters, A. C.'s reader is actually letting herself/himself be labeled and fit into one of those prototypical figures.[91] In this, the proposed readings are actually at odds with other important elements of the book such as the absence of dates in the letters for, if the latter "liberates" the reader from chronology, the former subjects her/him to a certain prescribed course of action. Castillo's "accomplice reader," therefore, would not be the one who follows any of the particular paths laid out for her/him but rather the one who "rebels" against the authorial force in the "prologue" while assuming an active role in the game s/he is being encouraged to enter. This reader will, no doubt, realize that reading possibilities are infinite or almost infinite in an open text like this[92] and that any ordering is nothing but a game, as Castillo herself acknowledges in her dedication. By choosing to write her novel in the form of (nondated) letters (thus invoking both the deferral of reading that any letter implies and a deemphasis of chronology),[93] Castillo advances one step further in Cortázar's goal of "[i]ntentar en cambio un texto que no agarre al lector pero que lo vuelva obligadamente cómplice al murmurarle, por debajo del desarrollo convencional, otros rumbos más esotéricos" (*Rayuela*, 447).[94] Thrown into the narratological side of Alicia, the actual reader (and, in particular, anyone who rereads the novel) is indeed whispered the possibility of other, more esoteric pathways as, at times, s/he would need to go back to reread a certain letter (while bypassing others) or to advance to the "end" to find out whether there is any type of closure.

An additional point of departure from Cortázar that I propose to analyze is the very terminology involved in creating the "game." Since Teresa's letters are intended to be from one woman to another, the male reader is not a narratological presence in Castillo's book. As a consequence, any male reader of the book must feel, to a certain extent, like an uninvited voyeur (a sort of Oliveira reading, this time, over Teresa's or Alicia's shoulders), not unlike the gods, the ghosts, and the scorpions who witnessed Alicia changing her tampon in the ruins of Monte Albán (or else he must feel like one of the mortals Teresa was watching for during that episode, an undesired mortal who somehow sneaks in). And this is where *Mixquiahuala* must be read as a response to Cortázar, even if it acknowledges him as a model. Because contrary to Cortázar's theory of literary reception, in the literary world of *Mixquiahuala* men are the passive receivers, the silent onlookers. Contrary to Cortázar's, Castillo's "lector hembra" is the privileged figure, the active correspondent and the active recipient, answering Teresa's letters and, in so doing, motivating further letters from Teresa. The "lector hembra," exemplified by Alicia, is thus a model for the reader of *Mixquiahuala* and a better one than any of those proposed by A. C. in the prologue (i.e., "the Conformist," "the Cynic," and "the Quixotic").

Furthermore, as Gonzales-Berry has noted, the dedication to Cortázar (coming just after the epigraph by Anaïs Nin that reads "I stopped loving my father a long time ago. What remained was the slavery to a pattern," n.p.) cannot be read without irony as Castillo "leads the reader to decode Cortázar's complicity with a code of patriarchal authority and her own subversive stance vis-à-vis that code" ("The [Subversive]," 117). In this manner, I would add to conclude, Castillo refuses to be Cortázar's "lector cómplice" inasmuch as that position would entail a disapproval of the "lector hembra." Instead, Castillo works to construct a revolutionary image of the "lector hembra" (Alicia) as her own, redefined "lector cómplice." As Castillo herself has said in an interview with Elsa Saeta,

> what I usually say is that "When I'm writing, I'm thinking about a woman who is very much like me reading it." Because that is the void that we have had in literature: a void in the representation in the literature of women who look and think and feel like me and who have had similar experiences in society. . . . When I think about who I would like to read what I write I think about another Chicana very similar to me. (140)[95]

Reaching the Women, Teaching the Men:
Erlinda Gonzales-Berry's *Paletitas de Guayaba*

In discussing Susan Glaspell's "A Jury of Her Peers," Judith Fetterley has made a key statement for understanding not only Glaspell's works but also many other texts written by women, including *Paletitas de guayaba*:

> Glaspell's fiction is didactic in the sense that it is designed to educate the male reader in the recognition and interpretation of women's texts, while at the same time it provides the woman reader with the gratification of discovering, recovering, and validating her own experience. ("Reading about Reading," 154)

Paletitas is, indeed, a novel characterized by its desire to fulfill both communicative missions: to share experiences with its female readers while teaching its male readers about being a woman and a Chicana. In that sense, and although perhaps not as explicitly as Castillo's *The Mixquiahuala Letters, Paletitas* is also a novel about gender and reading.[96]

A combination of letters, journal entries, notes to the reader, interior monologues, metanarrative asides, and other materials,[97] *Paletitas* chronicles its protagonist's (Marina or Mari) journey south to Mexico City by train, as well as her stay there as a student. Through memory, however, the narration goes back to Marina's childhood (and to a previous stay in Mexico during that period of her life), as well as forward to a point in the story's future when the "text" is finalized and assembled.[98]

As a text that engages in rejoicing with the female reader, *Paletitas* employs many of the same strategies we have seen in other works analyzed in this chapter. *Paletitas* assumes, for instance, a shared reading experience with its female audience, at least as it pertains to the realm of the fairy tales.[99] "Cinderella," in particular, is credited with forming Marina's views on marriage and adulthood. As in the fairy tale, Marina expects a fair prince to show up in her life and sweep her up to his castle in the clouds. This is the cultural baggage that Marina brings into her relationship with Steve, her first lover. But since *Paletitas* begins with a farewell letter to Steve, the reader understands this model to be a fallacy, an aspect later reinforced on pages 48 through 50, when Marina tells Sergio, her lover while in Mexico, the story of her affair with Steve.[100] In order to further repudiate the message of submission and lack of agency implicit in traditional fairy tales (and even their euphemistic language), *Paletitas* embarks shortly afterward on a more mature analysis of gender, narration, and language.

The first of two segments in which that critical reading of traditional discourses on women occurs can be found on page 52. In this interior monologue, Marina reflects on machismo and men's sexual obsessions. After a few lines of this, a parenthesis opens with a metanarrative aside in which Marina tells herself:

> (Andale, no te hagas la delicada; no me andes con eufemismos; dale nombre a ese instrumento sagrado, vehículo y portador del ego masculino, el verbo hecho carne, extensión obscena, motivo de nuestro pavor, objeto de nuestro deseo. . . .) (52)[101]

These lines are followed by a list of twenty-three names for the male sexual organ, after which the narrator concludes: "¿No ves lo mejor que se siente una al haberla-lo llamado por sus nombres? ¿Verdad que el nombrar las cosas es encontrarle un hilito a la libertad?" (52).[102] The connection between language, the "craving for utterance" (Thiebaux, 57), and freedom is a most important, self-reflective element of this novelistic reading of tradition. For Marina, female liberation requires such an appropriation of language, an appropriation that is both a narratorial prerogative and a search for a readership with whom to rejoice in the newly found/liberated language.[103]

The rejection of euphemistic discourse is, at the very same time, *Paletitas'* contribution to the feminist reinterpretation of the historical figure of Malintzin Tenepal (or Malinche, or Doña Marina). As *la lengua* (literally both "the translator" and "the language"—and conceivably "the tongue"), Malintzin is the link between the pre-Hispanic and the Hispanic world. As Hernán Cortés's lover, Marina is also the cocreator of the new (mestizo/a) race or the supreme traitress, depending on the interpretation. *Paletitas,* true to its desire to find and express women's voices, incorporates that of Malintzin in a dream in which Marina (the narrator) encounters her namesake. After defending her own personal choices (thus reinforcing her own sense of agency) and explaining to Marina how subsequent interpretations of history will turn her into a symbol of betrayal and promiscuity, Malintzin tells Marina about the veil of silence that will conceal women over the centuries. Like a heavy chain—Malintzin says—the ensuing oppression will asphyxiate the words of many silenced women, but other women—she predicts—will rebel against patriarchal silence and they will use their voices as a weapon against it. This, in turn, will create a new chain, not a chain of silence but one of communication, much as literature can be: "¿Te imaginas, Mari, si se uniera cada una de las cadenas de palabras de cada una de las mujeres del mundo, el poder que se generaría?" (76).[104] I would like to suggest that *Paletitas* becomes for its female readers what the dream of Malintzin had been for Marina, a link in the chain connecting all women: Marina (the recipient of Malintzin's narration) becomes the new speaker that continues the chain by telling her tale to her female addressees (much as Gonzales-Berry does with her female readers), thus inviting them to continue the chain.[105] This new awareness in Marina of the importance of creating a discursive family of women is also evident in a metaliterary fragment in which she articulates her reasons for producing the text that we read:

> Aunque ingénuos [los apuntes] . . . me parecía que revelaban cierta, qué sé yo, actitud interrogativa que quizá podria interesar a quienes se afanan actualmente en [des]cubrir la voz femenina (ni qué decir de la voz femenina chicana) que hasta hace poco había permanecido oculta tras las voces canonizadas de la cultura occidental. (33)[106]

The second passage in which sexuality and discourse are connected in order to propose an alternative reading of tradition will serve to introduce the discussion of the last aspect I want to analyze in this chapter, namely that of the feminist novel that addresses (even partly) a male reader. On pages 63 through 65 Marina explains to Sergio her theory about the differences between the male and the female orgasm and the cultural consequences derived from them. Marina's theory is that the female ability to enjoy multiple orgasms resulted in the male's anxiety to control her sexuality, reducing a "decent" woman's sexual activity to one vaginal orgasm and labeling any other practices as characteristic of nymphomaniacs or prostitutes. This critique of the social and cultural rules of patriarchy would stand in itself as a central moment in the novel. But what makes Marina's discourse doubly valuable, at least as far as reading is concerned, is the fact that it is addressed to Sergio, who serves as a narratee in many of the books' fragments.

As a male addressee, Sergio fulfills a very different role than the one performed by Alicia in *The Mixquiahuala Letters*. His presence allows Gonzales-Berry to turn *Paletitas* into a *novela para educación de hombres* (a novel intended to educate the male reader), not unlike Glaspell's "A Jury of Her Peers." He is, to a certain extent, an example of what I have called elsewhere (following Todorov) a "narratee man"[107]; that is, he exists almost solely so that the protagonist narrator can tell her story—in this case, as she would tell it only to a man, explaining many aspects that she would not need to make clear to a woman. This narratological existence of Sergio is clearly hinted at in a metanarrative aside in which we read the following about him:

> Se habrán preguntado más de una vez por qué es que no le he dado voz ni corporeidad a él. De eso no estoy totalmente segura. No obstante, les ofrezco algunas posibilidades. . . . 1) la técnica la vi en la novela de un escritor mexicano y me dejó muy impresionada; . . . 3) él es realmente el/la lector/a con quien desea Mari entrar en una íntima relación; 4) habrá entre ustedes quienes dirán que él nunca existió, que no es otra cosa que la proyección de su/mi/nuestra visión particular del varón ideal, o sea, el Segundo Sexo inventando al Primero tal como quisiera que fuera. (39)[108]

While the quoted segment is not exempt from a certain dose of humor, options 3 and 4 above confirm Sergio's main narrative role as that of a listener, a recipient, and, no doubt, an internal projection of the male reader Gonzales-Berry hopes to (in)form. It is in this sense that *Paletitas* can be interpreted as a partially didactic novel in which male readers are taught to unlearn certain inherited norms, both cultural and literary, and to assume a different kind of role in their relationships with women. In *Paletitas,* indeed, the Second Sex gets to invent an ideal First Sex.

In order to further delineate the figure of Sergio, he is counterbalanced by Beto, a minor character who shares with the former his political commitment but who is not free from misogynist behavior and patriarchal attitudes. While Beto, a Chicano militant who lives in Mexico City, is a reluctant learner (on page 35 we find out that he has accepted the idea that political liberation is inseparable from women's liberation), Sergio's permanent willingness to listen confirms him as the ideal male reader, to the point that Marina acknowledges her desire to be an open book for him ("Además quiero ser para ti un libro abierto," [61]).

Beyond the cliché, and in true postmodern fashion,[109] Marina's comparison must be taken at face value for, understood as a didactic book for the many potential Sergios out there, she and her story are—quite literally—nothing but an open book, at least while the reading lasts. In this, perhaps, resides the most innovative aspect of *Paletitas* as a feminist work of art, because Gonzales-Berry embarks on a daring challenge of (male) reading habits and of the dangerous inertia to which Annette Kolodny refers in her "Dancing through the Minefield":

> For, simply put, we read well, and with pleasure, what we already know how to read; and what we know how to read is to a large extent dependent upon what we have already read (works from which we've developed our expectations and learned our interpretive strategies). What we then choose to read—and, by extension, teach and thereby "canonize"—usually follows upon our previous reading. Radical breaks are tiring, demanding, uncomfortable, and sometimes wholly beyond our comprehension. (12)

Such a break is what Gonzales-Berry demands from her male readers. To be able, like Sergio, to "read" differently and from different texts. To be able to recognize and value the noncanonized voices of the chain of Marinas that, from Malintzin to her narrator, have tried to assert themselves against a silencing, self-perpetuating tradition. It may prove to be quite an arduous task for a reader to perform, but in it may rest our ability to really change things, *Paletitas* seems to suggest. After all, as Elizabeth Segel has speculated,

> In a society where many men and women are alienated from members of the other sex, one wonders whether males might be

more comfortable with an understanding of women's needs and perspectives if they had imaginatively shared female experience through books, beginning in childhood. (183)

Paletitas may not fully address the literary needs of boy and adolescent readers, but it is indeed a daring and masterful invitation for the adult male reader to learn (and unlearn) about the female and the Chicana experience.

CHAPTER 4

Querido Reader: Linguistic and Marketing Strategies for Addressing a Multicultural Readership

Quiero fer una prosa en romanz paladino
en qual suele el pueblo fablar con so vezino,
ca non só tan letrado por fer otro latino,
bien valdrá, como creo, un vaso de bon vino.
                    —Gonzalo de Berceo[1]

The previous three chapters have dealt with issues that pertain to a reader-oriented literary history of Chicano/a literature by analyzing some of the most influential books by Chicanos/as in recent decades, as well as by exploring the diachronic problematics of audience formation. With that context in mind, this chapter sets out to accomplish a double mission: first, it will examine an array of linguistic and literary strategies employed by Chicano/a authors in order to evaluate the diverse ways their texts succeed in addressing their monolingual and/or multilingual/multicultural readers; then I will analyze extratextual mechanisms that likewise work toward expanding the audience for Chicano/a literature, most important among them marketing and distribution techniques that have catapulted Chicano/a literature to new sales records in the past decade or so.

As my epigraph (taken from thirteenth-century Spanish poet Gonzalo de Berceo) suggests, emerging literatures—as well as those that are on the verge of a major change in direction—face the immediate task of defining the linguistic parameters of interaction with their envisioned readers. Berceo, who wrote in a Latin-dominant literary tradition, embraced the nascent vernacular Castilian ("romanz paladino") in which—as he said—people talked to each other. Strategically, he also embraced the rhetorical position of the vernacular oral tradition of *juglares*, as his anticipated compensation of a glass of good wine indicates.

The impact that Berceo had on medieval Spain in his reclamation of the vernacular for literary purposes is certainly comparable to that of the early contemporary Chicano/a writers in their assumption of a populist discourse and (rather frequently) a colloquial speech. Much as the Spanish friar did, authors such as Tomás Rivera, Rolando Hinojosa, Abelardo Delgado, Ricardo Sánchez, Carmen Tafolla, and José Montoya are to be credited for their literary vindication of the language "en qual suele el pueblo / fablar con so vezino." In doing so, they contributed to creating a sense of national unity among Chicano/a readers from different parts of the country, as analyzed in chapter 1. Likewise, the rhetorical assumption by Berceo of the role of a *juglar* is not unlike the reclamation of the oral tradition by contemporary Chicano/a authors, as seen, for instance, in Tomás Rivera's inclusion of the troubadour Bartolo in his . . . *y no se lo tragó la tierra.*[2]

Of course, there are significant differences between the case of Berceo and that of contemporary Chicano/a literature. Perhaps the most significant one with which this chapter is concerned is that Chicanos/as used either one or two different languages (Spanish and English, with varying degrees of other languages and Caló interspersed) to speak with their neighbors. In that sense, the relationship between English (as the mainstream language of institutions, etc.) and Spanish in the contemporary United States, while still hierarchically unbalanced, is dissimilar from that between Latin and early Castilian in medieval Spain. The contemporary Chicano/a writer who sat down, then, to compose a "prosa" in the language of his/her neighbor was first and foremost faced with deciding which of the several linguistic possibilities (including the bilingual text) to use.

The first part of my analysis in this chapter will deal with aspects pertaining to the linguistic evolution of Chicano/a literature as it relates to the ceaseless transformation of its readership. I am interested in exploring the ways language, marketing, and readership are interrelated and in how the choice of certain language registers reflects a desire to connect with a particular segment of the potential audience and/or a reaction to changed or changing marketing strategies. For this, I will elaborate on previous work of mine,[3] as well as on later studies by others, not available when that earlier work of mine was published.

A clear indication of the importance given since early on to the choice of language in contemporary Chicano/a literature is found in Juan Bruce-Novoa's book of interviews *Chicano Authors,* one of the first printed collections to allow readers an insight into the Chicano/a authors' opinions on the literary process. Two of the questions on Bruce-Novoa's questionnaire were directly related to language use and language choice. The first inquired about the language proficiency of each of the fourteen writers interviewed, focusing both on their childhood and on their contemporary usage. The second, more important for my purposes, asked the writers whether or not Chicano/a literature had a particular language to call its own. Most of the writers' replies emphasized the diversity of linguistic choices available, indicating that such diversity replicated the real-life speech patterns of Chicanos/as (i.e., the language in which people talk to their neighbors, in Berceo's terms). The connection that those responses established between the linguistic choices available for crafting a literary text, on the one hand, and everyday Chicano/a speech, on the other, was reflective of what kind of an audience writers were looking for during that crucial decade in the development of contemporary Chicano/a literature (roughly from the mid-1960s to the mid-1970s): Chicanos/as from their own communities or from other Chicano/a communities nationwide. In a sense, one could say that for these writers it was more important to reach a Chicano/a than to reach a reader in any abstract, undefined sense of the word.

Moreover, since most of their works appeared in nonmainstream publishing venues, these writers were left with an exhilarating freedom for exploring multifold linguistic combinations.[4] This freedom, in turn, translated into a linguistically diverse body of works such as Chicano/a literature had not known before and may not replicate at the same level again. In that sense, and although I disagree with the somewhat ominous tone of his conclusion, Miguel R. López's recent assessment of the narrowing of linguistic choices in recent Chicano/a literature is worth quoting at length, because it is indicative of the prevailing critical perception on the issue. In discussing the work of Ricardo Sánchez, López states:

> In his poems and essays, Sánchez improvises on the speech patterns of marginalized Chicano youths from the barrios and prisons of California and the Southwest. He combines these popular forms with a literate discourse gleaned from his own readings and formal and informal studies. This practice, which was typical of Chicano poetry in the 1960s and 1970s, has been in decline since the early 1980s, when writers, critics, and publishers more aggressively sought to integrate the writings of Chicanos and Latinos into a new broader concept of American literature. Chicano literature thus gained access to substantially larger

English-monolingual audiences, but at the cost of having to
abandon the linguistic diversity that characterized its renaissance
in the 1960s and 1970s. (8)

I do not believe that the linguistic diversity that characterized
Chicano/a literature has been abandoned. What has changed, however,
has been the relative weight acquired by publications in English vis-à-
vis those in Caló, bilingual, or in Spanish. While successful marketing
has catapulted works in English by Chicanos/as to the literary forefront,
community readings, small press publications, and all kinds of locally
distributed writings still reflect the linguistic diversity of earlier decades.
The visibility of these texts, nonetheless, is limited, which may prompt a
critic or a potential reader to dismiss their importance or even to ignore
their existence. The assessment of linguistic diversity in the most recent
Chicano/a literature is therefore complicated by the fact that a significant
split seems to be taking place at the core of this literature, a divide that I
propose to summarize (and somewhat simplify) as the tension between
"the market" and "*la marketa*," that is, between those works that are now
directed to the literary establishment and those that are addressed to the
(always elusive when it comes to definition) Chicano/a community. This
rift, in all likelihood a logical consequence of the institutionalizing drive I
explored in chapter 1, accounts for the apparent closing up of linguistic
(and even literary)[5] choices in Chicano/a literature. When Chicanos/as
wrote (and when they now write) with la marketa in mind, they could
(and can) indulge in linguistic diversification knowing that the target
audience would have no major difficulties with the language(s) used. The
U.S. literary market, however, seems to tolerate little more than a minimal
dose of non-English words for literary or cultural effect. But concluding
from this situation that a qualitative change in the linguistic fabric of
Chicano/a literature has taken place may be exaggerated.

Instead, and in contrast with the assessment by López and others,[6] I
would like to propose that both sides of the "split" I have just identified
(the market vs. la marketa) are equally active nowadays and that only
their respective audiences determine (as was always the case) the linguistic
choices available. In fact, I would also argue that what has resulted from
the progressive closing down of traditional spaces for multilingual
literature (a process that can be noted even by exploring the catalogs of
established small presses such as Arte Público Press and Bilingual Review/
Press) is the creation of alternative spaces and venues for those writers
who could not/would not participate in them. Thus, Chicano/a poetry,

for instance, has seen an invigorated return to community audiences with the creation of performance groups such as The Taco Shop Poets and similar collectives. Likewise, new small presses (Calaca Press being one of the most active among them, including spoken word CDs along with more traditional printed volumes in their catalog) have burgeoned to provide an outlet for bilingual as well as English and Spanish monolingual literature.[7] Even established small presses (such as Arte Público) have expanded the distribution outlets of Spanish-language Chicano/a literature toward nontraditional selling points, including supermarkets, in which Tomás Rivera's . . . *y no se lo tragó la tierra* and Daniel Venegas's *Las aventuras de don Chipote* are among the top sellers.[8] This new editorial movement also includes borderlands presses (some of them operating from Mexico) that publish works in Spanish by Chicano/a authors, hardly a new phenomenon in Chicano/a letters. Finally, even large mainstream presses seem to be opening up to linguistic diversity, as many of them have launched their own series in Spanish, in which some Chicano/a authors have been included along with Latin Americans and Spaniards.[9]

The question, therefore, is not one of reduced linguistic variety but rather of the different critical and marketing support granted to books written in languages other than English. This situation is in part the result of academic indifference and/or lack of commitment toward analyzing the works of nonmainstream, bilingual, or Spanish-speaking Chicano/a authors. As fewer Chicano/a literature critics and professors read (and have their students read) against the grain of commercially successful texts, the reading lists of Chicano/a literature classes begin to reflect a linguistic, and even stylistic and thematic, uniformity that is not reflective of the total body of works written by Chicanos/as. A consequence of this trend toward a new canon of mainstream, commercially successful literature is that many excellent books written in linguistic registers beyond English end up out of print and inaccessible for teachers and readers alike, as anyone who has tried to purchase Erlinda Gonzales-Berry's *Paletitas de guayaba,* Juan Felipe Herrera's *Akrílica,* or Margarita Cota-Cárdenas's *Puppet* in recent times knows.[10]

Contrary to appearances, then, what I propose is that Chicano/a literature continues to be linguistically diverse and that it enjoys a multilingual, heterogeneous audience, understood not as a block but as a series of diverse constituencies that will not (or could not) read all books written by Chicanos/as but only those accessible and meaningful for them. These diverse constituencies include Chicanos/as who are not regular readers but who may read (or listen to) Chicano/a literature occasionally, voracious Chicano/a readers of Chicano/a and other literatures, university and college students, professional readers (professors and critics), non-Chicano/a readers (including national and international audiences), readers who are attracted to a particular segment of Chicano/a literature (i.e., gay or lesbian fiction, women's literature, borderlands texts, detective stories), and others. In this sense, speaking of audiences plural might be more accurate, but for the purpose of clarity, I will use audience (or readership) singular with the proviso that I am referring to such an assorted collection of groups as described above. The title of the next section in this chapter is illustrative of this marked use of the term *readership*, since when I propose that Chicano/a literature creates (or has created) a multicultural readership, I do not mean to imply that every member of that audience is bilingual or bicultural but rather that the texts accommodate (in varying degrees) readers from different cultural and linguistic backgrounds and that they do so intentionally.

Linguistic and Literary Strategies for Addressing a Multicultural Readership

This part of my analysis will draw extensively on Wolfgang Iser's *The Act of Reading*. In the more than twenty years since the American publication of Iser's groundbreaking work, several theoreticians (including Iser himself, who has reworked many of his earlier postulates as he moved into the field of cultural anthropology) have questioned aspects of the German critic's very detailed phenomenological approach to the act of reading. There is no question, therefore, that some elements of Iser's theory of reading need revising, particularly as they are used to analyze bilingual or bicultural texts (even if I believe that many other aspects of his model remain as valid as when he first published it).[11] As I will explore in depth later in this chapter, the major challenge involved in that operation seems to be one of configuring a transcultural repertoire in order to make the text accessible for such a heterogeneous audience. This in turn entails the creation of a set of culturally appropriate strategies intended to secure the reader's uptake.

The task at hand for the bilingual/bicultural writer who wants to communicate with a similarly (or potentially) bilingual/ bicultural audience or with culturally different monolingual audiences is one of finding the appropriate means or strategies on which to base that literary communication, as well as one of creating a world that is (at least partially) understandable to the cultures involved in its reception. The Iserian concepts I will work with in this chapter, then, are those of the "repertoire" and the "strategies." The repertoire, according to Iser, "consists of all the familiar territory within the text. This may be in the form of references to earlier works, or to social and historical norms, or to the whole culture from which the text has emerged" (69). The strategies, on the other hand, "organize both the material of the text and the conditions under which that material is to be communicated" (86), thereby offering the reader possibilities of organization of the text rather than an already fixed structure.

In this understanding of the interaction between text and reader, Iser posits meaning not as a hidden content in the text that the reader has to "find" or decode, but rather as something that is created in the process of reading. For my own purposes, this idea is central since meaning in the transcultural text can only be constructed if the textual "instructions" for the reader are presented in an understandable way for her/him (even if the culture presented may not be entirely familiar to the reader). Furthermore, since blanks and negations will probably be increased in a transcultural text,[12] it is the (complex) task of its author to take the necessary steps to alleviate potential reader alienation.

To a certain extent, therefore, any successful bilingual and/or bicultural text that addresses itself to readers from outside one or both of those cultures (at the same time that it communicates with the bilingual and bicultural reader, of course) must engage in a process not unlike what critic Angel Rama termed "transculturación narrativa" (narrative transculturation) in a book by the same title. Rama's ideas in *Transculturación narrativa en América Latina* stem from his study of Latin American (in particular Andean) literature. He employs the concept of "transculturation" to explore the multicultural reality of Latin America, stemming from a colonization process that establishes "contact zones" throughout the continent, in which autochthonous and imported cultures coexist and modify each other.[13] Rather than using the more restrictive term "acculturation," Rama adopts Cuban anthropologist Fernando Ortiz's term "transculturation," along with Ortiz's reasons for proposing it:

> Entendemos que el vocablo *transculturación* expresa mejor las diferentes partes del proceso transitivo de una cultura a otra, porque éste no consiste solamente en adquirir una cultura, que es lo que en rigor indica la voz anglo-americana *aculturación,* sino que el proceso implica también necesariamente la pérdida o

desarraigo de una cultura precedente, lo que pudiera decirse una parcial desculturación, y, además, significa la consiguiente creación de nuevos fenómenos culturales que pudieran denominarse *neoculturación*. (Quoted in Rama, 32–33, original emphasis)[14]

Rama's approach to writing and reading, then, already presupposes a negotiation of cultures that is not part of Iser's understanding of the "repertoire" as defined above. In other words, where Iser speaks of the repertoire as (among other things) the sum of references "to *the* whole culture from which the text has emerged" (69, my emphasis), Rama's transcultural approach casts the shadow of a doubt over the independence of any one culture from other contact cultures, and that is one of the main reasons for my relying on Rama's ideas for an analysis such as the one I propose to undertake here.

Moreover, Rama's exploration of the tension between languages and cultures implicit in the process of transculturation is also worth mentioning for its useful application to the Chicano/a context as well. For Rama, the transcultural author "ocupa el papel de mediador, uno de los 'roles' característicos de los procesos de transculturación: en él se deposita un legado cultural y sobre él se arquitectura para poder transmitirse a una nueva instancia del desarrollo, ahora modernizado" (99–100).[15] In such a mediating role, it is not uncommon for the transcultural author to appropriate and reclaim popular culture in the vernacular and to transpose it into an artistic category of its own, as Mexican writer Juan Rulfo skillfully does, according to Rama's interpretation (112). Rama also suggests that the transcultural narrative process is different from traditional costumbrismo and regionalism, since what is at stake is not re-creating "local color" but rather an attempt to capture the culture's vitality and to codify it for the appreciation of a reader who may not belong to that culture and who inhabits a different historical circumstance (123).

This latest claim by Rama is worth keeping in mind for the rest of this chapter: transcultural literature is addressed to (or includes among its addressees) a reader who does not (or who does no longer) belong to the culture narrated or re-created in the literary text. In that sense, of course, not all Chicano/a literature engages in the type of transcultural translation that I will explore here, since many Chicano/a texts, in particular those written for *la marketa,* are addressed to a reader who can recognize her/himself as part of the narrated culture, as we saw. But what happens when a "distant reader" (to use J. Cazemajou's term)[16] picks up a transcultural book? And more importantly, what do transcultural texts do to avoid alienating potential "distant readers"? In chapter 1 we saw the ways Rudolfo A. Anaya's *Bless Me, Ultima* succeeded in addressing a multicultural audience. Chapter 3, likewise, provided examples from Chicana literature (e.g., Ana Castillo's *The Mixquiahuala Letters* and Erlinda Gonzales-Berry's *Paletitas de guayaba*). Here, my focus will not be the in-depth analysis of individual works that those chapters entailed but rather a contrastive examination of specific strategies, taken from different Chicano/a texts, and of the ways they relate to the social and literary repertoires of diverse audiences.

One of the most successful strategies employed by Chicano/a authors for approaching multicultural audiences is the use of children characters and/or narrators, as we saw in the case of Anaya's *Bless Me, Ultima* and in Sandra Cisneros's *The House on Mango Street,* among other texts. This should not be surprising, since in reading about a boy or a girl discovering his/her own world, the reader is allowed to share in the excitement of those discoveries, gaining understanding as the character/narrator does so. Values and norms are not taken for granted in this type of texts, as they may sometimes be in those with an adult protagonist, but rather they are to be learned and experienced by/with the character him/herself.[17] By way of example, *Bless Me, Ultima*'s young protagonist, Antonio, is exposed for the first time to the rites a curandera uses to combat black magic in chapter 10 of the novel. As he embarks on a journey to his grandparents' house with Ultima, he seems to wonder aloud as he tries to read the weather for omens:

> But why was the weather so strange today? And why had Ultima brought me? I wanted to help, but how was I to help? Just because my name was Juan?[18] And what was it about my innocent Luna blood that was to help lift the curse from my uncle? I did not know then, but I was to find out. (91)

Antonio's questions serve a double purpose. In the first place, they work toward creating suspense by interrupting the narration, by delaying the episode's resolution, and by making the reader pause and ponder about the very same questions that the character asks himself. But at the same time, Antonio's doubts and ignorance of the ways of witchcraft and curanderismo are helpful in bringing him closer to the culturally distant reader (and vice versa). Whatever the reader does not understand at this point, s/he knows s/he will learn by simply following Antonio's own learning process.[19]

Many other writers, including Arturo Islas in *The Rain God,* employ the same strategy. Islas begins his novel with a chapter titled "Judgment Day," in which the main character, Miguel Chico, is still a child. While this is hardly surprising given the chronological emphasis implicit in most stories of growing up, it is obvious that having a protagonist child in the first chapters of the novel is crucial for Islas, as it helps him in presenting the cultural context for the rest of the narrative in a way even the "distant reader" can understand. Thus, it is no coincidence that in a text so focused on death and its meaning, part of the opening pages are devoted to a cultural framing of this topic:

> They took him to the cemetery for three years before Miguel Chico understood what it was. . . . Mama Chona never accompanied them to the cemetery. "Campo Santo" she called it, and for a long time Miguel Chico thought it was a place for the saints to go camping. (9)

These lines in which, once again, the character is brought to par with even the most distant reader appear to have only minimal potentially unfamiliar cultural content for a multicultural readership (except for the Spanish term used by Mama Chona). But immediately, the narrator seizes the opportunity provided by the child's ignorance about the rituals and customs associated with a camposanto to provide the reader with a synthesis of what death signifies in a Mexican and Chicano/a cultural context: "His grandmother taught him and his cousins that they must respect the dead, especially on the Day of the Dead when they wandered about the earth until they were remembered by the living" (9). These lines, in turn, are followed by a description of activities and customs at the cemetery during the Day of the Dead. Learning with the character, then, the reader is little by little prepared to enter the novelistic world of Islas, which is rich in cultural symbolism in its treatment of death.[20]

Even when no child character or narrator is present, transcultural Chicano/a literature often includes what could be defined as an anthropological or ethnographic discourse that becomes a cultural explanation of sorts for the benefit of the distant readers (much as it happens in my last example from Islas's novel). In chapter 3, I already discussed Alvina E. Quintana's views on Ana Castillo's *The Mixquiahuala Letters* as a parody of the ethnographic journal. In a larger, nonparodic context, Ellen McCracken astutely suggests that this ethnographic discourse is often associated with the description of religious (and, I would add, other cultural) practices that may be foreign to the reader:

> An ethnographic dimension often underlies the description of religious practices in Latina narrative, for the writers embed explanations in the text to aid a variety of "outsiders," who range from non-Chicano or non-Catholic readers to Chicanos and other Catholics who themselves might be unfamiliar with certain popular religious practices. There are no privileged readers of these narratives who can be counted on to have "insider" knowledge of every aspect of religious culture in the accounts. (*New Latina*, 95)

While I believe that McCracken is absolutely right in interpreting this ethnographic dimension of the texts, I disagree with her statement that there are no privileged readers with "insider" knowledge of the narrated practices. Rather, I believe that the existence of such an ethnographic discourse only signals the existence of "unprivileged" readers in need of a cultural explanation, but the cultural exegesis does not preclude the existence of readers with a cultural capital similar to that of the narrator; in fact, close readings of many of these texts would reveal insider's comments or even jokes that the exegesis leaves untouched and that provide the cultural insider with a space of identification with the narrator not available to the distant reader. As a consequence, many of these "ethnographic" texts participate in a long tradition of double-conscious texts (in the W. E. B. DuBoisian sense) that manage to speak to two audiences at the same time, a tradition that includes the memoirs of nineteenth-century Californios,[21] nineteenth-century political novels such as María Amparo Ruiz de Burton's *The Squatter and the Don*,[22] mid-twentieth-century cookbooks,[23] as well as many more recent texts. Aesthetic enjoyment of these texts is thus dependent on the level of cultural proficiency of the reader, who may just grasp the immediate (ethnographic) explanation or rejoice in the feeling that s/he is communicating with the text at a level not available to the uninformed reader.[24]

Another set of strategies employed by Chicano/a authors as a means to familiarize the unacquainted reader with the text's repertoire is based on linguistic translation or transcultural explanation. When carefully done, this results in a meaningful opening up of the text to its cultural outsiders. Unfortunately, too often this practice is based solely on the immediate translation of a sentence in Spanish or of a culturally marked situation.[25] While the latter enables the most distant readers to get a grasp of what is going on (helping their mental ideation of a reality unknown to them), it often becomes a nuisance for the bilingual and/or informed reader and, as such, it is a controversial strategy of mixed aesthetic results. The resource allows for different degrees of translation and/or explanation, and a few examples could serve to illustrate their relative success in dealing with the transcultural reader.

At one extreme of the spectrum are those textual instances in which the nonproficient reader is given no explanation or clues as to what the particular character is saying. Examples range from brief utterances or isolated words in Spanish, usually referred to as ethnic or identity markers,[26] to elaborate sentences in which the reader's cultural and linguistic background is determinant in the construction of meaning. The former, the ethnic marker, is found throughout the history of Chicano/a literature, including those books published in mainstream presses, in which a sprinkling of Spanish is used to provide the reader with a sense of "authenticity." An example of the latter is found in Rudolfo A. Anaya's *Heart of Aztlán*, a text less accessible to the distant reader than his first novel, *Bless Me, Ultima:* "'Se robaron a la novia,' one of [the men] commented. They looked intently at the groom. What would he do?" (40). Unless the reader knows Spanish, he or she would be at a loss to understand why everyone is looking at the groom. The English language context surrounding this utterance is of limited help, but it is indeed possible for the reader to form his or her own (culturally marked) inferences and, perhaps, to imagine that something is wrong with the bride.

The narrative context is of extreme importance in cases such as the one quoted above, and a narrator can include enough clues in it to facilitate the reader's task in decoding an unfamiliar sentence or situation. This is the case in the following example from Ana Castillo's *The Mixquiahuala Letters.* The narrator, Teresa, is telling her friend Alicia about a family scene involving some of Teresa's relatives, including her uncle Chino ("he" in the second line of the quote):

> i said i was going to get a beer as an excuse to get away. He said, no thanks, he already had one. i said it wasn't for him, but for me. The look i got could've stopped a charging bull.
>
> "Y tráeme una para mí y el niño, hija," Tía Filo said, coming around the house with Peloncito by the hand. She gives Peloncito a beer now and then. (13)

No need to know Spanish to guess at the meaning of what Aunt Filo says in this example, even if the (English) monolingual reader would certainly be at a disadvantage when it comes to understanding the reasons for the code switching, as well as the actual contents of Aunt Filo's utterance. Yet the narrator manages to convey enough information to let the reader construct a meaning for this scene while avoiding the cumbersome immediate direct translations that we find in other texts.[27]

An example (among many) of the much more crude type of immediate linguistic translation is found in John Rechy's *The Miraculous Day of Amalia Gómez:* "She pulled away from him. 'Lárgate, desgraciado,' she said. 'Get out of my house, you bastard'" (189). To be sure, direct translation reveals the desire to avoid alienating the reader not fluent in Spanish, including a segment of the Chicano/a audience. But the echo effect that immediate translation creates for the bilingual or bicultural reader becomes too heavy a burden for his/her aesthetic appreciation of the text. Even when the translation is left for the narrator, the repetition of words or of whole utterances always poses a risk for narrative rhythm. Occasionally, Chicano/a writers have opted for narratorial paraphrasing rather than direct translation, a decision that appears to be a slightly more satisfying compromise between the needs of the informed reader and those of the distant one. The following example, from Celso A. de Casas's *Pelón Drops Out,* is illustrative in this respect: "'Vente Pelón, para que veas tu tierra,' beckoned his Papá Ricardo, inviting Pelón to visit the land of his ancestors" (134). The advantage of this type of translation resides in the way the distant reader is given the gist of what the character said while respecting the linguistic peculiarity of the character. In that sense, while the cultural/linguistic insider is still left to deal with narrative repetition, at least the writer allows him/herself a degree of linguistic freedom not encountered in other works to which I will refer again below, in which the narrator simply gives the reader information about which language is used at a particular time without allowing him or her to read the characters' words in their original form.

In truth, representing Spanish-speaking characters in a text written in English is one of the greatest challenges for any Chicano/a transcultural text.[28] This is in no way a unique concern of Chicano/a literature. Rama already explored how difficult it was to negotiate reported speech for José María Arguedas, the Peruvian writer who wrote in Spanish about the Quechuas and to whom many pages of *Transculturación* are devoted. Rama calls attention, for instance, to Arguedas's creation of a "literary language" to evoke (but not reproduce) the way Quechua Indians spoke in Spanish (219). He also analyzes less subtle strategies employed by the Peruvian, including a distortion of syntax to make Spanish sound like Quechua and the use of narratorial intrusion to let the reader know when the characters had said something in Quechua, even if the text was in Spanish (240).

These strategies, which for Rama were a sort of mixed blessing or productive failure, have also been employed in Chicano/a literature with equally mixed results. Syntactic distortion is not very common, but it appeared in some of the early texts of the contemporary period. José Antonio Villarreal's *Pocho* abounds in examples of this narrative tactic, as do others that entail a literal translation from the Spanish, as in the following quote: "'Your mother has given light,' he said to his oldest daughter. 'Go to the creek bed and bring the lamp and cover up the mess with sand'" (41).[29] More recent Chicano/a texts, however, seem to have all but discarded this strategy as an artistic option, although an occasional example is found in novels as recent as Alejandro Morales's *The Rag Doll Plagues:* "In that church I was baptized, made my First Communion and my Confirmation" (73–74).

But narratorial intrusion to let the readers know that the dialogue they are reading in English was supposed to have taken place in Spanish is not at all uncommon: "'Look at him one more time before we go,' Maria said to him in Spanish. 'He's dead now and you will not see him again until Judgment Day'" (Arturo Islas, *The Rain God*, 12). On occasion, as in Max Martínez's *Schoolland,* entirely written in English, the reader is asked toward the end of the novel to believe that the characters actually speak all the time in Spanish: "I had trouble making the connection that the Spanish we spoke all the time was written, too, just like the English in our textbooks. It had never occurred to me that Spanish was also a written language" (242). Appearing, as it does, toward the end of the novel, this comment is a bit surprising, since even direct speech is rendered only in English in Martínez's novel. The narrator, as transcultural mediator, is in this case at one of the most cumbersome positions possible, since the apparent direct speech is revealed (by the narrator) to have been translated, thus reducing the feeling of immediacy that direct speech normally creates in a literary text.

Given this set of difficulties in negotiating transcultural mediation, it does not come as a surprise that some Chicano/a authors have taken the question of translation one step further, beyond the purely linguistic domain. Some writers, such as Rolando Hinojosa, have shown that they are fully aware of the existence of multiple audiences for their books and have dealt with that situation in a more creative way. Hinojosa's work, furthermore, seems to have evolved from the realization that the intent to accommodate all readerships in a single text may prove impossible. Thus, rather than risking alienating his Anglo-American or foreign readership with too little explanation or offending his Chicano/ a audience with constant exegesis, Hinojosa has pursued an entirely different approach. He has effectively rewritten some of his texts, originally in Spanish or bilingual and clearly intended for a Chicano/a audience, in order to bring them closer to the experiences of his Anglo-American (and later, European) public.[30]

The originality of Hinojosa's approach resides in his apparent realization that different repertoires are needed in order to communicate with different audiences. The changes in the repertoire, in turn, have also modified some of the main strategies that he had previously used. For instance, while in *Estampas del Valle* (the first book of his multivolume Klail City Death Trip Series) one of the most prominent literary genres evoked was Hispanic costumbrismo, the English version (titled *The Valley*) reworks the original text and presents it as a description of a picture album, much in the way Michael Lesy had sought to chronicle the experience of Scandinavian settlers in Wisconsin in his *Wisconsin Death Trip* (Martín-Rodríguez, *Rolando Hinojosa,* 71–75).

But in the case of Hinojosa, the rewriting of the text for a new audience goes well beyond the use or recalling of a different literary genre. The whole set of social norms that Iser believes to form part of the repertoire is also altered when Hinojosa envisions a different, transcultural readership. Compare the following two passages. The first is from Hinojosa's *Klail City y sus alrededores.* The second is from the author's rendition of that text in English, now titled simply *Klail City.* The Spanish version reads as follows:

> Aquí no hay héroes de leyenda: esta gente va al escusado, estornuda, se limpia los mocos, cría familias, conoce lo que es morir con el ojo pelón, se cuartea con dificultad y (como madera verde) resiste rajarse. El que busca [*sic*] héroes de la proporción del Cid, pongamos por caso, que se vaya a la Laguna de la Leche. (*Klail City y sus alrededores,* 11–12)

A more or less literal translation of this paragraph would say something like: "There are no legendary heroes here: these people go to the toilet, sneeze, blow their noses, raise their families, know how to die when the time comes, are not easily broken, and (like green wood) will not split. He who looks for heroes like El Cid, for instance, may as well go to Milk's Lagoon." This type of translation would need, of course, some transcultural explanation that I have not provided. It would need, perhaps, to explain or hint at who El Cid was, it would definitely need to try to convey what "morir con el ojo pelón" implies in the vernacular Chicano/a Spanish, and more importantly, it would need to account for the cultural importance of the reference to wood in a rural Chicano/a society and, in this context, to the play on words implicit in "rajarse," meaning both "to be split" (referring to wood) and "to go back on one's word" or "to chicken out" (referring to people).

Rather than embarking on such a cumbersome process, Hinojosa opts for a complete change of repertoire. The previous passage appears as follows in the English-language version:

> Caveat: one shouldn't expect to find legendary heroes here; our taxpayers go to the toilet on a regular basis, sneeze on cue and blow their noses too, as the limerick says. Some raise families, and most of them know Death well enough, but (innocents that they are) they don't pretend to know what it is that usually happens to them *after* death. As a rule, the Texas Mexican, being a Texan, is a hard nut to crack, and this will be seen enough and throughout. (*Klail City*, 9, original emphasis)

"La gente," a culturally marked term for "people," becomes in the English version "taxpayers" and "Texas Mexican," a term of little usage among Texas Chicanos/as when they speak in English (Paredes, *Folklore and Culture*, 37–38). On the other hand, people's endurance is no longer associated with Mexican or Chicano/a culture (via the reference to "madera verde" and "rajarse") but rather is related to their being Texan. Finally, the mention of a limerick has substituted for the intertextual reference to El Cid. It is obvious that the text is courting a different public, and hence it has switched the parameters along which communication with that audience would be verified.[31]

While cultural nationalists might decry the loss of Chicanismo in the text, and perhaps they would accuse Hinojosa as translator of being a traitor to his own text, it is important to keep in mind that *Klail City* is not a translation but a transcultural version of *Klail City y sus alrededores*, and as such it entails change, conversion, and even destruction as its Latin etymology (*vertere*) conveys (Corominas, 604). In the process of re-creating the text in a different language and for a different audience, the transcultural operation also involves speaking about one culture in meaningful, understandable terms for another.

These are by no means the only strategies observed in Chicano/a texts for addressing a multicultural readership, but they are probably the most salient of all. What they reveal is the existence of a rather complex interaction between bilingual/ bicultural texts and their readers. This interaction, I believe with Iser, is made possible by their sharing a set or sets of norms (social and literary) transmitted via an assortment of acceptable procedures. But in the case of a text intended for a diverse multicultural audience, the configuration of the repertoire becomes a very different operation from that found in a text more or less grounded in a single national culture, since not one but several sets of norms are working at the same time in the relationship created between the text and the target audience.

Authors of transcultural texts, therefore, seem to be much more aware of their texts being different things to different people, as well as of their need to transcend barriers and borders that could impede the reader's interaction and thus the need to come up with novel strategies. From the early bilingual face-to-face editions typical of Quinto Sol and other Chicano/a presses in the 1970s to Hinojosa's transcultural reworkings, a long trend of experimental writing has been set.

In seeking to create and address a multicultural readership, Chicano/a texts are reacting to the changed environment in which we are living, one in which borders tend to become contact zones rather than geographical markers, cultures are understood as processes and not as essentially predefined, writers become (of necessity) transcultural mediators, and languages infiltrate other languages in everyday and literary practices.

Marketing and Labeling Chicano/a Literature:
On the Uses and Abuses of Magical Realism

After exploring some of the ways certain Chicano/a texts operate to meet their transcultural readers halfway, I will now concentrate on some of the extratextual resources that have been utilized to market and promote Chicano/a literature to a (mainstream) multicultural audience, in the sense defined earlier in this chapter. As I will describe below, many of these resources have resulted in the commodification of Chicano/a literature and in the creation of a visual and verbal code of (minimal) semiotic elements by virtue of which the reader can identify a particular book as Chicano/a or, at least, Latino/a. Even if, as McCracken suggests (*New Latina,* 12), this attempt at co-optation is never entirely successful, the fact remains that a whole "grammar" is used now to define and make identifiable the Chicano/a text in mainstream sources. Missing (or not mentioning) at times many of the salient aspects of the books they illustrate or comment on, reviewers, illustrators, and other analysts instead concentrate on a few traits that the mainstream reader either expects or is taught to expect in works by Chicanos/as. Robert Escarpit's well-known concept of the "multiplication of meaning" can be of help in exploring these elements, because it accounts for both the external appearance of a particular book or books as well as for the discourse associated with their presentation to potential readers. In the words of Cathy N. Davidson,

> Robert Escarpit has noted that a book (as opposed to a manuscript) is characterized by a "multiplication of meaning," a public and changing act influenced by material considerations (book morphology and production) and nonmaterial ones (the previous experiences readers bring to their texts). ("The Life," 173)

In the case of Chicano/a literature available in mainstream markets, the material considerations involved in this "multiplication of meaning" seem to revolve around two main elements: cover (and back cover) art, characterized for what seems to be a predefined set of colors and images, and critical sponsorship, in the form of quotes and blurbs from well-known figures of the (normally mainstream) literary world. I am purposefully leaving out of the discussion, at this point, the issue of the previous experiences readers bring to their texts, which I have explored in detail in earlier chapters. Suffice it to say that indeed the previous experiences (and preconceptions) of reviewers and commentators are in part responsible, along with marketing requirements, for the lack of variety in their comments. Even when mainstream successful Chicano/a and Latino/a authors are called upon to comment on the work of their fellow writers, their comments seem to adjust to what the press publicists are willing to emphasize, as we will see.

The artistic presentation of a Chicano/a book published by a mainstream press is highly consistent, and it tends to create an immediate visual identifier for the reader who is browsing around the shelves and display stands in a bookstore. The ensuing homogenization of forms and colors is meant to create an ersatz artistic "authenticity," aided at times by the insertion of highly recognizable Mexican curio images such as lottery cards, serapes, and the like. In turn, the discursive apparatus accompanying Chicano/a books in the mass markets is likewise reduced to a set of limited (but almost omnipresent) identification traits. Blurbs and review quotes seem obsessed with referring to Latin American magical realism and affiliating Chicano/a texts to that (by now old, tried, and tired) literary trend as belated by-products of the Latin American imagination. As I have explored elsewhere, this response is not only misleading from a literary history point of view but also politically charged, as it works to make a national (i.e., U.S.) literature appear foreign ("Border Crisscrossing," 197–99).

The label "magical realism" routinely applied to most Chicano/a texts that enter the mainstream is, in fact, the single most important solecism currently haunting the marketing of Chicano/a texts, as it works to reduce these texts to a quaint, facile imitation of what was a booming, revolutionary literary movement a few decades ago. When used by non-Latinos/as, as the term is mostly used, the label "magical realist" employed to define a Latino/a text suggests a reductionist approach to minority literature that actually works to make it meaningless and insignificant, much in the same way Paul Lauter has analyzed critical labeling with respect to race and gender ("Race and Gender").[32] As such, the magical realism definition is now being used to exoticize the texts to which the term is applied, to make them foreign rather than a product of the U.S. literary arena. A few examples from *The New York Times* will illustrate my point.

The first illustration I will use, in order to give the reader a sense of how the differences between Chicano/a and other Latino/a texts is consistently erased, is a graphic advertisement for the paperback edition of Cuban American writer Cristina García's *Dreaming in Cuban*. The ad reproduces the book cover, which presents a woman's face from the eyes up (thus suppressing her mouth and suggesting muteness). While two of the three critical excerpts reproduced in the ad sidestep the almost inevitable issue of magic, the main headline in the advertisement nonetheless reads: "The Magical Bestseller!," a claim further reinforced by an excerpt from a review in *The New York Times* by Michiko Kakutani, who describes García's novel as follows:

> DAZZLING . . . REMARKABLE . . . Fierce, visionary, and at the same time oddly beguiling and funny, [this] is a completely original novel. . . . [Garcia] has produced a work that possesses both the intimacy of a Chekhov story and the hallucinatory magic

of a novel by Gabriel García Márquez. [bracketed information appears as such in the original] (20)[33]

The originality attributed to the novel quickly fades away when mentions of Chekhov and, most importantly, García Márquez are later included in the excerpt from the review reprinted in the ad. The reference to García Márquez works to make *Dreaming in Cuban* a sort of generic novel (in the sense one speaks of a generic drug), which it is not. Mainstream presses' marketing departments seem to be caught between the rock of promoting a particular book's originality and the hard place of making it familiar to the reader. The normal outcome of this dilemma, when it comes to ads for Chicano/a and Latino/a books, is a feeble, unsubstantiated claim of originality, followed by a barrage of commonplace identifiers that include, at the very least, the word "magic" (along other praising adjectives that are not particular to this segment of the press's catalog) and a seemingly obligated comparison with Colombian novelist Gabriel García Márquez.

The critical affiliation of Chicano/a and Latino/a books to magical realism and to García Márquez's wake has become such a major burden for Chicano/a and Latino/a literature that it would give to a reader only exposed to mass-marketed texts the false impression that all valuable literature produced by Latinos/as is nothing but a continuation or imitation of that particular writer's work.[34] This rhetorical move deprives a whole body of literature of its own historicity and novelty, while (implicitly or explicitly) attempting to replicate a previous successful marketing strategy, the one precisely promoting the so-called Latin American boom, which included García Márquez among its best-selling authors. Mainstream commercial presses seem to care little about erasing several decades of Chicano/a literary production from the potential readers' minds, as there are no mentions in their ads of Chicano/a writers from the 1960s or 1970s, for instance, as possible influences or models for younger writers. Rather, the uninformed reader of mainstream reviews and blurbs will receive from them the incorrect idea that Chicano/a literature during those decades was either nonexistent or that it was taking place elsewhere, like Colombia and the rest of Latin America, where magical realism was an important literary trend then; this latter possibility would work toward making Chicano/a literature appear as an immigrant literature, a move that would counter, once again, its U.S. status and that could describe only some of its texts.[35]

The routine comparison with García Márquez's work can border at times on the literary insult, both to the source and to the alleged epigone. In an advertisement for Ana Castillo's *So Far from God*, also published in *The New York Times*,[36] the reviewers (and the ad as an overall text) indulged in such a slighting exercise of comparative literary analysis. The information, in this case, is of particular interest since this was Castillo's first book published originally by a non-Latino/a press and at the time of publication she was already a well-known figure in Chicano/a literary circles. The headline for this advertisement reads as follows: "Everyone loves ANA CASTILLO'S 'wondrous'* new novel!" (18). The adjective "wondrous," according to the asterisk attribution within the ad, is taken from a review by Patricia Holt that appeared in *The San Francisco Chronicle*. While the excerpt from Holt's review reprinted in the ad proclaims *So Far from God* "the breakthrough novel about Chicano life that Ana Castillo was born to write," a second reviewer, Barbara Kingsolver, goes far beyond when she decides to recommend the book as a gift: "Give it to people who always wanted to read 'One Hundred Years of Solitude' but couldn't quite get through it." Aside from the fact that *One Hundred Years of Solitude* is one of the best-selling books of all times (thus making it difficult to understand why the reviewer would suggest that people cannot somehow finish reading the book),[37] the comparison turns Castillo's work into less than a worthy epigone of magical realism, something we could call instead "magical realism lite." As such, the book is advertised as ideal for readers who are not able to digest what is normally considered to be the single most important magical realist novel but who would still be able to enjoy the "wonders" contained in a "lighter" narrative. Disregarding (by omission) the sheer originality of Castillo's *The Mixquiahuala Letters* (even if Castillo's first novel had been by then reprinted and repackaged by an East Coast press), as well as its significance for the history of Chicano/a literature, Castillo's reputation is here transferred from her position as a leading voice in the innovative contemporary Chicana/o literary arena to that of an undemanding late offspring of the highly patriarcal Latin American magical realist trend. Furthermore, if we conjoin once again Kingsolver's comment with that by Holt as they appear in the ad, a reader unfamiliar with Chicano/a literature may very well conclude that since this is supposed to be "the breakthrough novel about Chicano life that Ana Castillo was born to write" (in Holt's words), not much of importance must have happened in the recent history of Chicano/a literature that might be worth reading, thus once again diminishing the literary value of earlier works by herself and others.

The downsizing in importance of Castillo's work (and, by implication, of earlier Chicano/a literature) is a marketing ploy that may be part of a larger trend already noticed by N. Zill and M. Winglee in their book *Who Reads Literature?* According to Zill and Winglee,

> Among the trends that may be working to the detriment of literature appreciation are: . . . the advent of the so-called "lite-era," in which the mass media and commercial advertising have trained viewers and readers of all ages to be impatient with any work that requires serious and sustained attention. (77–78)

But it could also be interpreted as a crass attempt at co-optation that closes up the space for self-representation and agency (perhaps the foremost goal in the entire history of Chicano/a letters) while transforming the text into a sort of literary curio for the effortless consumption of a touristlike reader who is committed to nothing but having a good time and bringing home some eye-pleasing and fashionable exotic souvenirs. The commodification of these literary works is never complete, as McCracken asserts (*New Latina,* 12), in the sense that there are multiple layers in the texts themselves that resist co-optation. But for readers unfamiliar with Chicano/a letters who are brought to reading *So Far from God* (or any other Chicano/a text) through advertisements like the one quoted above, the information contained in the ads will play an important role (as part of what Escarpit called "previous experiences" or what Iser calls "repertoire") in whatever opinion they form of the book and even perhaps, by implication, of its author and her/his culture. Not surprisingly, the marketing strategies employed by non-Chicano/a or Latino/a controlled presses differ quite noticeably from those first started by Quinto Sol Press and then continued by Arte Público Press, the Bilingual Review/Press, and others, as discussed in chapter 1. Therefore, and in light of the commodification of the Chicano/a literary product that I am analyzing here, the question that begs asking is to what extent Chicano/a literature is being driven or, at least, conditioned by marketing practices that result in pressure on younger and even established writers as to what kinds of books they will be able to print and sell.[38]

In a Chicano/a context, Cecile Pineda, whose books have been published by non-Chicano/a presses, has been one of the first and fiercest voices in decrying the dangers resulting from the commercial pressure to write "lite" fiction and to abandon more serious projects:[39]

Today's marketplace, as well, with its glorification of the megabuck blockbuster, presents an ominous threat to the serious writer. There is a dwindling American audience for works of depth or darkness; but writers want to reach out. That is why we write. To reach large audiences, we are encouraged to create "popular" works, works that entertain and amuse. How can we manage to reach large audiences with more difficult works? And how does the marginalization we experience as Chicanas further separate us from the tyrannical and culturally straightjacketed self-identified mainstream? ("Deracinated," 66)

Pineda's assessment of the literary panorama seems accurate when one considers those books released by what she terms "the culturally straightjacketed self-identified mainstream." Her last question, in particular, is worth entertaining because of the dramatic shift in the reception and commercialization of books by Chicanas/os that has occurred in recent years (which may, in turn, reveal some of the marketing stratagems employed to package Chicano/a literature for mass consumption). As recently as 1989, Ellen McCracken denounced the lack of mainstream critical and popular attention accorded to Sandra Cisneros's *The House on Mango Street*. McCracken described Cisneros's book as follows: "Difficult to find in most libraries and bookstores, it is well known among Chicano critics and scholars, but virtually unheard of in larger academic and critical circles" ("Sandra Cisneros," 63); she then explored the main reasons for this marginalization, including gender and ethnicity and the treatment of women's issues, among other factors, and concluded that "Cisneros's text is likely to continue to be excluded from the canon because it 'speaks another language altogether,' one to which the critics of the literary establishment 'remain blind'" ("Sandra Cisneros," 63). Yet barely two years later, Cisneros had arguably become the most famous Chicana/o writer of all times, surpassing even Rudolfo A. Anaya and securing the attention of most literary circles and publications in the United States and even abroad. The tension between marginalization and commodification that Pineda identified as affecting Chicana writers is further problematized when books like *Mango*, originally celebrated for its contestatory and counterhegemonic impulses, are subsequently repackaged and reprinted for a larger market and when authors like Cisneros cease to be marginal and become central or, at least, evocations of the "presence of an absence" (de Certeau's term), as McCracken suggests is the case for mainstream successful Latina writers fifteen years after her article on *Mango* appeared.[40] Interestingly, in her more recent analysis of Cisneros's work, McCracken observes that the tension I have alluded to results in a different balance in the case of Cisneros's *Woman Hollering Creek,* a more recent collection of short stories, originally published by a mainstream press and therefore not subjected to the fight for recognition that *Mango* had to undergo:

> Both the hegemonic and the oppositional intersect in this text [*Woman Hollering*], not because Cisneros is politically ambivalent, but because in order to reach a wide audience, she is dependent on a mainstream publishing outlet bent on selling her as a commodity. (*New Latina*, 15)

While the mainstream-published Chicano/a text may still contain oppositional messages and politics, and while those messages may be understandable to a Chicano/a and to an informed reader, mass-marketing commodification has worked to ensure that a large segment of the potential readership may approach these books as commercial successes rather than as artistic commentaries on social issues. Warner Books editor Colleen Kapklein seems to acknowledge as much when commenting on Rudolfo A. Anaya's contract with her press:

> This author has a huge following, was poised to launch into the mainstream. . . . We saw him as having a strong track record, and he was taking a new direction in his work—telling more commercial stories, wanting to reach a wider audience—a direction we'd want him to take. (Quoted in W. Clark, "The Mainstream," 24).

What precisely constitutes a "more commercial story" is never defined at length by editors and agents. Only the reference to a wide or wider audience seems to be ubiquitous in statements such as that by Kapklein. But the attempt to reduce Chicano/a and Latino/a texts to the status of exotic commodities goes well beyond the expectation of a "commercial" plot line and is readily observable in the treatment given to book covers, authors' pictures, and other similar external details aimed to attract and (pre)condition the judgment of a potential reader. Even if they have been largely disregarded in the past, their analysis becomes a necessity for the contemporary literary critic.[41] To use Cathy N. Davidson's words, "[A]lthough one may not be able to judge a book by its cover, one can read what a given cover signifies" ("The Life," 171); in particular, I would add, when a given style or graphic treatment is repeatedly applied to books by authors belonging to a certain ethnic, cultural, or any other kind of group. In the case of Chicano/a and Latino/a literature,[42] a style of presentation that accentuates the childish, the naive, the colorful (with frequent recourse to pastel colors) is being used to create an immediately recognizable, "culturally marked" graphic image. Even if some of these elements may at one time have been part of a Latin American or Latino/a artistic language and discourse, their appropriation by outside institutions and their repeated use as ethnic markers work to transform them into a monological commercial language, producing what we might term a "Tacobellization" of the Latino/a image,[43] as books indeed assume the pleasant, nonoffensive, decorative appearance of a "southwestern" franchise restaurant. Since many books that were originally published by Latino/a owned and/or controlled presses are now available in new editions from mainstream houses, a comparison between presentation styles in both markets would be significant to illustrate that process.

A striking case is that of Sandra Cisneros's *The House on Mango Street.* The original Arte Público Press edition featured a quasi-expressionistic drawing of an urban setting by Narciso Peña, quite appropriate for the referential world alluded to in the novel. The Random House edition, by contrast, has opted for a painting by Nivia González of three women with their eyes and their mouths closed, clothed in pastel color shirts. Although the cover still recalls one episode from the book (the story "The Three Sisters"), the artistic idiom of the Random House packaging abruptly alters the reader's expectations that the Arte Público cover might produce, even if the painting used is by a Chicana artist. The impression that a reader familiar with Chicano/a books gets when seeing this cover is that of the much decried "'Festivals of Diversity,' in which women of color are exhibited as exotic dolls in native costume" (Ortega and Sternbach, 13). In addition, in the substitution of the disturbing agglomeration of buildings and overimposed faces found in Peña's cover by a much more soothing and serene composition in the Random House edition, one might find a visual correlative for the differences in the book's reception that I have illustrated between the 1989 article by McCracken and Cisneros's later reputation as the most recognizable name in Chicano/a letters.[44] The "threatening" aspects of the 1984 text, which provoked some harsh criticism even within Chicano/a circles,[45] are aptly reflected in the somewhat disturbing cover of the 1984 edition. By contrast, potential readers are not likely to be put off by the rather inviting

Random House cover, in which they can very well recognize the conventional forms and colors of an essentialized Latino/a look. To this end, even Sandra Cisneros's picture on the back cover appears to have been treated so as to make her skin darker than it actually is.

A similar manipulation of artistic registers is found in the Doubleday edition of Ana Castillo's first novel, *The Mixquiahuala Letters*. As was the case with Cisneros's *Mango*, *Mixquiahuala* has been presented to readers in quite a different fashion by the two presses that have published it. The Bilingual Review/Press original edition is austere, in blue, black, and gray tones, with just one image of what looks like a sheet of paper slightly off centered and inscribed with the novel's title and the author's name. This cover, designed by Christopher J. Bidlack , suggests a typed letter, thus making a connection with one of the most salient elements of Castillo's book, an epistolary novel, as we saw in chapter 3. By contrast, the Doubleday edition has opted for a much more colorful cover in which reproductions of Mexican lottery cards (used in a game somewhat similar to Bingo) are arranged around the cover, with the one representing number 27 (El corazón/The Heart) slightly bent.[46] While the cover still connects with elements of the book—part of *The Mixquiahuala Letters* takes place in Mexico—the implicit message in the cover is that this is a Mexican book and not a U.S. book. A second suggestion is that this book belongs to the ethnic curio type of consumable object as do the Mexican lottery cards reproduced on its cover (the cards are readily available from most curio shops along the U.S.-Mexico border and in the United States). In this sense, the Doubleday cover reifies and confuses the Chicano/a and Mexican cultures as it neutralizes the many contestatory elements in Castillo's novel by emphasizing in the book's wraps a folkloric and rather static image of one of the cultures that nurture it. Cultural reification is further accentuated by slightly bending the card that depicts a heart. The implication a bookstore browser might get from this visual clue is that the book must certainly be one of those stereotypical love stories about "romantic Mexico," a message further enhanced by some of the other cards represented on the cover (the drunkard, the bottle, the lady, the mermaid, and Death). The nontraditional love stories so carefully constructed in Castillo's novel are almost thus reduced by the graphical references in the cover to those of the dime novels in which Mexican and Chicano/a characters have frequently appeared in clichéd roles. Finally, it is ironic that for a book on letter writing the publishers have selected a cover representing the Mexican lottery, which uses images along the corresponding numbers so that an illiterate segment of the population, who could not recognize the numbers, would still be able to play the game by looking only at the pictures.[47]

Lest the reader think that this process of commodification only affects covers for books by women, it may be worthwhile to look at the covers of Ron Arias's *The Road to Tamazunchale*. This is an even more complex case, since *Tamazunchale* has been published by four different presses in the United States.[48] The first edition, issue 16 (vol. 4, no. 4), of the *West Coast Poetry Review* is the simplest of them all: an orange cover with the title and the author's name written diagonally across it. Only a drawing on page 2 is used to somehow give an ambiance to this edition: the drawing depicts two men with loaded burros in front of a mountainous background that one could easily associate with Mexico (perhaps Peru, although llamas or alpacas would have been expected in that case). This first edition comes from a non-Chicano/a press that clearly operates with the graphic (stereotypical) images associated with Mexico in mainstream America. Burros play no role whatsoever in Arias's novel, but they constitute a token image of Mexico and South America in many Anglo Americans' minds.[49] By contrast, the second edition, published by Chicano-owned Pajarito Publications, has a rather enigmatic cover by Desolina in which we see what looks like the figure of a woman (possibly Carmela) next to an enlarged picture of half of the face of a hairless man (most likely her uncle Fausto after skinning himself). Both figures are overprinted with a geometrical design that looks like a weaving pattern arranged in the shape of a fingerprint. This cover's foremost value resides in its evocative force that visually complements the rather enigmatic text by Arias and his fairly unpredictable and nonstereotypical characters and plot.[50] Likewise, the cover by Desolina refuses to depict any recognizable or folkloric image that might identify the characters as Chicanos/as and/or Mexicans; the implication, of course, is that the reader should treat the characters as individuals and not as types.

The third edition of Arias's *Tamazunchale* was published by Bilingual Review/Press, also a Chicano/a publishing house, and its cover was designed by Christopher J. Bidlack and based on a drawing by José Antonio Burciaga. The art on the cover represents a black-and-white sketch of a road, with a road sign that reads "TAMAZUNCHALE. 10 000 HAB." Simple enough to be a visual equivalent of the book's title (what we see in the cover is in fact the graphical road to Tamazunchale), this image is worth a second look, as it contains a few elements that supply additional information to the careful (and informed) reader. The letters "HAB" in the depicted road sign, for instance, may be wholly unintelligible for the English monolingual reader.[51] A Spanish-proficient reader, however, will know that HAB is an abbreviation of "Habitantes," the Spanish equivalent (in this case) to "population." While most readers would have no trouble guessing the meaning of this Spanish abbreviation, appearing as it does on a village road sign marker, non-Spanish-proficient readers would be forced to guess rather than read and thus feel a slight inadequacy when approaching the book. The resulting effect is important in two ways. First, the cover hints at a particular group (who may or may not be the same envisioned by Arias) as the target audience for this book: Spanish-proficient bilingual readers, thus suggesting a Chicano/a or Latino/a audience as the ideal readership. In addition, this minimal inclusion of Spanish on the cover is significant because of the way it serves the cover artist to represent Mexico.[52] While mainstream covers tend to use folkloric and touristically recognizable visual referents to signify cultural or geographical location, as seen, the Bilingual Review/ Press's cover avoids that kind of reification by using language instead to represent one of the action's locales. The understatement of this artistic strategy contrasts with the exaggeration of local color found in the mainstream covers already analyzed. As if to further prove the point, the cover for the fourth and most recent edition of Arias's *Tamazunchale,* by Doubleday, resorts once again to the colorful style that has become equated with Latino/a books in the mainstream publishing industry imaginary. The cover, illustrated by Robert Clyde Anderson and designed by Julie Duquet, represents a male figure (in all likelihood, Fausto) asleep over what looks like an iconographic cross between a bed and an open field (it has the appearance of grass). Several other figures can be seen in the background (representing a theater's proscenium), including a well-dressed woman (either Evangelina or Carmela) and an upright ladder with a parrot sporting a human face (a reference to Fausto's parrot, Tico-Tico, even if the human face is not part of the text). The parrot is perched on one of the steps in the ladder, and it holds a snow cloud. A walking skeleton peering from behind the curtain is also noticeable in the background. Most of the motifs and allusions in this cover do refer directly to the book or to the spirit of the book, so distortion is minimal in this case as compared to that of *The Mixquiahuala Letters.* But by virtue of its colors, the typeface employed, and its figurative language, this cover nonetheless positions the book as part of a homogenized marketable category of ethnic art and/or literature that, when so controlled by group outsiders, immediately becomes suspect as an objectification of difference that threatens to render it meaningless. As McCracken suggests,

> The optic of the assimilated Other who still affords a pleasing narrative exoticism—advanced both in reviews and in the imagetexts on the front covers—frames and helps to shape the interpretation of many fictional works by Latinas even before they are read. (*New Latina,* 27)

This can be said to be the case for the Doubleday cover, since it contains no individualizing or estrangement effects, like the Pajarito and Bilingual Review/Press covers.

What I am illustrating with these examples is my claim that the repackaging and marketing of Chicano/a literature that some of the U.S. mainstream presses have undertaken tends to create a homogenizing visual language to mark and identify the books as Latino/a. While this seems to be a successful marketing strategy, it implies nevertheless a dangerous essentializing of the culture(s) these books represent. In this sense, mainstream co-optation of and influence over this literature involves two dimensions whose effects on Chicano/a cultural production in the future are yet to be seen. First, by reprinting books already published by Chicano/a presses and widely respected in Chicano/a intellectual circles (*Mango, Mixquiahuala, Tamazunchale, Bless Me, Ultima*), mainstream presses can claim to be interested only in facilitating widespread access to these texts, therefore denying any editorial interference with Chicano/a literary production. Yet by manipulating the covers and creating the homogenized style I have briefly summarized, the presses are already interfering with the literature they reprint by altering the material conditions of reception—creating different expectatives in readers and appealing to a different cultural sensitivity, for instance. Second and more importantly, in thus acquiring the rights of publication for some of the best-known Chicano/a books and in subsequently creating an outlet for newer, unpublished Chicano/a literature, mainstream presses are ensuring themselves a prime spot in the development and marketing of future Chicano/a literature. The (important) difference in this second dimension is that while reprinted books have a history of their own prior to their publication in mainstream venues and are therefore less subject to commodification, new books have no previous exposure to Chicano/a and non-Chicano/a readers. The presses have, in this latter case, a more ample space for the marketing preconditioning of the readers and editorial intervention in the manuscripts. It would be difficult to discern whether or not this intervention is at the root of certain thematic and characterization trends observable in recent Chicano/a literature, but the fact remains that the appearance of characters who fly, magical or supernatural events, and many other traits that facilitate the identification and commercialization of this literature as part of magical realism have increased dramatically in the last few years.

By contrast, it is necessary to note that the term "magical realism" was never used for marketing purposes by Chicano/a presses and that it was virtually absent from the vocabulary of Chicano/a literary criticism until, at least, the late 1980s, when some critics started using it to account for some more recent novels such as Alejandro Morales's *Reto en el paraíso*.[53] Chicano/a literature critics who did so were more interested in the transgressive possibilities inherent in magical realist fiction than in its marketable appeal. Representative of that trend is the work of Carl Gutiérrez-Jones, who writes about the ontological transgressions typical of magical realism (i.e., the seemingly undisturbing appearance of ghosts and other such phenomena) as a form of counterdiscourse:

> This ontological blending is of course a critical technique used by many of the Chicano artists I have considered, artists who wrestle with the dictates of institutional denial by creating transgressive stories linked to magical realist techniques. (160)

But even if Gutiérrez-Jones is right in noting the narratological transgressive possibilities of nonrealist techniques, a look beyond the textual would reveal the issue to be more complicated at other levels. As I have suggested elsewhere, most of those magical realist techniques and ontological blendings are also part of postmodernist fiction's "grammar," yet no one would think of calling John Barth or Guy Davenport magical realists ("Border Crisscrossing," 198–99). The political danger of thus linking postmodernist traits in Chicano/a fiction with Latin American magical realism (while not doing so with works by other U.S. writers) is that of making appear as foreign what is in fact a U.S. literature. This is not to deny that Chicanos/as have cultural and historical connections with Latin America that are unlike those other groups may have. Rather, my intention is to suggest that the "magical realist" label in the United States and, in particular, since the 1980s has become too charged a term to be employed in the transgressive sense that it had in Latin America in the 1960s and 1970s or that Gutiérrez-Jones and others still assign to it. Thus, when employing the term to analyze recent works by Chicanos/as, critics need to be aware of the fact that "magical realism," in the 1990s and early 2000s, has become a reiterated commonplace by which the marketing departments of U.S. commercial presses refer to everything Latino/a or Latin American. As such, it has also become an expectation of Anglo-American readers who have been trained by reviewers and critics to expect every single book produced by a Latino/a or Latin American author to be "magical" in one way or another (while, again, the case is not the same for "postmodernist" writers such as Barth or Davenport). What was once a revolutionary way of writing is now (at least in the U.S. context) little less than a formula to exoticize books by Latinos/as. As Carlos Monsiváis suggests,

> [Cien años de soledad] desentierra, para mejor gloria del eurocentrismo, el término de Alejo Carpentier "lo real maravilloso," y pone en circulación el "realismo mágico," que no es sino el estupor "civilizado" ante los hallazgos del "primitivismo." (153)[54]

Continuing that line of reasoning, I would like to propose that the Anglo-American "civilized" are no longer stupefied by the Latino/a "primitive" but rather that they have found a way to enjoy whatever the "primitive" has to say by transforming counterhegemonic discursive challenges in their works into commercial formulas to sell them as the newest "hot" commodity.

Nevertheless, as I indicated earlier in this chapter while discussing Miguel López's views on the closing up of the linguistic spaces of Chicano/a literature, Chicano/a literature is not only that which accomplishes mainstream acceptance and visibility. A look at other books published by small or noncommercial presses reveals a much more complicated and diverse panorama of Chicano/a letters. For instance, Chicano/a and Latino/a controlled presses have started their own process of reprinting significant works from the recent past that were no longer accessible to Chicano/a readers, such as those by José Montoya,[55] Cecilio García-Camarillo,[56] and Raúl R. Salinas,[57] including those texts featured in the Bilingual Review/Press series Clásicos Chicanos/Chicano Classics. This suggests that many of those authors who (once) wrote for "la marketa" are still enjoying a following among part of Chicano/a literature's multicultural readership. At the same time, the presses just mentioned plus a myriad of others (M&A, Tía Chucha, Third Woman, Academia/El Norte Publications, MARCH/Abrazo Press, Calaca, Chusma House, Spanish Press, etc.) are publishing books by new authors and by those with a limited previous production (including Charlie Trujillo, Rosemary Catacalos, Alfred Arteaga, Miriam Bornstein, and David Rice, among many others). These authors open up alternative spaces in Chicano/a literature, spaces outside the reach of the mass-market expectations and constraints. Other writers, such as Kathleen Alcalá, Juan Estevan Arellano, and Ricardo Aguilar, among many, have found their niche in non-Chicano/a presses in the United States and Mexico. While some of them may end up publishing with mainstream presses, it is unlikely that the alternative spaces that they and others have opened would be closed as a result.

The split between what I have called in this chapter writing for "the market" and for "la marketa" confirms that, at least in terms of audience formation, the national unity that the Chicano/a Movement strove to create is no longer a possibility in this post-Movement era. Rather, Chicano/a literature seems to have embraced a multisegmented audience (a heterogeneous, multilingual, and multicultural community of neighbors, to continue and expand the epigraph I borrowed from Gonzalo de Berceo) that needs to be addressed in different ways and languages.

CHAPTER 5

Reading (in) the Past: Textual Recovery
and the History of (Reading) Chicano/a Literature

*Upon dusty shelves, frayed and forgotten, the books of this
history may still be hidden. By word of mouth, from time to
time, there is word of a lost literature, in reminiscences and
folk memories.*

—Stan Steiner (1970)[1]

*It is our belief that an effort should be made to trace the
historical development of Mexican American literature now that
it has been recognized as a subject worthy of serious study.*

—Luis Leal (1973)[2]

*¿Y cómo es posible . . . que tan ricas prosas hayan permanecido
ignoradas durante tantos años? . . . ¿cuántos más Ulicas no
habrá por allí enterrados en los empolvados anaqueles de las
bibliotecas o las amarillas páginas de los periódicos? Hasta que
no sean descubiertos, como lo ha sido Ulica, no podremos hablar
de una historia definitiva de la literatura chicana.*

—Luis Leal (1982)[3]

In this final chapter, I intend to address one of the most recent yet
dramatic shifts in the history of (reading) Chicano/a literature: the
recovery and reprint of forgotten and formerly lost literary works by
Chicanos/as, to which my three epigraphs refer. Since the mid-1980s,
approximately, numerous scholars have devoted themselves to
unearthing those texts, as well as to reclaiming their place in the history
of Chicano/a literature, thus belatedly heeding don Luis Leal's
recommendation quoted in my second epigraph. What were, at first,
isolated efforts by individual critics such as Juan Rodríguez (who in 1982
edited Jorge Ulica's *Crónicas diabólicas*), Nicolás Kanellos (editor in 1984

of Daniel Venegas's *Las aventuras de don Chipote*), and Genaro M. Padilla (who compiled and edited Fray Angélico Chávez's *Short Stories* in 1987) later crystallized into a series of organized collective projects to (re)construct the early history of Chicano/a letters. Salient among these ventures are the Recovering the U.S. Hispanic Literary Heritage Project at its Arte Público Press/University of Houston base (henceforth referred to as the Recovery Project), as well as the Pasó por aquí series of the University of New Mexico Press, which concentrates on reprinting texts from the New Mexican past. Through these and similar efforts, a reader of Chicano/a literature today can access an exponentially greater number of works written prior to the 1950s than was possible thirty years ago. In a sense, it could be argued that in the past two decades Chicano/a literature has expanded as much toward its past as it has toward its future.

In addition to the three titles mentioned above, for instance, a partial listing of works recovered and reprinted in recent years includes Jovita González's *Dew on the Thorn* (edited by José Limón), *Caballero: A Historical Novel* (written with Eve Raleigh [pseudonym of Margaret Eimer] and edited by José Limón and María Cotera), and *The Woman Who Lost Her Soul and Other Stories* (edited by Sergio Reyna); Adina de Zavala's *History and Legends of the Alamo and Other Missions in and Around San Antonio* (edited by Richard Flores); *The Collected Stories of María Cristina Mena* (edited by Amy Doherty); Miguel A. Otero's *The Real Billy the Kid* (introduction by John-Michael Rivera); Luis Pérez's *El Coyote the Rebel* (introduction by Lauro Flores); *Women's Tales from the New Mexico WPA: La Diabla a Pie* (edited by Tey D. Rebolledo and Teresa Márquez); María Amparo Ruiz de Burton's *The Squatter and the Don* and *Who Would Have Thought It?* (both edited by Rosaura Sánchez and Beatrice Pita); Leonor Villegas de Magnón's *The Rebel* (edited by Clara Lomas); Gaspar Pérez de Villagrá's *Historia de la Nueva México* (edited by Miguel Encinias et al.); Cleofas M. Jaramillo's *Romance of a Little Village Girl* (introduction by Tey D. Rebolledo); and Américo Paredes's *George Washington Gómez* (with an introduction by Rolando Hinojosa), *The Hammon and the Beans and Other Stories* (introduction by Ramón Saldívar), *The Shadow* (with a prologue by the author), and *Between Two Worlds* (also with a prologue by the author). In addition, bibliographical enterprises outside the field of Chicano/a publishing, such as The Friends of the Bancroft Library (in consortium with the University of California, Berkeley), have contributed to the recovery trend with volumes such as *Three Memoirs of Mexican California* (a collection of testimonials from Carlos N. Híjar, Eulalia Pérez, and Agustín Escobar, as told to H. H. Bancroft's assistant Thomas Savage); *The Diary of Captain Luis Antonio Argüello, October 17-November 17, 1821* (with an introduction by Arthur Quinn); and José Bandini's translated *A Description of California in 1828*. Finally, previously unpublished or unavailable works are now in print in such anthologies as *The Multilingual Anthology of American Literature: A Reader of Original Texts with English Translations* (edited by Marc Shell and Werner Sollors), *Nochebuena: Hispanic American Christmas Stories* (edited by Nicolás Kanellos), and *Herencia: The Anthology of Hispanic Literature of the United States* (also edited by N. Kanellos with a group of co-editors).[4]

Significant as these reprints or newly printed texts are, they seem to represent only the tip of the iceberg of what is now a massive database of original works recovered from the more than 1,700 extant periodicals published by Hispanics (many of them by Chicanos/as) in the United States, as well as from libraries and archives throughout the country and in Mexico. Arte Público Press's Recovery Project, for example, is currently working on indexing and cataloging a database of over 100,000 literary items.[5]

This felicitous circumstance does not come without its difficulties, however, as the task of rewriting the history of Chicano/a literature has become more complex—paradoxically—than it was when fewer works from the past were known to us. The complexity of this enterprise stems from the fact that, as I have suggested elsewhere and as I will explore in detail below,[6] the task of reconstructing the history of Chicano/a letters cannot be understood as the simple process of filling in the gaps in the sequence of known works and then tracing alleged lines of evolution from the past to the present. Rather, historiographic reconstruction involves a delicate process of interpretation that in effect results in a discursive construction of the Chicano/a past. Thus, the next pages will be devoted to analyzing the main tenets that have built that critical edifice to date. Toward the end, I will propose an alternative model for rewriting Chicano/a literary history as the textual recovery progresses.

The Chronological Urge: Shortcomings, Newer Critical Insights, and Their Relevance for Chicano/a Literature

Despite my and other similar cautionary calls for a more complex understanding of the Chicano/a past (which I will address in the penultimate section of this chapter), the predominant trend among Chicano/a literary historians so far has favored a chronological approach. This is not entirely surprising. Such a sequential ordering of known (or, at least, relevant) works has been the most common technique employed throughout the world by traditional literary historians, who would catalog books and authors by generations, groups, movements, or any other similar categories around the idea of literary evolution and sequential continuity.[7] I contend that this model's long dominance in the field of literary history has resulted in a sort of methodological inertia that has outlived its usefulness and that, in turn, demands the experimentation with newer approaches. In particular, in the case of transnational (or postnational) literatures and in the context of diasporic and globalized movements of cultural capital and human labor characterizing our times, clinging to the notion of the diachronic evolution of *national* literatures seems of limited use.

In fact, the chronological listing model had some very early critics, as the following quote from Hans Robert Jauss conveys:

> [A] description of literature that follows an already sanctioned canon and simply sets the life and work of the writers one after the other in a chronological series is, as Gervinus already remarked, "no history; it is scarcely the skeleton of a history." (*Toward an Aesthetic*, 4–5)

Other recent social and cultural changes in our understanding of history complement Jauss's (and Gervinus's!) reservations by opening up for questioning assumptions on which the chronological model rested. For one, Michael Foucault's thoughts on historical analysis in general, as expressed in *The Archeology of Knowledge* and other works, opened up a critical space for discussing the possibility of a historiographic discourse that would depart from the idea of history as a search for origins and as the permanent interconnection between eras. Foucault's warning, in this regard, was clear and straightforward, assuming the urgency of a mandate:

> We must renounce all those themes whose function is to ensure the infinite continuity of discourse and its secret presence to itself in the interplay of a constantly recurring absence. We must be ready to receive every moment of discourse in its sudden irruption; in that punctuality in which it appears, and in that temporal dispersion that enables it to be repeated, known, forgotten, transformed, utterly erased, and hidden, far from all view, in the dust of books. Discourse must not be referred to the distant presence of the origin, but treated as and when it occurs. (25)

The Foucauldian understanding of the historiographic task enables the writer to emphasize precisely "the question of discontinuities, systems and transformations, series and thresholds" (13) that would likely result in a debunking of the hidden tenets supporting the edifice of traditional history. Rather than embarking on the search for a definite origin (a manifestation of which I explored in chapter 1), Foucault forcefully advocates suspending "all [the] syntheses that are accepted without question" (25), including methodological and disciplinary assumptions that serve to legitimize a false "synthetic purity" (26) based on the notion of uninterrupted evolution.

Likewise, the authority by which the historian could order the past from a position of seeming detachment and impartiality has been reexamined in such works as Hayden White's *Tropics of Discourse* and some of his other works, in which the tropological construction of history and the notion of metahistory are employed to account for the way a history (of any kind) always speaks of itself as much as it does of its subject. History is understood by White as a discursive construct rather than as an unquestionable collection of documented events. In thus shifting the emphasis from the chronicled past to the chronicling present, this newer conception of the historiographic undertaking also suggests that the history of a nation (or a literature) is always as much the chronicle of its present as it is that of its earlier periods, as the New Historicists have claimed repeatedly as well.

In the realm of literary history proper, a similar understanding of the tensions between past and present, the narrated and the narrator was also implicit in Jauss's concept of the shifting horizon of expectations, as was explored in earlier chapters. More importantly, at least for the present discussion, Jauss also called attention to those moments in which the past is consciously revisited (and rewritten) by a new generation of scholars or readers. In examining the reasons behind such instances of cultural revisionism, the German theoretician claimed that

> a literary past can return only when a new reception draws it back into the present, whether an altered aesthetic attitude willfully reaches back to reappropriate the past, or an unexpected light falls back on forgotten literature from the new moment of literary evolution, allowing something to be found that one previously could not have sought in it. (*Toward an Aesthetic*, 35)

To illustrate this Jaussian concept of the altered return of the past and its importance for Chicano/a literature, one need only look at the way the 1970s *indigenismo* sought to adopt and adapt a pre-Hispanic aesthetics for the benefit of a contemporary Chicano/a audience.[8] From the Nahuatl-based identification of poetry as "floricanto" (flower and song) that later gave name to numerous literary festivals and publications, to the inclusion of other philosophical, ethic, aesthetic, and linguistic elements, Chicano/a literature in the 1970s was marked by its reinterpretation of its ancient past in Tenochtitlan (and, to a lesser extent, in the worlds of the Maya and other indigenous cultures). A poem such as Alurista's "las tripas y los condes," for instance, from his 1971 collection *Floricanto en Aztlán,* translates into contemporary imagery Aztec rituals and practices so as to poetically dignify life in the Chicano/a neighborhoods:

> "las tripas" y "los condes"
> "los tequilas" y "los coloraos"
> today in the barrio
> los clanes de mi gente
> incarnate gangs of caciques
> con plumas y navajas
> caballeros águilas y tigres.
>
> —(*Floricanto,* poem 50)[9]

The anachronistic poetical appropriation of the Aztec military orders in the last line quoted serves to instill a sense of pride and defiance in the barrio gangs, a rhetorical move further reinforced by the peculiar use of the terms "clanes" and "gangs" in lines 4 and 5: in Alurista's historical reconstruction, the indigenous chiefs are said to form gangs while the barrio dwellers are related as clans. By thus altering the reader's expectations (of a more normal association between "caciques" and "clanes"), the poet manages to deprive the word "gang" of some of its negative connotations (as pervasive at the time as they are now in media and sociological analysis) while suggesting that they are in fact—by virtue of this newly recovered genealogy—military orders of sorts for cultural and physical self-defense. This last aspect is further reinforced by conjoining the images of "plumas" ("feathers," but also "pens" in Spanish) and "navajas" ("knives") in the sixth line of the poem: in that way, Alurista symbolizes how these present-day street fighters with their knives (a metaphoric allusion to the tiger's claws) and the poets that sing about them with their pens (an allusion through the polysemic meaning of "plumas" to the eagle's feathers) are working together toward the survival of La Raza.[10]

Similarly, there are many instances of revisionist readings of the past at times when a changed cultural context has allowed Chicano/a literature critics and readers to go back to certain texts and to read them differently, thus changing their relative importance for the history of Chicano/a letters. In chapter 2, I examined the case of the shifting reception of José Antonio Villarreal's *Pocho,* perhaps the ultimate example of how diachronic cultural transformations allow readers to find *some things that one previously could not have sought in a particular text* (to paraphrase Jauss). But many other examples could be taken into account here, including how a more receptive cultural context to sexual and gender differences since the mid-1980s permitted the reclamation and reinterpretation of formerly shunned or overlooked works, such as the novels published by John Rechy more than two decades earlier.[11]

These and similar examples further confirm the ways (literary) history is necessarily dependent on the interplay between past and present and between the chronicled and the chronicler, rather than being predicated upon the existence of a more or less immutable past that the historian can record (or recover) without any further mediating intervention. Rather, as Jauss also suggested as typical of the history of reception, "the reappropriation of past works occurs simultaneously with the perpetual mediation of past and present art and of traditional evaluation and current literary attempts" (*Toward an Aesthetics,* 20). Because reception is always a subsequent phenomenon with respect to production and because of the "perpetual mediation" that Jauss identifies, it could be argued (as the parenthesis in this chapter's subtitle implies) that the history of a particular literature should also be the history of how that literature has been read in the different "presents" of enunciation of its diverse historians and readers.

In fact, within the Hispanic literary world, the idea of such a literary history of reception was already proposed in 1925 by the prolific José Martínez Ruiz (who published his works under the pseudonym "Azorín"). In a note on Lope de Vega, later collected in his *Lope en silueta* (*Profile of Lope*), Azorín first proposed his idea under the following terms as he devised a plan for such a history:

> No se ha escrito en España—sobre intentos y trabajos parciales—una historia de la evolución de los grandes autores en el concepto del público y de la crítica. *La Historia de las ideas estéticas* de Menéndez y Pelayo es otra cosa. Lo que pedimos aquí es un estudio en que se fuera viendo, época por época, siglo por

siglo, cómo la fama de un gran escritor ha ido formándose, modificándose, transformándose. . . . Y leyendo este libro—libro ejemplar—nos podríamos curar de muchos prejuicios y muchas vaguedades. (86)[12]

While Azorín's project was still marked by its reliance on the notion of the "great author," a notion that our own present has questioned, his ideas on methodology sound nonetheless fresh to this day. In fact, some fifty-five years after Azorín wrote his note on Lope de Vega, Annette Kolodny suggested employing a very similar analytical process to achieve almost diametrically opposed results. Kolodny demonstrated how documenting the diachronic changes in reception might serve not (just) to trace the changing estimation of the "great authors" but as a tool for canonical revisionism as well, with its attendant benefits for the (re)construction of historically marginalized literatures. Kolodny's essay reads not unlike a (much more modern) echo of Azorín's earlier claim, as it stresses the need for an acknowledgment of the presents from which literary history is constructed or revised:

[O]ur sense of a "literary history" and, by extension, our confidence in a historical canon, is rooted not so much in any definitive understanding of the past, as it is in our need to call up and utilize the past on behalf of a better understanding of the present. . . . To quote [David Couzens] Hoy fully, "this continual reinterpretation of the past goes hand in hand with the continual reinterpretation by the present of itself." (9)

Unlike Azorín, however, by thus invoking the notion of canon in a revisionist context, Kolodny was forced to question the very same process by which a certain standard emerges and is handed down through generations. In that sense, she was more interested in what literary histories have routinely qualified as "lesser authors" than in Azorín's "grandes autores." Kolodny's recollection of how she reread with her students forgotten texts by women writers is eloquent in this respect and her questions are largely applicable to the Chicano/a situation as well:

In reading with our students these previously lost works [by early women writers], we inevitably raised perplexing questions as to the reasons for their disappearance from the canons of "major works," and we worried over the aesthetic and critical criteria by which they had been accorded diminished status. (2)

While I will come back to the notion of "disappearance" immediately below, what interests me right now from Kolodny's second quote is her emphasis on the act of reading (rather than on that of writing) as characteristic of and responsible for canonical evolution. An opposite valuation of these two parameters has constituted the most blatant— yet concealed—contradiction in traditional histories of literature by making the historian's voice and tastes almost invisible under the veil of an alleged objective documentation of the writings of the "great authors" (with an occasional minor author thrown in for the sake of documenting the "decadence" of certain movements and/or periods). Likewise, I would like to stress in Kolodny's last quote the explicit displacement from the idea of the "great author" or the "major work" as an undisputable tenet, still prevalent in Azorín's mind, to an understanding of *literary relevance* (Jauss's horizon of expectations) as a critical construct: relevant to whom is the question with which our current literary histories rather need to deal.

An equally important challenge to the traditional dominance of chronology as the basis for literary historiography results from a complication of the notion of "disappearance" to which Kolodny alluded in her second quote; that is, the fact that unknown texts from earlier periods may be "discovered" at a much later date than that of their production, as in the Chicano/a case, with little or no record of their original reception left. In such situations, traditional historians have resorted to placing those texts in their chronological sequence and then to rewriting their histories to accommodate the newly discovered works in a thus restructured order. A telling example is found in the history of Spanish literature, in which the "discovery" of the *jarchas* in 1948 resulted in a rewriting of its literary history with the addition of an entirely new beginning for its lyric poetry, a literary prehistory of sorts that was then integrated into the otherwise unchanged teleological model of literary evolution.[13] But even if the dates of composition would reserve such a foundational role for the jarchas and other similarly unearthed works, literary historians cannot dismiss the temporality of their "discoveries" nor the present from which their new historiographical discourses emerge to thus rewrite the literary past. Jauss synthesized this idea eloquently when he signaled that "prehistories are always discovered *ex eventu* as prehistory of a *post-history.*"[14] In that sense, it should be apparent that the particular posthistory from which the prehistory is written into the literary annals would be determinant in whatever role is accorded to the newly found texts.

To give but a simplified illustration of how significantly this process operates in the case of the Chicano/a literary past, consider how different the interpretation of currently recovered works would have been if that process had taken place in the cultural context of the 1960s and 1970s instead of starting during the 1980s and 1990s. While the partially recovered memoirs of Mariano Vallejo and texts by other early Californios/as have been celebrated in the 1990s as the legitimate antecedents of twentieth-century Chicano/a protest literature, critics in the 1960s and 1970s were clearly dismissive of those very same figures (even if most of their works were not known at the time) as representative of an assimilationist stance at odds with Chicano/a militancy. While our interpretive present can benefit from the use of such theoretical concepts as the notions of positionality and articulation, strategic essentialism, or differential consciousness[15] critics in the 1970s were less inclined to consider in a positive light the notion of shifting or fluid identities, which then deserved the quick accusation of being *un vendido,* a sellout. A comparison between the following quotes, all of them centered around Vallejo in one way or another, would suffice to prove my point. The first quote is from Genaro M. Padilla's 1993 landmark study on Mexican American autobiography, *My History, Not Yours* (whose title is, in fact, a direct quote from Vallejo's memoirs):

> Vallejo, moreover, may help us to understand the competing social forces that have made a virtue of contradictory responses; a virtue, I say, because such necessary contradictions between public and private sentiments, between intra- and intercultural experience, may be seen as establishing a negotiatory consciousness for Mexican Americans like Vallejo—with Juan Seguín before him and Cleofas Jaramillo after him—which has enabled their (our) survival in North America during the last century and a half. (88)

Padilla's rhetorical strategy, including his careful choice of words ("virtue," "survival"), casts Vallejo's figure in the heroic terms intended to (re)situate this pioneer memoirist (as well as the other individuals he mentions) as the foundation stone of later Chicano/a literature, as his parenthesis further emphasizes. In this, Padilla's narrative is not unlike those of other recent readers of the Chicano/a past, such as Rosaura Sánchez and Beatrice Pita, who claimed (also in 1993) that Maria Amparo

Ruiz de Burton's *The Squatter and the Don* (the latter character in the title being modeled after Vallejo)[16] contains "an interpellation of today's readers, as citizens, or as descendants of Californios/as, to resist oppression" (51), while concluding that "such are the contestation and defiant discourse with which the literature of the population of Mexican origin in the United States emerges" (51).

The enthusiasm with which these highly respectable critics embraced the works of Vallejo and his contemporary Californios in the early 1990s sharply contrasts with the dismissive condemnation found two decades earlier, in 1972, in Raymond V. Padilla's critique of Leonard M. Pitt's *The Decline of the Californios:*

> [F]ew conquests can be maintained without the continuous collaboration of some native faction. California and the Southwest were no exception. In California men like Mariano Vallejo and Pablo de la Guerra . . . played important roles in bringing California and the Southwest under Gabacho [Anglo] control. These political opportunists had much to gain by way of land speculation, increased commerce, and the hopes of political aggrandizement. They were men of influence and power who hoped to continue in privileged positions and even increase their power through a Gabacho hegemony. (35)[17]

The radical disparity between these quotes is indicative of how different a history of Chicano/a literature written in the early 1970s would have been from that being written in the 1990s and early 2000s, even if the newly recovered texts (by Vallejo, Ruiz de Burton, and others) had been known at the time.[18] Indeed, literary critics and historians in the 1970s had not paid much attention to similarly "heteredoxical" known figures from their recent past such as Fray Angélico Chávez (later "rediscovered" in part by Genaro M. Padilla), John Rechy, and Fabiola Cabeza de Vaca.[19] Taking the case of José Antonio Villarreal's *Pocho* as our yardstick once more, it is very doubtful that a novel like *The Squatter and the Don* would have made many reading lists in Chicano/a literature courses back in the 1970s (if it had been known to critics then) unless accompanied by a significant commentary clarifying its "ambiguities and ideological confusions" (to quote—albeit slightly out of context—Ramón E. Ruiz's preface to the 1970 edition of *Pocho*).[20] By contrast, Ruiz de Burton's novel has generated a significant body of criticism since the 1990s (most of it overwhelmingly celebratory), and it has become required reading in many university courses, which has resulted in several reprints to date. All this in spite of the novel's marked elitism, which, as I signaled in 1996, contrasts with the more common working-class bent in twentieth-century Chicano/a literature, an aspect that has been often overlooked or avoided in the existing studies of this novel.[21]

As such, the reception of *The Squatter and the Don* provides us with a fine example of why a posthistory (in Jauss's sense) undertakes the task of (re)writing its own prehistory. In particular, the Nietzschean overtones of Jauss's ideas are of relevance here. For Nietzsche, especially in what he calls the *critical* historiographic model, history can become a fabrication of the past, "an attempt to give ourselves *a posteriori,* as it were, a new past from which we would prefer to be descended, as opposed to the past from which we actually descended" (107).[22] Even though I am not suggesting that available Chicano/a literary histories are such a blatant fabrication of the Chicano/a past, it is nonetheless undeniable that—as is also the case with the recovery of many other marginalized literatures— the Chicano/a reconstruction of its literary past is not done without a combination of empirical restoration (involving physically locating and [re]printing texts from the past) and interpretive assumptions, which may very well be altered in future readings of the past but that allow the historian to construct a narrative of filiation between the recovered texts and the historian's present. This, in turn, determines which texts are selected as the main antecedents of present-day Chicano/a literature, as well as what parameters are selected as relevant for the historical narrative under construction. Because the main drive behind the different Chicano/ a recovery efforts so far has been firmly directed toward restoring an uninterrupted chronological sequence, those features that would signal heterodoxy or even heterogeneity amid the Chicanos/as have been deemphasized so as to present a more cohesive picture of literary continuity.[23]

Yet as I have suggested elsewhere ("Textual and Land Reclamations," 54) and as I will explore in more detail below, the history of Chicano/a literature cannot be written without taking into account those differences;[24] stressing them, rather than attempting to overlook them for the sake of constructing a teleological picture of continuous cultural evolution, must be the historian's ambition if s/he is to succeed in chronicling a collective experience that reaches back several centuries and cuts, at one time or another, across the political borders of at least four countries.[25] Otherwise, the homogenizing effort would prove in the field of Chicano/a letters as limited in use as similar attempts in the case of other minority and marginalized literatures. The ambiguities and the silences with which many critics have treated certain aspects of Ruiz de Burton's *The Squatter and the Don,* in that sense, are not unlike those that Andrew Lakritz finds in the reception and rereading accorded to Zora Neale Hurston's *Their Eyes Were Watching God.* According to Lakritz,

> Hurston's novel is an allegory of what happens when we try to return to origins and what we find there—not something upon which to build a stable, unifying sense of identity. We have taken this novel into the canon as a lost masterpiece. . . . Now that it is central to many American literature survey courses, American Studies courses, not to mention African American studies, women's studies, and others, it is harder to see that in fact the book was written from the point of view of an elite returning to find a home for herself and having to face the difficulty of seeing it. (24)

Implicit in Lakritz's criticism is the idea that a certain critical consensus can be reached at particular times (such as in instances of canonical revisions) that would overlook specific aspects of a text or texts, thus resulting in an un/intentional manipulation or distortion of the past. While acknowledging that many readers may not see in Hurston's novel those aspects that Lakritz identifies (or those I signaled in relation to Ruiz de Burton's novel), it is clear nonetheless that the literary past cannot be perceived without the mediation of an interpreting present and that, consequently, the motivating force behind a particular reading of the past (e.g., finding one's origins, restoring a broken sequence, building a sense of identity, or creating a past from which one would like to be descended) would play a major role in defining the actual outcome of such reconstruction. It may be an exaggerated popular truism that one only finds what one is looking for, but after examining most contemporary rereadings of the past, one cannot deny that revisiting history is seldom (if ever) an ideological- and methodological-free enterprise. Rather, as discussed at some length by David Perkins,

> [t]he classification is prior, in a sense, to the literature it classifies, for it organizes perceptions of literature. The validity of the classification confirms itself every time the texts are read, for the classification signals what to look for and therefore predetermines, to some degree, what will be observed. (72–73)

The ensuing tension between a heterogeneous past and the attempt
to homogenize it through historiographic discourses (the classifications
to which Perkins alludes) is felt with particular force in postcolonial
cultures or in the case of historically marginalized and suppressed
literatures, suggesting that many Chicano/a literary historians are
following in this sense a well-established, albeit questionable, path.
Among the most articulate detractors of the reductionist classification
as an intellectual enterprise is Mohammed Arkoun, a professor at the
Institute d'Études Islamiques of the Université Sorbonne Nouvelle-Paris
III, who focuses his criticism on the prevalent histories of postcolonial
North Africa:

> La historia del Magreb tiene lagunas y dispersiones,
> discontinuidad, rupturas culturales de las fuentes y de las fases
> romana, bizantina, árabe, turca, francesa y nacionalista. Lo que
> urge ahora es pensar en estas discontinuidades, sobre todo las
> que afectan al pensamiento árabe e islámico, en lugar de seguir
> construyendo una continuidad ilusoria, deseada por las élites
> nacionalistas. (99)[26]

The connection between elite, nationalism, and the homogenizing
historiographic discourse is far from accidental, as Arkoun suggests, and
in the Chicano/a—as in the North African case—it seems to be at the
root of most current interpretations of its literary past.

Indeed, many of the documented efforts to reconstruct the Chicano/
a literary history seem to have favored a search for links between the
recovered texts and our own cultural present so as to construct a sense
of unsuspended continuity despite the changes that time has brought to
language, urbanization patterns, population trends, religious and folk
practices, aesthetics, tastes, etc. This resulted in a series of "conceptual"
historiographic accounts, in Perkins's sense,[27] that characterized the initial
phase of the recovery enterprise, as critics attempted to present the newly
recovered texts in a familiar light for the modern reader. Nicolás Kanellos,
for example, made this the focus of his 1984 introduction to Daniel
Venegas's *Las aventuras de don Chipote,* which he qualified as the first
Chicano/a novel (an assertion repeated in the 1999 Spanish-language
edition by Arte Público Press),[28] while pointing out how the novel "ofrece
un nuevo indicio de la continuidad de producción cultural del mexicano
al norte de la frontera" (4).[29]

Kanellos's statement about the landmark status of *Don Chipote,* which in 1999 would otherwise sound even more inaccurate than it might have been in 1985, is not as much a chronological datation as an ideological interpretation, as the fact that he acknowledges the existence of earlier novels by conservative authors indicates (5).[30] In this, of course, we see yet another example of how the mediation of the literary historian works to mold and shape the reconstructed canon of Chicano/a literature. For the purpose of the literary history that Kanellos and others were starting to reconstruct in the mid-1980s, a proletarian novel was, no doubt, the ultimate text on which to found the edifice of Chicano/a letters. Literary history became, at that point, a genealogical enterprise, confounding into a discourse of filiation what was more than anything a case of heuristic affiliation for, as Perkins has signaled, "[a]ny conceptual scheme highlights only those texts that fit its concepts, sees in texts only what its concepts reflect, and inevitably falls short of the multiplicity, diversity, and ambiguity of the past" (51). The fact that Venegas's work was not known to Chicano/a Movement and post-Movement writers becomes irrelevant for Kanellos's historical reconstruction; in his analysis, Venegas becomes a sort of absent father who returns, almost six decades later, to reclaim his place at the head of the Chicano/a literary table.

The idea that Chicano/a literature has been marked since "the beginning" by one or several particular characteristics (e.g., its working-class status or its position as a site of direct or covert resistance) became— after Kanellos's edition—a major topos for the initial stages of the recovery of the Chicano/a literary past, and it dictated the shape that the reconstructed history would take. As I have demonstrated elsewhere, this strategy works only when individual texts from the past (or some of their aspects) are compared with a select corpus of works from the present; by contrast, when the recovered texts are compared among themselves or when one expands the corpus of our own contemporary works, the differences are as telling as the similarities, and the critic would be at pains to ignore them ("Textual and Land Reclamations," 53). This is not to say that there has been no continuity. On the contrary, a cultural continuity that encompasses folklore and the oral tradition, everyday practices, religion, and even to a certain extent printed literature is undeniable, and it has been documented extensively.[31] However, as is the case with other peoples who have been historically subjected to a pattern of conquest, marginalization, and exclusion from power positions, there have also been in the Chicano/a past many factors that resulted in disruptions and ruptures in the continuity of cultural evolution, including alphabetization patterns, lack of free time for reading and writing, limited printing and distribution opportunities, class and gender differences, and regional versus (inter)national awareness. For the task of (re)constructing the Chicano/a literary history, therefore, continuity may not necessarily be the leading indicator to pursue. Rather, the historian may gain more in registering the interplay between the connections and the interruptions reflected in the literary activity throughout the years, as I will explore toward the end of this chapter.

The Encyclopedic Trend in Chicano/a Literary History

A second dominant impulse in the recent rewriting of Chicano/a literary history has resulted in an attempt to compensate for the general lack of knowledge of the literary past that characterized the Chicano/a Movement era by filling in as many "empty boxes" in the literary chronological sequence as possible. If we look at those chronologies accompanying modern reference works on Chicano/a literature, even as late as 1985,[32] it is obvious that the gaps in the sequence of known works used to span in certain cases well over a century. The pedagogical utility of attempting to cover those "holes" by listing as many of the recovered texts as possible is therefore undeniable.[33] But aside from its didactic role as a visual aid, such an ex eventu reconstructed listing would be misleading, since it would include many of these works *as if they had been always known to us,* thus erasing precisely the history of displacement and marginalization that resulted in the temporary "disappearance" of those texts in the first place and that is, in itself, meaningful.

Therefore, I contend that instead of glossing it over with the help of the newly recovered texts, Chicano/a (literary) history needs to record the sense of loss and disjuncture that characterized its immediate past until recently and that Luis Valdez, one of the foremost cultural leaders of the 1960s and 1970s, conjured up in the following testimonial (as recorded in 1970 by Stan Steiner):

> "We have to rediscover ourselves," says Luis Valdez, the director of the Teatro Campesino. "There are years and years of discoveries we have to make of our people. People ask me: What is Mexican American history in the United States? There is no textbook of the history of La Raza. Yet the history of the Mexican in this country is four hundred years old. We know we pre-date the landing of the Pilgrims and the American Revolution. But beyond that? What really happened? No one can tell you. Our history has been lost. Lost!" (218)

As Steiner astutely reflected immediately after Valdez's statement, "[u]pon dusty shelves, frayed and forgotten, the books of this history may still be hidden. By word of mouth, from time to time, there is word of a lost literature, in reminiscences and folk memories" (218).[34] What I am claiming in this chapter (and, in effect, throughout this book) is that dusting those shelves and bringing to the fore those lost and forgotten books can only account for half of Chicano/a literary history: that half which concerns literary production; the other half, literary reception and literary tradition, will always be marked by the tensions between permanence and disappearance. By "dusting off the shelves," Chicano/a literary historians are uncovering a massive number of works whose existence was not recorded in previous annals, but Chicano/a literary history cannot be rewritten as if those texts had played then (i.e., in the periods when they were written) the significance that the historian can attribute to them now.

Rather, as I have advocated before, in rewriting Chicano/a literary history it is imperative to focus on both what I called the "gaps" and the "knots" in that "net full of holes" that the Chicano/a literary past has proven to be. Taking my title from a beautiful metaphor from the 1528 *Manuscript of Tlatelolco*,[35] I proposed that historians (and, in particular, those interested in the process of literary recovery) should approach the task of reconstructing the Chicano/a literary past not only with the sole intention of restoring a lost or forgotten sequence but also with the kind of cultural analysis that would account for a *disrupted and marginal(ized)* history; that is, with attention to what James Clifford has called "discrepant temporalities."[36] I propose, therefore, that we analyze *both* the connectors that have kept Chicano/a literature alive through the years *and* the discontinuities that have marked its existence and that are likewise charged with significance, since, as I suggested before, they are the result of geographic, social, linguistic, cultural, technological, and educational history. They are the parameters which serve to discuss questions of hegemony and marginalization; of nationalism versus regionalism, transnationalism, and the borderlands; they help to analyze printing and distribution conditions; they also serve to look at alphabetization patterns among Chicanos/as. They lead to the analysis of school segregation, linguistic marginalization, social constraints for women writers, gender patterns of historical audiences, and so on and so forth (17).

Ignoring those fissures by adopting an encyclopedical literary history model could only result in a distorted construction of the Chicano/a

literary past. At the same time, however, Chicano/a literary history can and
needs to trace the lines of continuity in the transmission of cultural capital,
whether that transmission occurred physically—through the inheritance of
private libraries, for instance—or intellectually—in the way Chicano/a
writers received and reacted to the works of earlier writers that may have
been known to them even if their works never reached a larger audience.[37]
The documented continuities reveal creative strategies for cultural survival
and intervention, and they are indicative of the transformative resilience of
Chicano/a printed culture, an element that was habitually overlooked by
earlier scholars of the Chicano/a past, who preferred to privilege in their
studies oral forms of resistance and cultural transmission.

If it is to continue to play a role in Chicano/a literary historiography,
the encyclopedic effort cannot be supported upon an acritical or non-
self-reflexive chronological listing model. The recovered works belong
as much to the time of their recovery as they do to the era in which they
were first published or conceived. Subsuming their multiple temporalities
into the date of production or publication constitutes a double
reductionism: first, it diminishes the social and aesthetic significance of
literary works by stressing their status as documents or artifacts; second,
it erases the history of their marginalization and/or disappearance, a
literary category of particular relevance for nonhegemonic literatures,
as discussed earlier in relation to Annette Kolodny's thoughts on
canonical revisionism.

Nationalism and Chicano/a Literary History

Because of the intense nationalism that has dominated Chicano/a critical
discourses since the late 1960s until very recently, a third element that
has characterized the reading and reconstruction of the Chicano/a literary
past has been the emphasis on the idea of Chicano/a literature as a
national literature. During the Chicano/a Movement, the rallying cry
"we are a nation" strove to instill a sense of national unity and
distinctiveness among Chicanos/as.[38] Aztlán, the term preferred by most
to symbolize that nationality, is found in the title and in the spirit of
many of the publications dealing with the Chicano/a literary past.[39]
Chicano/a literary history is not alone in this respect, as we saw in the
beginning of this chapter, since the combination of chronology and
nationality has been the base for literary historiography at least since
the German romantics. Literary history, in that context, was conceived
as the process by which to chronicle the continuous progress in the realm
of letters from the nation's origin to the chronicling present. Such process

entailed the notion of constant evolution toward an ever more refined and developed stage that would correspond with the consolidation of the national state. In the Chicano/a case, however, two objections need to be raised as a cautionary note against the nationalistic approach to literary history. First, the Chicano/a culture(s) and experiences transcend geographical borders. This is the result not only of shifting geopolitical boundaries but also of the cultural permeability of the historically rearranged limits between countries. Chicano/a literature, like the cultures from which it springs, is transnational, multicultural, and multilingual, and therefore the reliance on a nationalistic model to construct its history seems, at the very least, constrained.

In addition, and because of its transnational, borderlands nature, Chicano/a literary history presents a second challenge to the traditional reliance on the concept of nation. As the frequent debates on "who is Chicano/a?" have proven, biological and even experiential factors have never been entirely effective in writing the history of Chicano/a letters.[40] In fact, if we were to apply those criteria rigidly, one could even question Mexican-born Daniel Venegas's membership in the group as much as others question the status of figures such as Mexican-born Rubén Medina, despite the fact that he has resided in the United States for most of his life and that other Mexican-born writers (such as Alurista, Sergio D. Elizondo, and Abelardo Delgado) have been unquestionably accepted as Chicanos by critics.[41] I do not intend to enter into nor resuscitate those debates here.[42] Rather, my interest is in considering the actual existence of those debates so as to show their conceptual and historiographical limitations. Their existence, as far as literary history is concerned, is predicated on a rather fixed idea of cultural identity and nationality as well as on literary production or textuality as the sole parameters for the conceptualization of the body of works that has come to be known as Chicano/a letters. In successive (and, to a certain extent, overlapping) moments during these debates, the Chicano/a-ness, or what I would rather call Chicano/a-nicity, of a particular text has been determined by either its author's identity or by its contents.

The first preference (and its attendant problems) was well summarized by Luis Leal in his introduction to Trujillo and Rodríguez's *Literatura Chicana* when he noted that during the 1970s "[i]t was the consensus of opinion among critics that Chicano literature was that literature written by authors of Mexican background born or residing permanently in the United States" (1), but as Leal also acknowledged immediately, in many cases it was very difficult to determine the background of a particular writer, which resulted in the questionable inclusion or exclusion of certain writers. Thus, Leal's introduction discusses the well-known cases of Danny Santiago (pseudonym of Daniel James) and Amado Muro (Chester Seltzer in real life), but he forewarns that many other authors may be improperly classified in the existing bibliographies. As if to confirm Leal's suspicions, and to pinpoint the shortcomings of using the author's background as the main criteria for inclusion and exclusion, Trujillo and Rodríguez's bibliography lists Andrés Ramón Rodríguez (a Spaniard) as a Chicano poet while relegating Justo S. Alarcón (another Spaniard) to the category of "literatura chicanesca." Likewise, Mexican-born Luis Arturo Ramos is included among Chicano/a short-story writers, a classification that may not be universally shared by other critics or even by the author himself.

The second position would be to look in the text itself for a Chicano/a content. This is, then, a much more narrowly defined categorization, since it allows for the fact that "[j]ust as there are biological and cultural aspects to being a Mexican American, it must be understood that not all Mexican Americans call themselves Chicano" (Huerta, "Looking for the Magic," 37). For proponents of this classification, such as Jorge Huerta,

> [n]either the ancestry of its author, nor the fact that it is written in a particular language, determines whether or not a play is Chicano. If the theme explores the nature of being Chicano, I would call it Chicano and more particularly, ethno-specific theatre. ("Looking for the Magic," 39)

While biological and thematic issues cannot simply be dismissed, I suggest that the exclusive emphasis on the authorial and/or textual elements of the Chicano/a literary work results in a narrower literary history than is needed. On the one hand, these approaches would have to set more or less artificial borders where experience reveals a much more flexible reality. Because of that restrictive, normative stance, the resulting histories would always be plagued by questions that have proved irresoluble: why should a certain author born in Mexico be considered a Chicano/a while another should not? When can we say that a text has "enough" Chicano/a content, and how do we measure the degree of Chicanism in a particular book?

If, on the other hand, we were to seriously conceive Chicano/a identity and literature as transnational phenomena and if we were willing to analyze the entire literary experience rather than limiting ourselves to production and textuality, then it would be possible to circumvent these and similar dilemmas by acknowledging what are truly porous borders in the Chicano/a literary space. Furthermore, this transnational, multilingual aspect of Chicano/a literature would be better served by incorporating into its literary history parameters of reading patterns and empirical reception alongside textual and authorial considerations. Indeed, in order to (re)write Chicano/a literary history in its fuller dimension, one would need to look not only at what Chicanos/as wrote at different times but also at what they read. Traditional literary histories have all but ignored reading patterns and other reception-related aspects, but it is hard to deny that what authors and readers of a particular society consume becomes part of their cultural heritage as much as what they produce.

As I have proposed before, by way of example, late-nineteenth-century Mexican American poetry cannot be separated from the fact that its authors and their audience were knowledgeable and appreciative of romantic poetry from Mexico ("'A Net Made of Holes,'" 18), not to mention the fact that many felt themselves to be part of the same cultural continuum. Even clearer evidence of how tenuous these national literary borders have been historically is found in *Breve reseña de la literatura hispana de Nuevo México y Colorado,* a rather peculiar book published in 1959 by José T. López, Edgardo Núñez, and Roberto Lara Vialpando (respectively a native of Colorado, a Peruvian, and a New Mexican). This short tome combines literary criticism with bibliographical listings and, more importantly for my purposes, an anthology of poetry. In this latter section, poems by two of the volume editors are printed alongside others by fellow New Mexicans and Coloradoans *as well as* several poems by Juan de Dios Peza, one of Mexico's most popular and revered romantic poets. No indication is made in the book of the fact that Peza is not from the New Mexico–Colorado area, which strongly suggests that despite the regional focus indicated in this book's title, literary boundaries were not particularly relevant or exclusive in the authors' minds. And the same is true of most literary genres, including drama and other performative genres, as suggested by the research of Elizabeth C. Ramírez, who has studied theatrical touring companies in the Southwest, and has concluded:

> Above all, these [touring] dramatic companies were able to establish a reconnection between Mexican Americans and México. Rather than isolating themselves in the United States, the Spanish-speaking communities were able to continue cultural relations with México. (15)[43]

What this evidence confirms is that the nationalistic paradigm that brought much political strength to the Chicano/a Movement is inadequate for writing the literary history of Chicanos/as. Thus, when writing the history of this literature, it would be of limited use to differentiate categorically between north and south of the border and to ignore the transnational scope of literary trends, experiences, and tastes. Chicano/a literary history needs to keep itself open to such phenomena by engaging in a transnational analysis of the entire literary process rather than by restricting itself with self-imposed parameters of nation and literary production.[44] To a certain extent, some of the most recent publishing efforts seem to be leaning already in that direction, as reflected in Nicolás Kanellos's introduction to the anthology *Herencia* (2002):

> [I]n its variety and multiple perspectives, what we will call "U.S. Hispanic" literature is far more complex than the mere sampling of the last forty years would lead us to believe. This literature incorporates the voices of the conqueror and the conquered, the revolutionary and the reactionary, the native and the uprooted or landless. It is a literature that proclaims a sense of place in the United States while it also erases borders; it is transnational in the most postmodern sense possible. (1)

Moreover, as the above quote indicates, newer bridges are being built between Chicano/a and present-day Latino/a literatures, which is resulting in yet newer parameters of expansion of and interaction across traditional literary borders. This trend, which started to be noticeable in the San Francisco Bay Area during the 1980s and is only now gaining national attention, cannot simply be dismissed as a marketing fad or as political maneuvering (even if marketing forces are at play, as I explored in the previous chapter).[45] Rather, it works to confirm that insisting upon nationality as the central parameter around which to describe Chicano/a literature may not only be historically inaccurate (given the constant border crossings involved in the Chicano/a social and cultural experiences) but outdated as well (in the context of the diasporic movement of workers and other immigrants in the new globalized economy, in which newer alliances between immigrants and former immigrant groups are constantly refashioned).

Telling the Story: Chicano/a Metaliterary and
Metahistorical Discourses

In the preceding sections of this chapter, I have alluded to some of the best-known interpretations of the Chicano/a literary past. I have also discussed some of the assumptions underlying those analyses, as well as the critical parameters within which those interpreters have worked. In this section, I will concentrate on more recent metahistorical and metaliterary discourses that have emerged since the textual recovery projects started to take a more cohesive shape.

After the pioneering efforts noted at the beginning of this chapter, Chicano/a literary historiography received a major impulse through the biannual conferences of the Recovery Project at the University of Houston. In particular, the edited volumes with selected critical contributions from those conferences stand out as the most extensive and concerted body of thoughts on how to read the Chicano/a literary past. In them, one can detect the beginnings of a serious questioning of how Chicano/a literary history had been written to that point, as well as a series of proposals for nuancing future studies of the past. None of the critics and historians participating in those edited volumes has offered a comprehensive rethinking of the historiographical task, though, and therefore their influence is better felt in partial rereadings of specific works and periods than in a general or systematic approach.

Many of the contributions included in the first volume of *Recovering the U.S. Hispanic Heritage* (by far the richest of the three published volumes so far in metahistorical discourses and reflections) were authored by critics interested in discussing the overall implications of the recovery task ahead.[46] In the words of Erlinda Gonzales-Berry, the process of recovering and reinterpreting lost works needed to be seen as a delicate one with significant consequences for future interpretations of Chicano/a letters:

> This long over-due project, Recovering the U.S. Hispanic literary heritage, by its very nature places us in the rather uncomfortable position of creating a literary canon, that is to say, in the position not only of codifying an ethnic literary identity, but also of assigning a standard of value to a corpus of texts. ("Two Texts," 129)

Very much aware of the possible consequences of canonizing formerly marginalized works, Gonzales-Berry strongly urged literary historians

not to ignore parameters of difference when assessing the Chicano/a past
("Two Texts," 129), a position also echoed by Charles Tatum, who, quoting
an earlier essay by Rosaura Sánchez, suggests that

> [a]ny consideration of nineteenth-century literary works must
> take into account the fact that while the writers may be of Mexican
> origin, "this population is as diverse as any other living group of
> people. There can be no simple labeling which can encompass
> the diversity represented by this population despite the fact that
> there are certain general social changes which have affected the
> entire population." (200–01)[47]

But by far the most radical criticism of previous literary
historiography (and, in that capacity, a warning as well for future similar
endeavors) was launched by one of the volume editors, Ramón A.
Gutiérrez. Gutiérrez compared recent historiographic discourses to those
of 1920s Hispanophiles, and he found fascinating and, at the same time,
disturbing similarities:

> Like those histories of Hispanic literature written several
> decades earlier by the *hispanidad* advocates, Chicano, Puerto Rican
> and American Indian scholars created a past that relied heavily
> on identifying key writers and key texts. In many ways there was
> very little difference between these scholars who sought the first
> Chicano novelist, the first Chicano poet, the first Chicano short
> story, and *hispanidad* scholars who sought the purest and earliest
> Spanish literary forms in the United States. Both groups were
> intent in creating a canon of sacred texts. The histories of Chicano
> literature that were produced were premised on a monolithic
> concept of community and on the idea of political progress.
> ("Nationalism," 246)

To a certain extent, the similarities between the *hispanidad* trend and
the recent Chicano/a literary historiography to which Gutiérrez alluded
have grown even deeper since he wrote those words, inasmuch as colonial
texts by Spanish explorers, friars, and soldiers have been incorporated
into the new canon of Chicano/a literature through recovery and
publication efforts. In that sense, the publication by Arte Público Press
(in 1993) of Alvar Núñez Cabeza de Vaca's *Relación* and that of Gaspar
Pérez de Villagrá's *Historia de la Nueva México* in the *Pasó por aquí* series

of the University of New Mexico (in the emblematic year of 1992) is very much in line with Gutiérrez's findings, as well as with the hispanidad historiographic impulse itself, as a consideration of works such as Juan Francisco de Cárdenas's *Hispanic Culture and Language in the United States* would prove.[48] In that 1933 book, de Cárdenas postulated the notion that Spanish-American nations were a continuation of Spain—"each after its own fashion," he conceded (19)—which he followed with a list of reasons why the United States should make Spanish its second language. In point of fact, de Cárdenas's reasons were not entirely unlike those adopted by Chicano/a literary historians some sixty years later, namely the presence in what is today the United States of Spanish writers since shortly after 1492 (Cabeza de Vaca, of course, among them) and their treatment of an autochthonous reality. While few would probably agree with de Cárdenas today in his restrictive view of the role of the indigenous American cultures, inevitably (and perhaps somewhat ironically) the attempts to (re)write a chronological, encyclopedical history of Chicano/a literature have led many Chicano/a literary historians to very similar positions.

Furthermore, as R. A. Gutiérrez's quote implies, the temptation to rely on the idea of "key writers and texts" (e.g., María Amparo Ruiz de Burton, Jovita González, Américo Paredes) would bring Chicano/a literary historiography back to utilizing the very same questionable methodology by which the recovered texts were marginalized in the first place, and it would of necessity result in the marginalization of other "less key" writers and texts, a danger against which Erlinda Gonzales-Berry cautioned future critics as well, as we saw. If—as Audre Lorde has suggested—the master's tools will never dismantle the master's house, then Chicano/a literary history would do well in exploring alternative routes and mappings for its product, rather than relying on obsolete historiographic formulas.[49]

An innovative approach to thinking about history, methodology, and identity is already visible in the works of Chela Sandoval and Emma Pérez. Benefiting from the insights of feminist and postcolonial cultural criticism (as well as from Foucauldian and Deleuzian thought), the works of Sandoval and Pérez have opened up alternative lines of approaching the study of the past that may be beneficial for literary historiography as well. First, by developing the idea of differential consciousness in a Chicano/a studies context, Sandoval has translated and adapted Homi Bhabha's notions on positionality to the culturally specific context in which it could benefit historians of this group's literature. The mobility of identities that the differential consciousness model presupposes serves as a potential corrective to the essentializing implicit in nationalistic ideology. Moreover, as studies like Genaro M. Padilla's *My History, Not Yours* and my own "'A Net Made of Holes'" have made clear, at most historical junctures Chicano/a literary identities have proven to be extraordinarily fluid.[50] Consequently, newer Chicano/a literary histories could benefit from a concept such as Sandoval's differential consciousness to rethink parameters of identity and allegiance.

Likewise, in *The Decolonial Imaginary,* Emma Pérez has advocated for historians of the Chicano/a experiences to challenge the current status of the discipline, in which "traditionalist historiography produces a fictive past, and that fiction becomes the knowledge manipulated to negate the 'other' culture's differences" (*Decolonial,* xviii). Instead, Pérez proposes a Foucauldian archaeology based on the notion of the "decolonial imaginary" "as a rupturing space, the alternative to that which is written into history" (*Decolonial,* 6), in which the rupture rather than the causal becomes the organizing trope for her transnational, nonlinear historical account. In doing so, Pérez refuses to construct another master narrative in which localities and differences are subsumed into the main argument of community and progress.

Pérez's understanding of history finds a recent echo in Louis G. Mendoza's *Historia,* a monograph that attempts to read literature and history side by side. Mendoza's claim that literary works should be read as valid historical evidence (19) may recall earlier reductionist positions that relegated works of art to the status of documents, but his counterbalancing affirmation (following Hayden White) that history should be read as a literary genre produces enough of an equilibrium to bring the two disciplines into a much more complex dialectical relationship. This leads Mendoza to problematize the relationship between Chicano/a literature, on the one hand, and historical narratives on the other. For Mendoza, "Chicano/a literary production . . . exists independent of the formation of Chicano historical narratives and often contests the representation of a historical generation by shifting the focus of concern away from narrow definitions of power and identity" (61–62). While I disagree with Mendoza on the alleged discursive independence of literary production, his emphasis on addressing the assumptions that inform historical narratives remains essential. In this sense, analyzing Mendoza's own stated guiding principles is quite instructive, as his narrative reveals the mark of a certain intentionality that (like Pérez) favors the selective over the comprehensive approach but (unlike her) adopts a chronological model along a generational axis. The former, in a rather original interpretive move, allows him to renounce the kind of encyclopedic history I analyzed above and to denounce it as a masculinist project (36), but the latter threatens his narrative with the kind of selective comparative approach I criticized in "Textual and Land Reclamations" and again in this chapter. In acknowledging that he "selected authors and texts that lent themselves to a comparative analysis with the historical master narratives" he calls into question (36) and in clearly privileging Texas and California over the rest of the Hispanic United States, Mendoza fails to open his text up to the kind of counternarrative he attempts to construct, while walking an extremely tight rope over the problem of selective reductionism that Perkins exposed (see p. 153 above).

An Alternative Model: Toward a New Chicano/a Literary History

Given the limitations of chronology, nationalism, and encyclopedism as the possible bases for organizing Chicano/a literary history, alternative models need to be explored in future readings of the Chicano/a past. While the task is yet to be performed, I have advocated elsewhere for a decentered, rhizomatic type of history to undertake this most pressing need ("'A Net Made of Holes,'" 18), and I will briefly expand on my model here. I am taking the term "rhizomatic" from Gilles Deleuze and Félix Guattari's *A Thousand Plateaus* without necessarily subscribing to other concepts put forth by these critics nor entering on the polemics of the scientific/botanical accuracy of their ideas. What interests me about their theory on the rhizome is the possibility it affords to conceive literary history as a decentered assemblage with multiple lines of entry, rather than as a monumental, unidirectional entity. Conceived in such a rhizomatic sense, Chicano/a literary history opens itself up to a more flexible approach that need not rest on a traditional notion of order (the chronological) and boundaries (the national) to aim for a sense of encyclopedic (the entire body of literature) or exemplary (the great authors and books) completeness. Rather, the literary historian can now enter this body of literature at any given point of significance, have certain texts (re)appear at different times (according to the respective literary appreciation accorded to them at those times), cross and transgress national or linguistic borders, and, most important of all, consciously acknowledge her/his role as interpreter/reader of this literature. Traditional literary history would have its narrative start at the "beginning" (e.g., the Spanish jarchas, *Beowulf,* Fray Marcos de Niza's

Relación) and then follow through the centuries all the way up to the present. A rhizomatic literary history, by contrast, would allow the historian to start, if s/he so desired, with the Chicano/a Movement (or with any other point in time) and then move backward (to situate the newly recovered texts in their original time, for instance), forward (toward post-Movement literature), sideways (toward Mexican or other relevant literatures—like the Latino/a, the feminist, or the gay and lesbian in the United States), or even to proceed by a combination of these and other possibilities, as I have done in a minimal exemplary attempt in my "'A Net Made of Holes.'" As suggested above, a rhizomatic literary history would also be flexible enough to allow its writer to account for the appearance and/or disappearance of texts beyond their date of production.

The advantages of such an approach for writing Chicano/a literary history are many, since the historian could insert the recovered texts (for example) in at least two different temporal junctures: that of their production and early reception and that of their reappearance in our present Chicano/a literary world. This would ensure that the texts are accorded a multiplicity of meanings and artistic status so that we may read them now as they relate to our own aesthetics and politics without doing violence to what they could have meant then for their contemporary readerships. In the case of unpublished texts or of those works that failed to reach their audience, we can certainly reconstruct the horizon of expectations of its intended readers *then* while studying the actual reception of the published book *now*.

A rhizomatic literary history, furthermore, would allow its creator to account for more recent "disappearances" of authors and books that were at some point vastly read and quoted but that have now all but faded away from critical and even popular discourses. Movimiento poets as diverse as Sergio D. Elizondo and Reymundo "Tigre" Pérez and narrators such as Saúl Sánchez and J. L. Navarro, among others, are seldom mentioned or read these days, but there is no reason to predict that their works could not be reclaimed or "recovered" at some point in the future (as Cecilio García-Camarillo's poetry has been).[51]

Last but not least, multiple lines of entry into the rhizomatic literary history of Chicano/a literature will guarantee that novels such as José Antonio Villarreal's *Pocho* are not read solely as what they signified at any one particular time in the history of their reception, but rather that they are allowed to be approached as evolving entities that transform and are transformed by its readers.

The model I am proposing would also problematize the very notion of readership. If, as I have proposed in this book, Chicano/a literature is "life in search of readers," then it becomes imperative not to impose on the reader the same kind of restrictive definitions that have been used in the past to determine whether an author was Chicano/a or not. As should be clear from my analysis, Chicano/a literature's audiences have been diverse and multifarious. From the double audience of Ruiz de Burton and other Californias/os to the transcultural readerships of Rolando Hinojosa and even more recent writers, the role played by intended, potential, and actual readers has been determinant in ensuring not only the survival but also the shape Chicano/a literature has taken.

A Chicano/a literary history, therefore, would need to examine readerships with as much care as is used to investigate its authors, for these audiences are also transnational, multilingual, and multicultural. Furthermore, the audience's physical (as well as cultural) mobility would need to be taken into account to analyze certain periods in Chicano/a literary history. To give but a brief example, much has been written about how the Mexican Revolution displaced a cadre of intellectuals and writers to the United States, where they resumed their literary activity in community periodicals and in other media. It has also been noticed how these writers (Jorge Ulica, for example) observed Chicanos/as "from the outside" in their *costumbrista* chronicles and other satirical pieces, yet very little attention has been given to their audiences, among which we can presuppose a great number of equally displaced readers whose enjoyment of these pieces would be possible precisely because of their status as cultural "outsiders" as well. As we recover texts originally printed in periodicals across the United States, much would be gained from researching who subscribed to those periodicals, what their implied audiences were like, and how they were shaped and influenced by those they needed to reach in order to survive.

In closing, then, a new type of literary history needs to be devised to account for as complex a case as that of Chicano/a literature. This history must be prepared to address both historical continuities and ruptures. Because the history of Chicano/a literature has been marked by social and material conditions resulting from war, colonialism, and economic and political subordination, any account of this literature would need to address both the links that have kept literary activity alive among Chicanos/as and the gaps that have resulted from those experiences of marginalization and disenfranchisement. Chicano/a literary historians should resist the temptation to write master narratives that portray this literature's history as a heroic succession of congruent steps from "the beginning" to the present. Rather, internal contradictions and differences (resulting from gender, class, ethnic, sexual, and linguistic factors, among others) should be given as much weight as commonalities. Likewise, the recovered texts' former erasure from the history of Chicano/a letters should not be ignored when restoring them to new historical accounts: their previous disappearance needs to be accounted for inasmuch as it has value for understanding those forces that have shaped literary production and reception.

In consequence, Chicano/a literary historians must be careful not to do violence to a text's multiple temporalities and historical contexts by ascribing it solely to its period of composition or publication. Since the history of Chicano/a letters should address issues of reception as well as those related to literary production and textuality, it should be open to the changing significance of literary works for successive generations of readers as well. In that sense, any Chicano/a work of literature belongs to all of those periods in which it has had relevance for its readers. Furthermore, because many of the texts to be included in this history are now being recovered after a long period of oblivion, historians should not reduce them to historical documents by inserting them only in the time in which they were composed or published. At the very least, Chicano/a literary historians should aspire to analyze these works both in their original time of production and in the time in which they were recovered and made available to readers once again.

A third element of importance in the kind of literary history that I am proposing is the need to address both the regional-case scenarios and the transnational experience of Chicanos/as. The history of Chicanos/as has been marked by the long-standing presence in more or less self-contained areas (e.g., New Mexico, the Valley in South Texas) as much as by migration, immigration, and other forms of diasporic movements (including exile and deportation). Any account of the Chicano/a literary past should be flexible enough to account for those local particularities while keeping in sight transnational developments. Chicano/a literary history, therefore, should not be approached as a national enterprise but rather as a regional, national-driven, or transnational phenomenon depending on the areas, periods, readerships, authors, and movements studied.

Other internal differences need to be observed when chronicling Chicano/a literary developments. Salient among them is the fact that Chicano/a literature has been written in Spanish, in English, and in varied combinations of both languages. In addition, other linguistic forms (Caló, pre-Hispanic tongues, foreign words) have played a role in shaping Chicano/a texts and their target audiences. Chicano/a literary histories, on the other hand, tend to be written in English and published in largely monolingual outlets where the original linguistic richness of Chicano/a texts may not appear at all or be relegated to translations in the endnotes. If they are not to be accomplices to historical processes of marginalization, Chicano/a literary historians must strive for respecting the original language(s) in which the different works are written and consumed by linguistically proficient readerships. If translations into any other languages are needed, they should not take preference over the original; Chicano/a literary histories should not suppress Chicano/a multilingualism for the sake of an academic community of readers that is mostly monolingual.

Because of the peculiarities noted above, Chicano/a literary history can ill afford to depend on a master narrative constructed from any one particular vantage point. A rhizomatic approach, on the other hand, would minimize the risk of constructing a history that exerts rhetorical violence over its subject in order to mold it into a particular shape or to prove a particular theory. This innovative, flexible structure would also allow the historian to explore the connections between Chicano/a and other literatures as they become of relevance for particular works or audiences. Finally, it will ensure that literary works are studied as organic structures with a life beyond their dates and places of publication and, in so doing, that they are not treated as documents but acknowledged as artistic objects permanently open to new aesthetic consumptions (or, in other words, life in search of readers). Chicano literary history, in effect, should not restrict itself to the analysis of literary production only but should be open to exploring readers' response and reception as well.

As explored throughout this book, Chicano/a literature has been formed historically by the continuous interplay of authors and readerships, from the early colonial writers who wrote both for the metropolis powers and for the local communities to present-day transcultural writers who need to address Chicano/a and non-Chicano/a readers alike. Readers have had a determinant effect on the generic shape of literary works (by providing authors with admissible familiar genres from which to depart, for instance), on their thematics (by providing a social base of relevance), and on the linguistic choices available to Chicano/a authors. A history of Chicano/a literature would be ill served by neglecting to study one of the two poles on which literary activity hinges. Rather, the history of Chicano/a letters must account for the evolving significance of texts and genres as their interaction with successive generations of readers alters their aesthetic status. Only then can we aspire to truly chronicle the changing evolution of what has proven to be life in a constant search of readers.

Notes

Introduction

1. *The Complete Works*, 327.

2. The only exception to this norm will apply when I quote from translated texts originally published in languages not directly related to Chicano/a literature (e.g., Italian or German).

3. CHICLE, a Chicano/a literature discussion list, was housed at the University of New Mexico, where librarian Teresa Márquez was in charge of maintaining and moderating the postings. Although literature and literary criticism were not the only subjects discussed, there were lively debates and contributions on Chicano/a literature until the list's closing, many of them by individuals who were not literary critics.

4. Moreover, as many decry the growing split between Chicano/a intellectuals and their communities, the idea of accessibility becomes a major subject of concern for a project such as mine. I am not advocating transforming scholarly monographs into popular texts (although I see my contributions on literature to community papers as a natural extension of my training), but if complex works of literature can be appreciated by un-trained readers, there is no reason why the critic should not strive for the same level of comprehensibility.

Chapter 1

1. *The Complete Works*, 327.

2. Boxed announcement on last page of inaugural issue. *El Grito* 1.1 (1967): n.p.

3. "To(o) Queer the Writer," 269. Anzaldúa's essay also touches upon issues of reading and its effects on identity formation.

4. As I will explore below, journalistic expansion and periods of intense literary development in certain localities are evidence of more organized literary activity. For an example of one of those local "booms," see F. A. Lomelí, "A Literary Portrait," especially 142–44.

5. Among the many studies devoted to Chicano/a folklore, the pioneering work of Américo Paredes is still the major point of reference. Of particular relevance for their treatment of issues of audience formation and transformation are *With His Pistol in His Hand* (especially chapters 2 and 5) and the recently compiled *Folklore and Culture.*

6. As I have explored in further detail in "Textual and Land Reclamations," the question of Ruiz de Burton's implied audience is somewhat more complicated, since she seems to have had two readerships in mind as she wrote *The Squatter*: the main one was that sympathetic Anglo audience I am referring to here, but there is a subtext in her novel that suggests that many passages were coded for a Mexican American readership as well.

7. She was not an entirely unknown figure, though. As early as 1890, Bancroft acknowledges (albeit in passing) an earlier work of hers in an essay on early California literature: "Mrs Burton reveals her innate Spanish taste in the five-act comedy of Don Quixote" (638).

8. [I dedicate these pages to my friend Lic. D. Félix Baca. They are a creation of my own imagination, and they are not stolen nor borrowed from Americans nor foreigners. I dare to plant on the New Mexican soil the seed of creative literature so that, if some others with a better ability than mine should follow the road I am opening, they could look back and point at me as the one who first undertook such an arduous task] (my translation).

9. Several publications have dealt with the colonial past of Chicano/a literature. See, for example, Herrera-Sobek's edited volume *Reconstructing a Chicano/a Literary Heritage.*

10. The first edition, from 1959, went largely unnoticed. When the text was reprinted in 1970, it was immediately surrounded by a critical apparatus that, starting with Ruiz's introduction, proclaimed it to be the first Chicano novel.

11. The treaty of Guadalupe-Hidalgo ended the war between the United States and Mexico in 1848. By that treaty, Mexico lost almost half of its territory to the United States. Mexican residents were given the choice of crossing the new border to the south or staying on their land, now part of a new country. Through legal schemes and outright harassment, most landed Mexicanos ended up losing their property shortly afterward. For more on the treaty, see Griswold del Castillo.

12. For examples relevant to the turn-of-the-century period, see Lomelí ("A Literary Portrait"), 147–48.

13. For an analysis of Chicanos/as as characters in non-Chicano/a books, see C. Robinson.

14. Interestingly, neither Mercedes nor Luciano seems to have read any books by a fellow Mexican American, as Mercedes concentrates on foreign books and Luciano is fond of European romantic writers and Hispanic dramas. Non–Mexican American writers likewise acknowledge reading as a favorite pastime for Californios. Consider, for example, the following quote from Gertrude Atherton's Rzánov: "Concha had a larger vocabulary than other Californians of her sex, for she had read many books, and if never a novel, she knew something of poetry" (100).

15. See San Miguel, "Let All of Them Take Heed," for an analysis of Chicanos/as and the school system in Texas, for example.

16. For general assessments of the Hispanic press in the United States, see Kanellos ("A Socio-Historic Study") and Chabrán and Chabrán. Regional studies abound, with examples ranging from New Mexico (Meyer and Meléndez) to the Midwest (Myers and Cortina). A comprehensive bibliography is found in Kanellos and Martell's *Hispanic Periodicals in the United States.*

17. Meléndez describes how *La Voz del Pueblo* and *El Independiente* (from Santa Fe, New Mexico, and Las Vegas, New Mexico, respectively) "claimed large readerships and good advertisement revenues, with subscribers lists for each in excess of three thousand names" (77), a number only surpassed by *La Revista de Taos,* whose readership Meléndez describes

as over five thousand. These figures strongly suggest that the papers were read beyond Santa Fe and Las Vegas, most likely through the efforts of La Prensa Asociada (Meléndez, 87–97).

18. This practice is also documented in literature, which further stresses its cultural relevance. For an example, see Aristeo Brito's *El diablo en Texas:* "Entonces cayó en la cuenta que la mejor manera de ayudar y ayudarse a sí mismo sería por medio del periodismo, y de inmediato circuló *El Fronterizo,* un periodiquito que leían no tanto los que necesitaban leerlo sino otros editores del suroeste. Su negocio cobró vigor cuando para su sorpresa, empezó a recibir periódicos de California, de Trinidad, Colorado, de Laredo, de Nuevo México, y de partes que ni sospechaba hubiera gente mexicana." (134) [Then he came to realize that the best way to help others and to help himself would be through journalism, and he immediately began to publish *The Frontiersman,* a small newspaper that was read not only by those who needed to read it but also by other publishers in the Southwest. His undertaking grew strong when to his surprise he began to receive newspapers from California, Trinidad, Colorado, Laredo, New Mexico, and from places where he never even suspected there were Mexicans] (*The Devil,* 37, trans. by David W. Foster).

19. McWilliams attributes this regional isolation to the patterns imposed by the Spanish conquest and settlement of the region, a discontinuous model that he terms "the broken border" (82). Acuña, in turn, stresses how that pattern prolonged itself until the Chicano/a Movement by focusing on regional leaders, or "caudillos" (338–42).

20. On the role of the Imprenta Lozano and of La Prensa see Hinojosa-Smith ("'La Prensa'"), Munguía, Ríos-McMillan, Bruce-Novoa ("'La Prensa'"), and Parle.

21. Details on the original publication of *Don Chipote* can be found in Nicolás Kanellos's introduction to any of the novel's modern editions. For additional bio-bibliographical information see Kanellos, "Daniel Venegas."

22. This is not to suggest that internal differences simply disappeared overnight but rather that the dominant rhetoric strategies deemphasized difference for the sake of unity. Thus, even if Movimiento rhetoric united Chicanos/as in a common nationality, differences in class, gender, and sexual orientation soon became tools of analysis that complicated the nationalistic language of unity.

23. Technological innovations and the improvement of communications need to be taken into account as well. For an analysis of how these factors influence American literature in general, see R. J. Zboray's "Antebellum Reading," especially pp. 192–94. On the GI Bill and other postwar transformations in Chicano/a society, see Meier and Ribera, 169–71.

24. This label has been used before by Lomelí in his "Contemporary Chicano Literature."

25. Rivera's agenda, as discussed by Olivares, is not unique, nor is it exclusively found in the field of literature. In the visual arts, Carmen Lomas Garza expressed a rather similar intention in a 1994 interview with Alicia Gaspar de Alba: "I felt I should concentrate . . . [on] everyday life, so that ordinary people could look at it and recognize themselves in the artwork and start to feel proud of their culture and their heritage" (cited in Gaspar de Alba, *Chicano Art,* 100).

26. For a reading of Rivera's work as autobiography, see Juan Rodríguez's "The Problematic in Tomás Rivera."

27. Quinto Sol started publishing *El Grito* in 1967. Soon afterward, it launched into an ambitious publishing agenda that included literary landmarks such as the 1969 anthology *El espejo/The Mirror* and the establishment of literary prizes of national scope. For more on Quinto Sol, see below in this chapter.

28. Another interesting example of this drive toward creating a national readership is Ernesto Galarza's *Todo mundo lee,* one of the chapbooks in his series Colección Mini-Libros. First published in 1973, *Todo mundo lee* combines images of people from different ages and ethnic and professional backgrounds (many of them, of course, Chicanos/as) engaged in public or private reading, thus demonstrating that reading is not the special privilege of any particular social or ethnic group. Among the readers so pictured and described were Teresita, *los obreros,* and *los braceros.* The seventies were also characterized by many community literacy drives, for which Galarza's book must have functioned as an inspirational tool.

29. A fourth prize was awarded in 1973 to Estela Portillo-Trambley, from Texas, and to Abelardo Delgado, a Mexican-born long-term resident of Colorado. The awarding of this prize was somewhat tarnished by the dissolution of Quinto Sol, split afterward into Tonatiuh Quinto Sol and Justa Publications.

30. This phenomenon—in itself—is not new, as the educational market has been deemed responsible for previous literary successes as far back in time as that enjoyed by French fabulist Jean de La Fontaine (Lyons, 494). My claim is that Quinto Sol was the first Chicano/a enterprise to capitalize on the educational market.

31. Notice also, in the quoted promotional text from Quinto Sol, the reference to international publishers. Chicano/a books started to be read and studied in European universities as well, mainly in Germany, France, and Spain, and the internationalization of Chicano/a literature has continued ever since at a steady pace.

32. My understanding of the models of identification with the hero is based on H. R. Jauss's *Aesthetic Experience and Literary Hermeneutics.*

33. For further analysis of Hinojosa's work in light of Iser's theory, see my book *Rolando Hinojosa y su "cronicón" chicano.*

34. The interested reader may also want to consult my *Rolando Hinojosa y su "cronicón" chicano,* where I analyze Hinojosa's multivolume Klail City Death Trip Series from a reader-oriented perspective. Chapter 4 of that study already utilizes the formula "vida en busca de lector" ("life in search of reader") as a subtitle.

35. I speak of the "ideal reader" not without taking into account Jonathan Culler's reservations when he points out that "[t]o speak of an ideal reader is to forget that reading has a history. There is no reason to suggest that the perfect master of today's interpretive techniques would be the ideal reader or that any trans-historic ideal could be conceived" ("Prolegomena," 53, note 3). However, I do believe that historically situated ideal audiences are definable and that they change across periods of time (even if the material text remains "the same"), as this and the next chapters will illustrate. While my analysis will be historically and culturally grounded, I will not engage in details about empirical audiences of the kind found in D. P. Nord's "A Republican Literature" or in N. Zill and M. Winglee's *Who Reads Literature?* Even if the information they present is quite valuable (particularly so in the latter case), a comprehensive empirical analysis of Chicano/a

literature's audience is beyond my purposes here.

36. [That year was lost to him. At times he tried to remember and, just about when he thought everything was clearing up some, he would be at a loss for words.... He tried to figure out when that time he had come to call "year" had started. He became aware that he was always thinking and thinking and from this there was no way out. Then he started thinking about how he never thought and this was when his mind would go blank and he would fall asleep. But before falling asleep he saw and heard many things . . .] (83). This and subsequent translations quoted from this book are by Evangelina Vigil-Piñón.

37. See Olivares's "The Search for Being," for example.

38. [Smiling, he walked down the chuckhole-ridden street leading to his house. He immediately felt happy because . . . he realized that in reality he hadn't lost anything. He had made a discovery. To discover and rediscover and piece things together. This to this, that to that, all with all. That was it. That was everything] (152).

39. [When he got home he went straight to the tree that was in the yard. He climbed it. He saw a palm tree on the horizon. He imagined someone perched on top, gazing across at him. He even raised one arm and waved it back and forth so that the other could see that he knew he was there] (152).

40. Without further elaborating on it, Gutiérrez Martínez-Conde has reached the same conclusion (83).

41. This connection becomes of greater interest through Rivera's admission (in an interview with Bruce-Novoa) of a long-term passion with painting that started in childhood (*Chicano Authors,* 141–42).

42. Bartolo becomes a character in *Tierra* and, as such, has been privileged by critics (cf. A. Morales's "'Y no se lo tragó la tierra'") as a figure representing the community and the oral tradition, as the following passage would suggest: "Bartolo pasaba por el pueblo por aquello de diciembre . . . vendiendo sus poemas. . . . Recuerdo que una vez le dijo a la raza que leyeran los poemas en voz alta porque la voz era la semilla del amor en la oscuridad" (74). "Bartolo passed through the town every December . . . selling his poems. . . . I recall that one time he told the people to read the poems out loud because the spoken word was the seed of love in the darkness" (154). Leaving aside the symbolism of terms such as "seed" and "darkness," I would like to suggest that Bartolo, a character related with the protagonist's (and the author's) childhood, represents the moment prior to the Chicano/a Movement and to contemporary Chicano/a literature when even reading was often a collective enterprise, involving a reader and his/her listeners. Bartolo's poems are, in this sense, very much like the "talking objects" of classical Greece that Svenbro analyzes: "[I]n a culture which practiced an oral reading, any inscribed object was necessarily a 'talking object,' . . . provided, of course, it could find one reader" (74, my translation). As I will demonstrate next, that reading pattern is no longer operative (or, at least, not the dominant one) when Rivera and his protagonist grow up.

43. I am using the term *metahistorical* in the sense in which H. White defines it in *Metahistory* (x). However, I also consider to be metahistorical those narrative fragments that comment on the form of narrating, something White does not include in his definition.

44. The only book not included in the series (for obvious reasons) is *This Migrant*

Earth, an English version by Hinojosa of Tomás Rivera's *Tierra.*

45. *Cronicón* has a slightly humoristic connotation in Spanish. Although it could be used as a derogatory term for a too big or pompous chronicle, Hinojosa's narrators seem to use the term more with a dose of bemused affection that the *-ón* ending can also convey.

46. For an analysis of orality and print in Hinojosa's series, see Broyles ("Hinojosa's").

47. The series *Dallas* ran on television from 1978 until 1991, thus coinciding in time with Hinojosa's works such as *Mi querido Rafa* (1981)—later translated by Hinojosa as *Dear Rafe* (1985)—and *Rites and Witnesses* (1982), in which this connection is better seen.

48. See Brox for an example of this criticism.

49. In this sense, the interplay of genres works to secure reader participation in a way not unlike that which Iser has identified as proper for what he calls "negations" (212 ff.); that is, a paradigmatic choice that eliminates all other textual possibilities without canceling them entirely. Rafa's experiences in Korea are re-created in the form of diaries in *The Useless Servants* and, to a lesser degree, in *Estampas del Valle;* the poetic version is found in *Korean Love Songs.* The incident at the "Aquí me quedo" occupies an entire section of *Estampas del Valle,* under the title "Por esas cosas que pasan."

50. For an analysis of Hinojosa's versions as representative of "how Hinojosa is evolving as writer" (92) see Akers ("From Translation"). While Akers's essay focuses on authorial intention, my reading here stresses reader's response as a reason for Hinojosa's versions. I have also developed this argument in my "Act of Reading Chicano/a Texts," 24–26.

51. "The repertoire consists of all the familiar territory within the text. This may be in the form of references to earlier works, or to social and historical norms, or to the whole culture from which the text has emerged" (Iser, 69).

52. On myths and their effect on the novel's reception, see Jean Cazemajou's "The Search for a Center" and Enrique Lamadrid's "The Dynamics of Myth."

53. The words in quotes are Padilla's (as quoted by Calderón). The manuscript that Calderón quotes was later published by Padilla as "Imprisoned Narrative?"

54. On the psychological pleasure of reading or listening to a familiar story, see Nell, 59–60.

Chapter 2

1. In J. Bruce-Novoa, *Chicano Authors,* 40.

2. "Reading about Reading," 147.

3. For two of the most well-known studies, see Bruce-Novoa's "Portraits of the Chicano Artist" and Eysturoy's *Daughters of Self-Creation.*

4. In this, Chicano/a literature is not unlike the rest of American and many other literatures. Judith Fetterley, as this chapter's second epigraph suggests, has argued the case for American literature in general, although she does not acknowledge any Chicano/a texts in her essay.

5. Even as late as 1975, Chicano/a reader characters appear at times if not as oddities, definitely as standing out for their knowledge and habits and, because of them, as bordering on insanity. Such is the case of Lupe, a character from Estela Portillo-Trambley's *Rain of Scorpions:* "Fito admired the fact that she had read so many books and had educated

herself beyond anyone he knew in the barrio. . . . What Fito saw in her was a form of education that was a kind of madness. The reading of too many books had grown into a madness, and that madness had grown wings" (*Rain of Scorpions*, 127–28). In this case, of course, Fito's perspective dictates the association between reading and madness, while we sense the narrator (and the implied author) siding with Lupe on her views of the liberatory role of reading: "These wings took her to places she dared not go before. She visited libraries, museums, and free concerts by herself. . . . She had the wings of a searcher and that was all that mattered" (128).

6. See Bruce-Novoa's "Portraits of the Chicano Artist" and R. Saldívar's *Chicano Narrative*.

7. In my criticism of a reading that considers literary texts as documents, I am follow-ing Wolfgang Iser, for whom a "theory of aesthetic response" would consider the text "not as a documentary record of something that exists or has existed, but as a reformula-tion of an already formulated reality, which brings into the world something that did not exist before" (x).

8. My reader may recognize in this question the dilemma posed by the theories of reading proposed by Stanley Fish and Umberto Eco, respectively. The former has advocated a quasi-total independence on the reader's part (see his *Is There a Text in This Class?*), while the latter advocates a more restricted set of possibilities based on textual strategies employed in a text to guide its readers (see his *Open Work*). While I would not attempt to resolve this issue, I am closer to Eco's position, in the sense that I believe that the text delimits to a certain extent successful and (possible but) unsuccessful readings (e.g., through the metaliterary information it may contain).

9. On aisthesis and poiesis as, respectively, the receptive and productive aspects of the aesthetic experience, see Jauss, *Aesthetic Experience*, chapters 5–6.

10. This tension between utilitarian reading and reading for pleasure dates back to the sixteenth century in the Anglo-Saxon world, as Victor Nell has noted (32), and could have deeper origins in the changes in reading patterns that scholasticism brought about (170). Nell's book is particularly useful as a frame of reference for analyzing Richard as a reader often "lost in a book."

11. On the Protestant ethic background of the dilemma of doing versus reading, see Nell, 31–32.

12. The movie referred to is, in all likelihood, Warner Brothers' *Juarez* (1939), starring Paul Muni as the Mexican president. See Hadley-García (70–76) and Pettit (147–48) for complementary analyses of this film.

13. While the views on gender and ethnicity contained in the above quote from *Pocho* would open themselves to a fascinating discussion, I must restrict myself to signaling how women (even in a novel that dramatizes a rather radical change of cultural paradigms) are still seen as the least-critical "readers," capable of cathartic readings but not visibly so of aisthetic or poietic enjoyment. As such, the misogynist discourse in *Pocho* dismisses passive consumption/reading and the young Richard, as the embodiment of the ideal, active reader that Villarreal seeks, is never again to be found at the movies.

14. [Melodramatic films aid their viewers in traveling from rural to urban traditions and back. In the 1940s, a demographic boom will populate Latin America with a relentless pro-

fusion; in the ensuing crash of mores, melodramas will be responsible for safe-guarding tradition. Everything changes around you, oh, viewer!, would be the message, but if you watch these movies, you will keep achieving a cathartic experience] (my translation).

15. Ong, *Orality and Literacy*, 108.

16. In this sense, the scene is also an inversion of the patriarchal familial type of reading described by Cavallo and Chartier in discussing idealized representations of the same during the eighteenth century: [The motif of a patriarchal, rural, biblical, evening reading in which the head of the family read aloud for all of the house dwellers gathered as an audience—a much repeated topic in the works of turn of the century painters and writers–expressed the grief for a lost type of reading] (42, my translation).

17. This is most explicitly explored in pp. 91 ff., among several other passages in the novel.

18. See p. 29, for instance.

19. For more on how certain texts were excluded from the Chicano/a canon in formation at this time, see Bruce-Novoa, "Canonical and NonCanonical Texts," 119–20.

20. For a discussion of similar questionings of "beginnings" and chronology by Michel Foucault and others, see chapter 5.

21. "En la frontera del lenguaje," on which this analysis is based.

22. To avoid unnecessary confusion, I will refer to Miguel Méndez by his name, reserving the term "The Author" (in quotation marks) for this authorial figure that signs the "Preface." On Booth's notion of "implied author," see his *Rhetoric of Fiction*, 71–76.

23. [I wrote this book with a plan and structure in order to move exquisite sensibilities, with the additional desire to win a smile of approval from the many academicians of the Spanish language, as many of them are devoted to ridding words of their fleas. I confess that my preconceived plan failed, not by design but because of a strange rebellion on the part of the words] (*Pilgrims*, 1). I will quote the Spanish original in the text while providing translations in endnotes. All translations are by David W. Foster.

24. [The sufferings, feelings, and anger of the oppressed] (*Pilgrims*, 1).

25. For Rivera, this was connected to remembering not only the stories that people used to tell but also the way they told them. See chapter 1 for details.

26. "I truly laughed when I saw that the words of the down-and-out struggled to reach the sacred stage of literature with dirty faces and the torn and tattered clothes of peasants" (1).

27. It is important to note that this reference to 1968 as the date of composition for *Peregrinos* appears in a paragraph added to the prologue in the latest edition of the novel. It is not clear why this date was not mentioned in earlier editions (by Editorial Peregrinos and by Justa Publications), although it may have been added simply because the Bilingual Press printing is more of a critical edition, including an introduction by Francisco A. Lomelí, a bibliography, etc. In any case, I see no reason to doubt the general accuracy of that statement as far as my reading of the novel is concerned, particularly since Méndez alluded elsewhere to works he had authored since 1948 (see Rodríguez del Pino, 40). For my purposes, then, 1948, 1968, 1974, and 1991 will be key dates to remember, referring, respec-

tively, to the beginning of Méndez's literary career, to the finishing of the manuscript of *Peregrinos*, to the novel's first printing, and to its reprinting in the Clásicos Chicanos series of Bilingual Press, with several (minor) additions.

28. This summary of criticism does not attempt to reflect the entire bibliography on *Peregrinos*. For a more extensive listing, see the Bilingual Press edition of the novel.

29. [The other Chicano was a tall and heavyset type, prematurely gray. The legendary Yaqui shone forth. He represented the stereotype of ignorance, making fun of the ostriches dressed like peacocks and writing books no one read] (117).

30. This fragment starts on p. 124 of the translation with the sentence, "The brothels in this lost area . . ." A typesetting problem in the translation italicizes that page from the beginning, but the first paragraph should not be in italics.

31. [Méndez wrote his first novel at the age of eighteen [in 1948]. That text, according to its author, "was a short novel of 120–150 pages, still unpublished and without a title." The need to publish was not there for Méndez at the time, because he thought that his stories about the people he knew would not interest anyone] (40, my translation).

32. [Méndez saw the break he needed to make public his artistic creations in that new movement which advocated the emancipation of the Chicano people in order to preserve their cultural tradition] (40, my translation).

33. [Read this book, reader, if you like the prose dictated to me by the common speech of the oppressed. If you don't, if it offends you, do not read it, for I will consider myself well paid just by having written it in my condition as a Mexican Indian, a wetback, and a Chicano] (*Pilgrims*, 2). This paragraph was the last one in the 1974 "Preface." The 1991 edition adds two more paragraphs outlining the novel's printing history.

34. [With all the fervor of Saint Isidore, he had sown the good seed in our tender minds. A stimulus that would not grow, that would fade away, diminished, but one that would subsist like a thirsty plant] (*Pilgrims*, 124).

35. ["[Y]ou are lying! Neither poetry nor poets exist, and everything is a masquerade so we can't see human tragedy. Only the slobs who ignore suffering and crime, those who toady to power, sing to the flowers with the eloquence of beggars, show no embarrassment as they pay homage to the powerful, and they repay flashiness and riches with a prostituted art. Fools!"] (*Pilgrims*, 126).

36. ["[M]aking fun of ostriches dressed like peacocks"] (*Pilgrims*, 117).

37. ["Flickering light, alive, radiant—dead! Mercury for the deceived, a disk of howling, scales, rings, strands of sand hair. Whirl, deceitful moon, whirl! Symphony of symbols, whirl in your immense coffin"] (*Pilgrims*, 49).

38. [[A]lways veiled by a sadness that came from deep within him] (*Pilgrims*, 51).

39. ["Now I understand why the poet loves the moon, because the moon is like poetry: both shine with the light of others. As long as there's no one to read the verses, they're probably dead"] (*Pilgrims*, 52). The word "probably" that Foster has chosen here to convey what in the Spanish original is expressed by a grammatical future tense does not do justice, in my opinion, to the force of "estarán muertos." A more literal, perhaps more accurate translation would be "they will be dead," which I prefer for my interpretation here.

40. [[A] falling star dragging along a tail of orphan words'] (*Pilgrims*, 70).

41. I am interpreting this fragment as one penned by El Vate because he is the only character who participated in that march whose name or nickname does not appear in the text. For this and all other texts I attribute to El Vate, I will give the page numbers of the Spanish original first and then the English translation pages separated by a slash.

42. Attributing this fragment to El Vate is more risky. Nonetheless, I think there are several elements in support of such attribution, among them the use of italics (as in the previous text I attributed to him), the desert as a subject, and the organic relationship between this fragment and the narrative of the crossing of the desert on pp. 86–88. A counterargument would be that El Vate is a poet, not a narrator. In reading his elegy to Lorenzo, however (see below), it is obvious that, if anything, El Vate writes poetic prose, not traditional metric poetry.

43. [In the desert, virgin in the absence of any will toward the creative, my words threaded their way among the dust storms. . . . Any innovation [sic] was answered by nothingness with its dead bell towers. And I was God writing pages in the wind so that my words would fly away. . . . Now I know that He creates life and that I invent the language with which one speaks. Nevertheless, I lose myself in the tangle of vocabulary and the words that still are not born of thought and that make one's heart ache] (Pilgrims, 82). The word "innovation" in the translation seems to result from a typo or a misreading of the original "invocación," which could have been translated as "invocation."

44. [He wished to make the desert flower with poems. Ecstatically, he went forth to plant metaphlowers and fountains with jets of polychrome letters. . . . On the canceled page of creation, he heard the cries that silence buries. . . . Cursed desert! You have drunk the language and the breath of my people of yore, Nahuatlaca majesty] (Pilgrims, 138).

45. The two quotes are translated as follows in Pilgrims: ["Here the voices travel far because no one holds them back"] (49); ["As long as there's no one to read the verses, they're probably dead"] (52). On this last translation, see note 39.

46. [Lencho had taught himself with pretentious and ready-made sentences. His clichés were not extracts from great literature, but sentences repeated by generations of politicians and ass-licking journalists, blind in their imaginations] (Pilgrims, 74).

47. [At meal time, with the whole family seated at the table, Mr. MacCane read the Bible. With a strong voice and pointing with his finger, he seemed to give off sparks] (Pilgrims, 144). On the significance of patriarchal, familial type of readings, see note 16 in this chapter.

48. ["You know what? Now it's almost like I felt ashamed, always scrounging around like an animal. You know what I mean, you've read a lot of comics. Are we just a bunch of slaves?"] (Pilgrims, 20). Granted, the irony is bittersweet, as it points out socioeconomic conditions in which books were not easily acquired by Chicanos/as. One need only consider the testimonies of Tomás Rivera and Sandra Cisneros to ascertain the continuity of this situation among Chicano communities. Rivera, for instance, recalls his first introduction to books by a friendly librarian during summers in Iowa. But acquiring reading materials was difficult for a farmworker family: "My dad knew I liked to read, so he would go knocking on doors, asking if they had any old magazines, which he then brought home to me. . . . We also used to go to the dump to collect reading materials" (Bruce-

Novoa, *Chicano Authors,* 143). This experience of the young Tomás Rivera has been re-created, in turn, by Pat Mora in her book for children, *Tomás and the Library Lady.* Cisneros, on the other hand, expresses in the following quote how absolutely unthinkable it was for her (even in an urban context much different from that to which Rivera alludes) to dream of owning her own books, as she reminisces on how she and her brother had plotted to keep a book on loan from the library: "I didn't know books could be legitimately purchased somewhere until years later. For a long time I believed they were so valuable as to only be dispensed to institutions and libraries, the only place I'd seen them" ("From a Writer's Notebook," 71). Margarita Cota-Cárdenas, furthermore, has written in *Puppet* about comic books as learning devices used by Chicano/a children, as her protagonist is introduced in the opening sentence of the novel as follows: "Aprendió a leer y escribir, leyendo el Pepín de Mexicalli" (1, [*sic*]) [She learned to read and write by reading the Pepín from Mexicali]. For a testimonial on reading El Pepín, see also Abelardo Delgado's interview with J. Bruce-Novoa, in *Chicano Authors,* 95–114 (especially 98).

49. [It was then that he invoked the legendary idols that inhabited the heart of his countrymen. Superman destroying planes in midair by merely spitting at them, lifting convoys with his baby finger, winning the war in a wink. Batman with his genius and strength overcoming the stupid Asians who did not know how to fight because they're cowards and short on smarts. And if these ultrapowerful beings did not dominate the unjust enemy, ah!, there was the great, the sublime, the invincible, and moreover exquisitely beautiful Great Cowboy!] (*Pilgrims,* 147).

50. For further analysis of Chicano/a reactions to white supremacist scholarship, see J. D. Saldívar, *The Dialectics,* 49–84; Martín-Rodríguez, *Rolando Hinojosa,* 27–67; and Pettit, 22–60 and 111–30.

51. For a more detailed analysis of these recovery efforts see chapter 5.

52. [Thus the story, like a bad dream, left us stranded suddenly in the island of forgetfulness, prisoners. Not only that, but the genes that guard our culture, the essence of our history, have been left chained up, clogging the arteries that carry the impetus of the blood that animates the voice and soul of our people like rivers. Neither dignity nor education for the slaves, the masters said, only ignominy, prejudice, and death. At best, the tragic slobber of demagoguery, the counterfeit money of the perverse] (*Pilgrims,* 178). In my reading of the Spanish original, I interpret "la historia" to mean "history" rather than "the story."

53. [When amnesia began to sow shadows in our memory, we went to our ancient lakes, seeking in the depth the faces we had lost] (*Pilgrims,* 178).

Chapter 3

1. [Basically, what I want to say is that for me being a woman means to have reading]. "Encuentro entre escritoras chicanas y mexicanas," 222.

2. "Silence at Bay," 29, original emphasis.

3. For an analysis of this context, see G. Padilla, *My History,* chapter 6, especially p. 198.

4. For recent, thorough accounts of this issue, see G. Padilla (*My History*) and R. Sánchez (*Telling Identities*).

5. On the role of *Holland Magazine* see Padilla, *My History,* 224.

6. In *Romance* she regrets her "appalling shortage of words, not being a writer, *and writing in a language almost foreign to me*" (vii, my emphasis).

7. For an assessment of the early reception of Chicana novelists see Lomelí, "Chicana Novelists," 46, endnote 6.

8. The name has since been changed to National Association for Chicana and Chicano Studies.

9. A similar complaint was still issued, almost a decade later, by María Herrera-Sobek, for whom "[i]f women's issues and concerns are not taken seriously by a male-dominated society, then works with a female perspective will not be published; and if indeed these works get published, critics (who are generally male) will ignore or lightly pass over these books" ("Introduction" to Herrera-Sobek, ed., *Beyond Stereotypes*, 10).

10. Author Denise Chávez has also credited Black women writers with addressing social and cultural taboos in their narratives, something that Chicana writers would do as well (quoted in J. Mena, 2).

11. In thus privileging gender over the other elements I just outlined, I am not suggesting that the foregrounding of gender is done at their expense or in absolute independence from them. Rather, I agree with McCracken when she suggests that although many Chicana and Latina narratives "ultimately emphasize the role of gender politics in the construction of identity, they often pass through the mediations of class, race, ethnicity, and sometimes sexual preference" (*New Latina Narrative*, 179). I would only add that the same is true for their attempts at audience formation and that the mediating factors at times include some of the others I have delineated, such as linguistic preference and geographic (and cultural) location.

12. I will not try to define what a Chicana practice of writing (or reading, for that matter) is. Rather, I will engage in the exploration of the ways some Chicanas write and of the audiences for whom they write. In this, of course, I am heeding H. Cixous's warning against attempting such a definition: "It is impossible to *define* a feminine practice of writing, and this is an impossibility that will remain, for this practice can never be theorized, enclosed, coded—which doesn't mean that it doesn't exist. But it will always surpass the discourse that regulates the phallocentric system; it does and will take place in areas other than those subordinated to philosophico-theoretical domination. It will be conceived of only by subjects who are breakers of automatisms, by peripheral figures that no authority can ever subjugate" ("The Laugh of the Medusa," 253, original emphasis).

13. For some of the most recent studies to explore these issues see Rebolledo's *Women Singing* and Martín-Rodríguez's "The Raw and Who Cooked It."

14. Herrera-Sobek's "The Street Scene" provides an interesting analysis of the street as a liberating space of self-assertion for Chicanas.

15. [my beans got burned / for I lived / in some other world of verses / for I wanted to tell someone / that I am not a legend / for thinking and feeling / a world that exists / yes it exists / in the air / water / fire earth / and a few lines from a poem].

16. On Nell, see chapter 2, note 10.

17. For additional analysis of the food images in this poem see my "The Raw and Who Cooked It."

18. For an early assessment of this issue, see P. Gutiérrez-Revuelta, "Género e ideología."

19. As the correspondence between Cisneros and Arte Público Press publisher Nicolás Kanellos demonstrates, at one point during the planning stages Kanellos suggested including poems as well. The poems originally considered were the following: "South Sangamon" (which Cisneros links with the *Mango Street* story "Minerva Writes Poems" in a handwritten note not dated), "Joe," "Good Hotdogs," "Traficante" (Cisneros casts doubt on its appropriateness, and Kanellos feels it is not appropriate), "Velorio," "Arturo Burro," "Abuelito Who," "I Told Susan Reyna," "Curtains" (same feelings as for "Traficante"), "Mexican Hat Dance," and "Muddy Kid Comes Home." Eventually, all poems were dismissed. Some of them had appeared in the chapbook *Bad Boys,* and most of them were later reprinted in *My Wicked Wicked Ways.* Of interest is Cisneros's reference (in a letter dated 10/1/82) to another poem, "Roosevelt Road," which she feels is too close to *Mango Street.* I would like to thank Nicolás Kanellos for granting me access to the Arte Público Press archives, which house copies of the correspondence between Cisneros and Kanellos as well as many other documents. A published, partial chronicle of the editing stages is found in Cisneros's "Do You Know Me?"

20. As Cisneros's readers will, no doubt, recognize, I am paraphrasing here the opening lines of the story "A House of My Own": "Not a flat. Not an apartment in back. Not a man's house. Not a daddy's" (108).

21. While odd at times, the punctuation throughout the book is intentionally so, as Cisneros reminds Kanellos in a letter dated 11/1/82. Not intentional are several typos, which affected the book's first printing and which were not corrected until Arte Público's second edition in 1987.

22. On a different level, this desire has also been made explicit by Cisneros in "Notes to a Young(er) Writer": "There are so few of us writing about the powerless, and that world, the world of thousands of silent women, . . . needs to be, must be recorded so that their stories can finally be heard" (76). Most likely, Cisneros's commitment is in part born out of her administrative experience at Loyola University in Chicago, as she recalls in "Do You Know Me?": "From that experience of listening to young Latinas whose problems were so great, I felt helpless; I was moved to do something to change their lives, ours, mine. I did the only thing I knew. I wrote . . ." (78).

23. That is the position adopted by Juan Rodríguez's early review in *The Austin Chronicle.*

24. In this and previous similar assertions I am suggesting that Cisneros's book enters into an intertextual dialogue with such major landmarks of feminist writing as Virginia Woolf's *A Room of One's Own* and Gilbert and Gubar's *The Madwoman in the Attic.* I am also aware of the fact that relegating the bums to the attic can be perceived as a classist act. Nonetheless, I believe that in the context of this "paper house" constructed in the book, the attic is more of a "paper attic" as well; i.e., an example of the intertextual dialogue to which I referred above.

25. Cisneros's epiphany here is extremely close to that of Tomás Rivera's character in *Tierra* (as discussed in chapter 1). For further comparison between Cisneros and Rivera

see the next section of this chapter.

26. See chapter 1, note 51.

27. For further analysis on nonconforming female heroes (as opposed to heroines) see Salazar Parr and Ramírez's "The Female Hero in Chicano Literature."

28. This delineation of a feminine space in literature needs to be read in the context of contemporary debates on women-only or women-of-color-only zones in academic (and other) gatherings. For the role of these male-gaze- or White-gaze-free zones, see D. J. González, especially 48–55.

29. Among them, I have already mentioned Virginia Woolf's work and that by Gilbert and Gubar. Another more or less obvious connection is with Gaston Bachelard's *The Poetics of Space*, a point of contact that Cisneros makes explicit in "Ghosts and Voices." While this list is not intended to enumerate the many other books with which *Mango Street* is connected, it provides a complementary balance to the book's marked sense of orality. I will return to the issue of intertextual dialogism below.

30. This episode is even more closely connected to the Cinderella story, a connection that Cisneros makes explicitly on page 40. As a story of little girls venturing into dangerous territory, I think that a connection with Little Red Riding Hood (or Shoes, perhaps) is also possible.

31. The correspondence between Cisneros and Kanellos housed in the archives of Arte Público Press suggests that the final ordering of the stories was a collaborative project in which Cisneros insisted on the relative placement of certain stories based on the narrator's sophistication and on the need for internal coherence of events (in a letter dated 11/1/82) but left room for editorial ordering by Kanellos (Kanellos suggested a final order in a letter dated 12/28/82).

32. See note 21 in this chapter.

33. In doing so, this narrative device of apparent circularity explores once more the conflict between Esperanza's desire for a house "clean as paper before the poem" (108) of the preceding story ("A House of My Own") and the fact that the paper in which she communicates her desire cannot be blank in order for her to do so.

34. On the notion of "resisting readings," see Fetterley, *The Resisting Reader,* in which she talks about the need "to become a resisting reader rather than an assenting reader and, by this refusal to assent, to begin the process of exorcizing the male mind that has been implanted in us" (xxii).

35. In this, *Mango Street* had a powerful predecessor in C. Moraga and Gloria Anzaldúa's edited anthology *This Bridge Called My Back*. As Moraga acknowledges in her foreword to the second edition, "We created a book which concentrated on relationships *between women*" (n.p., original emphasis). While Cisneros does not restrict herself to relationships between women, it is clear that her feminization of the repertoire seeks a special communication with her female readership.

36. See chapter 1.

37. In an e-mail communication (2/29/00) through her agent, Susan Bergholz, Cisneros recently told me that she had not read Rivera until 1984 or 1985, at least two years after finishing *Mango Street*.

38. Cisneros's position vis-à-vis writing the body seems to take into account both Hélène Cixous's gendered call for such an écriture as well as the culturally situated history of violence against Chicanas, exemplified by her texts just quoted and later succinctly articulated by Gloria Anzaldúa's opening remarks in *Making Face:* "Because our bodies have been stolen, brutalized or numbed it is difficult to speak from/through them" (xxii). For further analysis on Anzaldúa's position on this issue, see A. Keating, 118–44. As for Cixous, the following quote contains in a nutshell her position on writing and the body: "We've been turned away from our bodies, shamefully taught to ignore them, to strike them with that stupid sexual modesty. . . . But who are the men who give women the body that women blindly yield to them? Why so few texts? Because so few women have as yet won back their body. Women must write through their bodies, they must invent the impregnable language that will wreck partitions, classes, and rhetorics, regulations and codes . . ." (256).

39. The poem appeared first in *Third Woman* 4 (1989): 19–23. Some significant typographic features of that printing were not continued in the book edition. If anything, the original typography further confirms my analysis, but I have decided to use the *Loose Woman* version nonetheless, judging it not only more accessible for my readers but also a revised (maybe final) one. The three lines I consider to be central in the poem appear as follows in *Third Woman:* "Yes, / I want to talk at length about MEN-/ struation. Or my period" (22).

40. This syllabic similarity should not be pushed too far, however, as the lines do not follow the traditional 5-7-5 syllable symmetrical scheme of the classic haiku.

41. This feminization of the repertoire is not unlike the female imaginary of which Emma Pérez speaks in her reading of Irigaray: "By placing women, women's bodies, and their sexualities at center, the feminist essentializes to achieve a specific task—the female imaginary" ("Irigaray's Female," 91).

42. A footnote on p. 82 identifies the poem as John Updike's poem "Cunts," published in the January 1984 issue of *Playboy*. The complete reference reads as follows in Cisneros's poem: "Baby, I'd like to mention / the Tampax you pulled with your teeth / once in a *Playboy* poem / and found it, darling, not so bloody" (82).

43. See note 42 for the lines in Cisneros's poem with that reference. Most likely, Cisneros is also playing here with the traditional image of the "vagina dentata" and its associated fear of castration.

44. [for those who think with their penis . . .]. The poem appears in *Thirty an' Seen a Lot*.

45. Needless to say, much of this "writing the body" had already taken place in *Mango Street*. Even the most cursory look at the table of contents (where we find stories such as "Hairs," "The Family of Little Feet," and "Hips" among others with less obvious titles) would confirm this. In this double process of writing the body and rewriting traditional discourses, Chicana writers such as Cisneros or Margarita Cota-Cárdenas (one of the first poets to take on classical myths, in her *Noches despertando inconciencias*), are very close to French feminists such as Hélène Cixous and Monique Wittig and the associated concept of écriture féminine. However, as my discussion of *Mango Street* should have made

evident, Chicana writing cannot be disassociated from its specific social and cultural conditions.

46. I am borrowing this title from Martha P. Cotera's seminal analysis of Chicana history.

47. "Mitólogos y mitómanos," 8.

48. The bibliography on Aztlán and its significance for Chicanas/os is extensive. The most accessible introduction is found in Anaya and Lomelí, eds., *Aztlán.*

49. Mayan cultural references were also incorporated, to a lesser extent, most of all by Alurista and Luis Valdez. A "dissenting" voice in the indigenist ranks was that of Miguel Méndez, who concentrated on Yaqui myths and legends.

50. El Sol's first words after greeting La Luna and La Tierra set the tone for La Luna's subordination to male characters: "SOL: Luna! How goes my eternal war with the stars? ¿Cuidaste mi cielo por toda la noche? [Did you take care of my heavens all night long?] / LUNA: Simón [yes], Jefe, the heavens are fine. / SOL: ¿Y tu hermana? [How about your sister?] Did you watch over her?" (162).

51. For her maternal side, see the last lines of the play: "BERNABE and LA TIERRA appear in a cosmic embrace. He is naked, wearing only a loincloth. She is Coatlicue, Mother Earth, the Aztec Goddess of Life, Death, and Rebirth" (167). Earlier, La Tierra is compared to a whore (part of the play takes place in a bordello) by her father, the Sun: "Billions of men have loved her.... Look at her, Bernabé, this is la Tierra who has been all things to all men. Madre, prostituta, mujer [Mother, prostitute, woman]" (163).

52. On a different note, Valdez's changes in sexes and roles sidesteps another element of the original story: Coyolxauhqui's dismemberment by Huitzilopochtli as a punishment for her attempt at matricide. For more on the significance for Chicana literature of Coyolxauhqui's dismemberment, see below my interpretation of Gloria Anzaldúa's poem "Holy Relics." Although she does not discuss "Bernabé," Broyles-González's *El Teatro Campesino* is the most comprehensive study on women and/in El Teatro Campesino.

53. Del Castillo's lead has been followed by many others whose works I have no space to discuss here. For the interested reader, other substantial contributions to this critical reassessment are Norma Alarcón's "Chicana's Feminist Literature" and "Traddutora [sic], Traditora."

54. The entire poetic section of *Borderlands* is titled "Un agitado viento/Ehécatl, The Wind." In Aztec mythology, Ehécatl is a manifestation of Quetzalcoatl and, in fact, Quetzalcoatl and Huitzilopochtli play an important role in Anzaldúa's analysis in her chapter 3.

55. Cultural nationalism had been the subject of attacks from Marxist critics because of its alleged detachment from the most immediate realities. This critique, however, was based on class and not gender parameters as is Anzaldúa's. For more on cultural nationalism and the Marxist critics see my "Aesthetic Concepts," 113–14.

56. Cherríe Moraga, for instance, criticizes the way those two chapters become disjointed, self-conscious, and laborious in their prose ("Algo secretamente amado," 152) while further reproving some of the more metaphysical poems in *Borderlands*, which, in her opinion, "become 'mini-essays,' convoluted with 'new age' and psychological jargon" (154).

57. Notice, in the final lines of this quote, the parallel with Esperanza's wishes for a

house of her own (not a daddy's, not a husband's).

58. For another line of connection with religious/literary traditions in *Borderlands,* see Gaspar de Alba, "The Politics of Location," 150.

59. [In this dark mount of cacti / Something secretly loved / Is hiding in my womb / And in my heart / A love not from this world incubates].

60. A name Anzaldúa uses throughout the book to refer to Coatlicue.

61. "Y ahora por todas las tierras vulnerada te busco. / Antigua, tu hija errante no puede alcanzarte" (189) [And now, wounded, I look for you through all lands. / Antigua, your wandering daughter cannot reach you].

62. "En medio de un chillido de trenes / veniste [*sic*] a las ruinas de Brooklyn / con tu sonido de cascabeles" [In the midst of a trains' howling / you came to the ruins of Brooklyn / with your bell's sound]. Notice how skillfully Anzaldúa fuses the images of the sounds of the bells and the trains' whistling, which point, respectively, to Coatlicue's daughter Coyolxauhqui, earlier referred to in the book as "She With Golden Bells" (27)—at the same time, the bells are also a reference to the rattlesnakes on Coatlicue herself, thus connecting mother and daughter through the symbol of the serpent— and to Coatlicue's manifestation as Cihuacoatl, la Llorona. The trains as metaphors for the serpent (a similar comparison had been used before by Rudolfo A. Anaya in his *Heart of Aztlán*) are effective in the literal context (one cannot help but think of the underground trains of the subway) as well as in the mythopoetic one (as a further connection with Coatlicue).

63. "Mira como [*sic*] me has arruinado. / No tengo remedio" (189) [Look how you ruined me. / I am hopeless].

64. There are a few other elements of mystic poetry in "Antigua," such as the description of the goddess/lover as a farmer who plants her seed in the speaker, only to flee at harvesttime. I think that the ones I have already mentioned are sufficient in any case to document my point.

65. Anzaldúa is very close here and elsewhere in *Borderlands* to the poetry of Alurista, with whom she shares an interest in reviving pre-Hispanic mythologies. In particular, Alurista's "must be the season of the witch" (from *Floricanto en Aztlán*), in which he describes the alienation felt by many Mexicans and Chicanos in the United States, reverberates as a clear intertextual presence. In that poem, Alurista paints an image of La Llorona looking for her lost children in the United States. In Anzaldúa's poem, La Llorona/ Coatlicue arrives in Brooklyn as a serpent/train. This intertextual presence is felt even more directly in the chapter "Entering the Serpent," where Anzaldúa summarizes her views on La Llorona, and she concludes as follows: "I'd like to think that she was crying for her lost children, *los Chicanos/mexicanos*" (38, original emphasis). Even the didactic, motivational aspect of Alurista's poetry finds a feminized counterpart in Anzaldúa, as a comparison between the former's "Tortilla Host" (from *Nationchild Plumaroja)* or many other poems in that book and in the earlier *Floricanto* and the latter's "No se raje, chicanita" (from *Borderlands*) would prove. Much as Rivera was a powerful intertext for Cisneros, Alurista can be said to be the Chicano author closest to Anzaldúa.

66. Santamaría notes both "cantil" and "cantil de agua" as terms designating snakes; regional differences in the animals these words identify are also noted in his dictionary.

67. The letters, as I will discuss below in more detail, have been arranged by Castillo (loosely following the model of Argentinian writer Julio Cortázar) in four different reading orders corresponding to "the Conformist," "the Cynic," "the Quixotic," and "the reader committed to nothing but short fiction" (for whom the author notes that all letters can be read separately). A fifth ordering, not explicitly suggested by Castillo but nonetheless obvious judging from the sequential presentation in the book, is to read the letters *continuously* from number 1 to number 40. Following this peculiar arrangement, the "Conformist" and the "Quixotic" readers will encounter letter Three as their second letter; for the "Cynic," letter Three is the first.

68. In her 1988 book of poems, *My Father Was a Toltec,* Castillo plays again with the reader's expectations, as the Toltecs to which the title refers are not the pre-Hispanic people but an urban gang in Chicago.

69. Alarcón has analyzed sarcasm as it relates to the erotic discourse in *Mixquiahuala,* exploring both the intertextual origins of Teresa's erotic illusions and ideals (i.e., romance, telenovelas) and the "sarcastic, pragmatic, and even distant tone" ("The Sardonic," 99) that she assumes in retelling those experiences.

70. Chicana authors have mostly been wary of these excursions/searches into Mexico, and their critique has normally centered upon sexuality and/or societal roles expected of women. In one of the most well-known poems to deal with this issue, "Oaxaca, 1974," Lorna Dee Cervantes ponders issues of identity while in Mexico, only to be confronted by a feeling of foreignness thrown at her in (un)ambiguous sexual terms: "But Mexico gags, / ¡Esputa! / on this bland pochaseed" (*Emplumada,* 44). The equation between "pocha" (acculturated Mexican American) and "puta" (whore) with which Mexico rejects the poetic persona in Cervantes's poem is not entirely unlike the equation between "gringas" and "liberated women" that the engineers of *Mixquiahuala*'s letter Twenty-two use to try to bed with Teresa and Alicia. As Teresa explains: "In *that* country, the term 'liberated woman' meant something other than what we had strived for back in the United States. In this case it simply meant a woman who would sleep nondiscriminately with any man who came along" (79, my emphasis).

71. Letters Twenty-three and Twenty-five, among others, contain narrative details about the physical violence they are subjected to.

72. This letter, written as a poem, was first published as "From 'A Letter to Alicia'" in Castillo's *Women Are Not Roses* (19–20).

73. Roberta Fernández has synthesized as follows the cultural atmosphere that I suggest Castillo is demystifying: "Male critics created their 'criticism of anticipation,' defining what Chicano literature should be like before it was actually written. During those years, . . . a patriarchal umbrella hovered over Chicano literature written by men about male rituals. It referred to Aztec warriors and male heroes in the barrio. It dealt with the land and with the working class according to male values" (76–77).

74. For more on how the reader's expectations are aroused by the text, see S. Fish, *Is There a Text,* 21–67.

75. The imagery also recalls the myth of Aztlán as retold by Fray Diego Durán. The friar explains how the Aztecs were forced to migrate south from their paradisiac island

(Aztlán) and how "después que salieron de allí a la tierra firme y dejaron aquel delicioso lugar, todo se volvió contra ellos: las yerbas mordían, las piedras picaban . . . todo lo hallaron lleno de víboras y culebras y sabandijas ponzoñosas" (*Historia de las Indias* I, XXVII. Quoted in Leal, "En busca," 23) [after they came to the mainland and abandoned that delightful place, everything turned against them. The weeds began to bite, the stones became sharp, . . . everything became filled with vipers, snakes, poisonous little animals], trans. Doris Heyden; Leal, "In Search," 9.

76. More recently, Cherríe Moraga has also engaged in a similar feminization of the sacrificial locus that also subverts traditional expectations from the reader. In her poem "Credo" ["The Apostle's Creed"; literally "I believe" in Latin], from *The Last Generation,* the orthodox Catholicism implied in the title (which is that of one of the most important Catholic prayers) immediately derives into domestic synchretism in the first verse ("Frente al altar de mi madre" [In front of my mother's altar], 65). Several lines later, the synchretic balance is lost again, this time as we enter the world of pre-Hispanic religion filtered, as in the case of Castillo, by eroticism: "I believed and dreamed / my body stripped naked / like the virgin daughter / splayed upon your altar. / Not that you, my priestess / would wrench from me / my heart sangrando / but to feel your hand heavy / on that raised hill / of flesh / my breast / rising / like a pyramid / from the sacred / walls of this templo / my body" (65–66).

77. This "prologue" has been called the "real beginning" of the book by N. Alarcón ("The Sardonic," 105), who rightly points out that "the first letter is to the reader, penned by Castillo" (105). To avoid confusion with Teresa's letters, however, I will refer to Castillo's letter to the reader as the prologue (my term). This prologue is placed after the dedication to Cortázar and an epigraph from Anaïs Nin and before a disclaimer and Teresa's letters (which in all Doubleday's printings—but not in the original Bilingual Press edition—are also preceded by a second title page, which reads "The Mixquiahuala Letters," thus suggesting the preliminary role of all preceding materials).

78. A. Quintana has also perceived this effect, which she interprets as a mediating discourse intended to raise "questions regarding the issue of authority and interpretation, an issue which has become problematic in the disciplines of history and anthropology" (82).

79. These categories have been further analyzed in P. Rabinowitz's "What's Hecuba to Us?"

80. A foremost Chicano/a example of literary recycling is *The Road to Tamazunchale,* where Arias borrows freely from Gabriel García Márquez's story "El ahogado más bello del mundo." See E. Martínez's "Ron Arias" and Martín-Rodríguez's "Border Crisscrossing" for further analysis.

81. In fact, Cortázar refers to three types of reader: the "lector alondra," or lark reader, who identifies him/herself with the characters in the text s/he is reading (*Rayuela,* 112); the "lector hembra," defined in *Rayuela* as one that "no quiere problemas sino soluciones, o falsos problemas ajenos que le permiten sufrir cómodamente sentado en su sillón" (496) [the type that doesn't want any problems but rather solutions, or false and alien problems that will allow him to suffer comfortably seated in his chair] (this and all other translated passages I will quote are from *Hopscotch,* trans. Gregory Rabassa); and the "lector cómplice" for whom the author creates a dis-organized or dis-ordered text that forces her/him to forgo the cathartic aspects of reading in favor of an active role as,

almost, cocreator: "Intentar en cambio un texto que no agarre al lector pero que lo vuelva obligadamente cómplice al murmurarle, por debajo del desarrollo convencional, otros rumbos más esotéricos" (447) [To attempt on the other hand a text that would not clutch the reader but that would oblige him to become an accomplice as it whispers to him underneath the conventional exposition other more esoteric directions] (396). Although Cortázar scorns both the female and the lark reader, in the past chapter we saw how effective and even revolutionary a mimetic reading could be for a marginalized literature (see my discussion on Tomás Rivera), and in thus we can see how the "female" reader is a less than felicitous term. Cortázar's views on reading should, therefore, be applied carefully to the analysis of Chicana/o literature, as historical and cultural circumstances need to be taken into account.

82. Even a cursory glance at the text would reveal numerous passages such as the following from letter Three to support my claim: "*Our* first letters were addressed and signed with the greatest affirmation of allegiance . . ." (24, my emphasis), or the following opening of letter Twenty-seven, which strongly suggests a direct response to a letter from Alicia: "Alicia, I too suffer from dreams" (101).

83. This episode, in chapter 34 of the novel, is where criticism of both the "female" and the "lark" reader is more fully developed in *Rayuela*. Horacio Oliveira's thoughts occupy the even lines while Galdós's text is printed on the odd lines. The resulting "critique of la Maga's retrograde reading habits" (Debra A. Castillo, "Reading Over Her Shoulder," 148) is not exempt from a marked chauvinistic discourse in which Oliveira shows an absolute disregard for how reading in itself can be a form of resistance, regardless of the text being read, as Radway—among others—has shown (see her influential *Reading the Romance*). D. A. Castillo provides a useful synopsis of the "female reader" as both a disdained figure in the Christian tradition and as a subversive figure in Latin American female narratives in *Talking Back*, 47–54.

84. These terms are M. M. Bakhtin's. For further elaboration see his *The Dialogic Imagination*, 278 ff.

85. In "Yes, dear critic" Castillo has poked fun at critics pondering this dilemma: "As to the ingenuous opinion of one of your colleagues, who wrote in a review that it is 'unclear as to why anyone would write such elaborate letters simply to retell, without analysis, what the recipient already knows,' I would have to suggest . . . to kindly take the time for a more careful reading of the text" (157).

86. Heiner Bus has suggested a parallel between Alicia and the potential unfamiliar Anglo reader: "Alicia emerges from this letter [One] as a fairly naive outsider who needs assistance like the well-intentioned liberal Anglo reader even farther removed from the clash of cultures under investigation" ("'i too,'" 129). While provocative, this comparison is not without problems as (*a*) letter One is absent from two of the proposed readings (Conformist and Cynic) and only appears as the last letter for the Quixotic, thus minimizing its potential guiding effect; (*b*) all forty letters painfully set out to explore how both Teresa and Alicia are, at some point or another, cultural outsiders to a certain extent. My own reading of Alicia as an addressee of and an addressor to Teresa would emphasize the way both women negotiate relative cultural positions in a constant exploration of change

and multiple subjectivities. This, I believe, is further confirmed in letter Twenty-five, when Teresa adds a parenthesis addressing both Alicia (as a figurative reader) and the actual reader as a virtual narratological presence: "(Now, dear Alicia, i know you are cynically recalling that after all we two brave, but not always wise, heroines had been through, there was no way we should have contemplated one more risk.... Years later, only hindsight causes us to look upon the engineers' proposal as ludicrous, but we are not those of then, and if anyone else happens to read this account and would like to give us the benefit of the doubt, i warn him/her not to put money on it)" (94).

87. As Carolyn Heilbrun has further punctualized, "reading as a woman" does not take place every time a woman reads, since women may read (and have indeed read) as men in the past (39). Judith Fetterley suggests a way to read as a woman by becoming a resisting rather than an assenting reader (see note 34). This is, I believe, what Castillo is trying to accomplish with *Mixquiahuala*. J. Culler provides an interesting analysis of what reading as a woman has meant for different waves of feminism in his *On Deconstruction,* 43–64.

88. See note 81.

89. The situation is, perhaps, comparable to that of biblical interpretation in the Middle Ages, when the moral, allegorical, and anagogical readings were first devised as complements for a literal interpretation. As Umberto Eco has explored, this apparent diversification of approaches was misleading in its presumable openness: "What in fact is made available is a range of rigidly preestablished and ordained interpretive solutions, and these never allow the reader to move outside the strict control of the author" (*The Role of the Reader,* 51). While Castillo's control is certainly not as complete, the parallel is still valid inasmuch as her lines of reading are an obtrusion of the reader's ability to engage in her/his own reading of *Mixquiahuala.*

90. Yarbro-Bejarano, after noticing that the book (as printed) ends by foregrounding "the bonding between the two women through failed relationships with men" (67), goes on to characterize the other different endings as "ways of living out different strands of Teresa's subjectivity—the confirmation of maternal and cultural dictates in the conformist ...; the confirmation of women's betrayal of women in the cynic ...; and the quixotic preparations for yet another trip to Mexico" (68). Inasmuch as she reads them as "strands of Teresa's subjectivity," Yarbro-Bejarano's reading confirms Alarcón's views, particularly so when she claims that "the text's meaning is in no one of these endings and in all" (68). For my own reading, however, the notion of a "meaning" of the text is largely irrelevant, particularly for a text like *Mixquiahuala.* Rather than emphasizing the importance of the (multiple) endings, I think *Mixquiahuala* emphasizes the significance of the multiple (or infinite, see below) reading processes.

91. Others, like Gonzales-Berry, have chosen to interpret this as "Castillo plac[ing] her reader in the very uncomfortable position of having to make a choice based on an act of self-scrutiny and self-definition" ("The [Subversive]," 116).

92. This is what Carlos Fuentes proposes with respect to *Rayuela* when he suggests that, once the reader realizes that the novel can be read from beginning to end or following the alternative ordering, there is nothing to stop her/him from concluding that there could also be a third reading, and so on and so forth, ad infinitum (*La nueva novela,* 69).

The term "open text" is, of course, borrowed from Umberto Eco's *The Open Work*.

93. Gonzales-Berry has expanded on this point when she notices how "gradually there begins a breakdown of this [letter genre] pattern: failure to date letters, a confusing mixture of pronouns, a missing greeting here, an absent farewell there, no signature. The very conventions of the genre which traditionally have marked the boundaries between self and others begin to disappear and ambiguity shows her tantalizing face" ("The [Subversive]," 119).

94. See note 81 for a translation of this passage.

95. This clear description of her ideal audience, while acknowledging the centrality of that Chicana-to-Chicana communication, does not mean that Castillo is unaware of multiple audiences who might enjoy the book at other levels or in other ways. In the same interview, she goes on to say the following: "**Interviewer**: You've probably characterized your ideal audience as "another woman of color" or more specifically as a "friend who was a budding feminist . . . had some consciousness . . . and needed to work things out." Is that still your ideal audience? **Castillo:** I still think so. If I focus on my perspective and what I feel I've needed to explore as a social being, as an entity in this society, that guides me on what I write. For example, in *Massacre of the Dreamers*, a book about Chicano and Mexican women, I have that focus. I said in the introduction that when I spoke of men and women, I was specifically talking about Mexican men and Mexican women unless otherwise specified. My editor, my agent, and my publisher—all said, 'You know, Ana, although you are directing yourself to this woman, there are a lot of people who are interested and will be using that work.' I would like to think that anybody in my time right now will pick up my work and say 'there's something in there for me.' People have been asking me for the past 5 years, white students at universities for example, 'I really identify with your poetry or with *The Mixquiahuala Letters*, does that bother you?' and I always respond 'No that doesn't bother me. I'm very delighted that you enjoyed it and that it speaks to you.' So, now I'm much clearer on the importance of acknowledging that there is a wider audience in the country and abroad. In fact, I welcome it because by welcoming it it's not that I personally get accepted, but that we are communicating as a culture to other people. That's making it acceptable to other people instead of historically being foreign and strange and therefore something they could reject" (140–41).

96. Needless to say, *Paletitas* has other interesting points of connection with the texts and authors studied so far in this chapter. Like Cisneros's *The House on Mango Street*, *Paletitas* is a novel about growing up and achieving a state of consciousness and understanding, even if Marina is no longer a child. *Paletitas* also shares a borderlands problematics with Anzaldúa's text, along with an investigation of language and mestizaje. Finally, a point of contact with *Mixquiahuala* is the motif of the journey to Mexico, which forms the bulk of this novel. The most salient difference with all three of them resides in the fact that *Paletitas* is entirely written in Spanish.

97. In one of the numerous metaliterary asides to the reader, the narrator refers to the text as a combination of "los apuntes del viaje y las memorias de postviaje" (32) [notes taken during the trip and after-the-trip memories] (my translation).

98. This moment is chronicled on pp. 32–33.

99. Of interest, likewise, are references in passing to works by Chicano authors, Sergio Elizondo among them.

100. The different sections of *Paletitas* are not numbered or titled, so I will refer to them by page numbers.

101. [Come on, don't be a sissy; enough with the euphemisms; name that sacred instrument, the vehicle and the carrier of the male ego, the word become flesh, that obscene extension, the cause of our terror, the object of our desire] (my translation).

102. [Don't you see how much better you feel after calling it by its names? Isn't it true that naming things is like finding a thread of freedom?] (my translation).

103. I have witnessed, in several public readings, the delight of the female audience when this fragment is read.

104. ["Can you imagine, Mari, the power that would result from the union of all chains of words from all women of the world?"] (my translation).

105. In a metaliterary aside right after the dream I am analyzing, Marina asks herself how to narrate the dream, given the fact that she is both inside the dream (as a character) and outside of it (as the narrator). The last line of that fragment, "¿Qué diferencia hay entre el sueño y la narración?" ["What is the difference between dream and narration?"] (78) is a question for the reader to ponder. For my own purposes here, I believe that the question reinforces my interpretation of *Paletitas* as a chain link in that string that connects—or should connect—all women: inside the dream, Marina listens to Malintzin; outside of it, she tells the story to her readers.

106. [Despite their [the notes] naiveté, . . . I thought that they revealed a certain inquisitive attitude, perhaps, that might be of interest for those who currently labor in discovering the feminine voice (not to mention the feminine Chicana voice), which, until recently, had remained hidden behind the canonical voices of occidental culture] (my translation). As I have suggested elsewhere ("En la lengua materna," 83), the original reads "encubrir" (to hide), which will not make sense in the context of the quote. In both cases, therefore, I have substituted "encubrir" for "descubrir" (to discover), which appears to be more appropriate.

107. See my "En la frontera del lenguaje," 59. For Todorov, see *The Poetics of Prose*, 70.

108. "You may have wondered more than once why is it that I have not given him a voice or a body. I am not entirely sure myself. However, I will offer you some possibilities. . . . 1) I saw the technique in a novel by a Mexican writer, and I was quite impressed by it; . . . 3) he really is the reader with whom Mari wants to establish an intimate relationship; 4) some of you will say that he never existed, that he is only a projection of your/my/our particular vision of the ideal male, that is, the Second Sex inventing the First at its will." The second option, which I am not quoting verbatim, suggests that she does not remember him properly or that the act of remembering is too painful for her to embark on a narrative retelling.

109. On postmodern metaphors, clichés, and literalization, see McHale, 134–40.

Chapter Four

1. [I want to write a story in the vulgar romance / in which people normally talk to their neighbors / because I am not wise enough to write it in Latin; / I believe it will be

worth a glass of good wine.] *La vida de Santo Domingo de Silos,* 35. My (functional rather than artistic) translation.

2. On the tensions arising from the rhetorical connection to the oral tradition and the written media, see Bruce-Novoa's "Dialogical Strategies," especially pp. 237–38.

3. "Lenguaje y poder" and "The Act of Reading Chicano/a Texts," primarily.

4. This is not to suggest that presses and editors did not curtail, at times, this freedom. Alejandro Morales's crude language and distorted syntax in *Caras viejas y vino nuevo* (along with the type of situations he creates in that novel) may have played a major role in the difficulties that the author encountered in publishing it (see Morales, "Dynamic Identities," 17). Likewise, the editors of Quinto Sol allegedly rejected Alurista's early bilingual poetry at first, only to accept it for publication shortly afterward; the mixing of languages that Alurista practiced seems to have been the disturbing element then (see Alurista's interview in J. Bruce-Novoa's *Chicano Authors,* 271–72).

5. As I will explore below, "mainstream" Chicano/a literature not only suffers from a market-driven linguistic uniformity but also from the conscious or unconscious imposition of certain stylistic and generic formulas that make it recognizable and therefore sellable.

6. José A. Gurpegui, for instance, presented a paper at the Primer Ciclo Hispanos en los Estados Unidos: Los Chicanos (Universidad de Sevilla, Spain, May 23–27, 1994), titled "La delicada salud del español en los Estados Unidos" ["The Poor Health of Spanish in the United States"]. Gurpegui's comments were partly a criticism of what he termed my "optimism" on the future of Spanish in Chicano/a literature in my essay "Lenguaje y poder."

7. A small list of them, in no particular order and without any attempt at being comprehensive, would include the following: Calaca Press (San Diego, Calif.), Chusma House (San Jose, Calif.), Red Salmon (Austin, Tex.), Moving Parts (Santa Cruz, Calif.), We Press (Santa Cruz, Calif.), Red Age (Detroit, Mich.), Tía Chucha (Chicago, Ill.), Spanish Press (Sacramento, Calif.), Third Woman (Berkeley, Calif.), MARCH/Abrazo Press (Chicago, Ill.), Cinco Puntos Press (El Paso, Tex.), Academia/El Norte Publications (Albuquerque, N.Mex.), Spinsters/Aunt Lute (San Francisco, Calif.), Wings Press (San Antonio, Tex.), the veteran M&A Publications (San Antonio, Tex.), Lalo Press (La Jolla, Calif.), Canto Norteño (Grandview, Wash.), Focus Communications (Madison, Wis.), Casa de Unidad (Detroit, Mich.), MediammiX (San Francisco, Calif.), West End (Albuquerque, N.Mex.), Leyenda (Greeley, Colo.), Curbstone (Willimantic, Conn.), Pecan Grove (San Antonio, Tex.), Floricanto (Encino, Calif.), Solería (West Covina, Calif.). To this should be added other large and small presses that are still (or are now) publishing bilingual texts at times, including Chronicle Books (San Francisco, Calif.), Children's Press (San Francisco, Calif.), the University of New Mexico Press, and Arte Público and Bilingual Review/Press, as well as foreign presses that have published Chicano/a books in recent years (e.g., Osuna and Bassarai in Spain and Cactus in Mexico).

8. Along with the two books just cited, Arte Público Press's best-sellers in supermarket stores include the immigration-related works by Salvadoran Mario Bencastro and children's books. Supermarket chains where Arte Público books are for sale include Kroger, Fiesta, and HEB in Houston, Austin, and Dallas, with a contemplated expansion into stores in San Antonio and southern Texas. My thanks to Arte Público's publisher,

Nicolás Kanellos, for this information (e-mail message dated September 4, 2001).

9. Among the presses that have launched new series in Spanish most recently are Houghton Mifflin (Nuestra visión series) and HarperCollins (Rayo series).

10. Conversely, critical and public demand for texts like the ones mentioned can change the trend in significant ways. Recently, *Puppet* is once again available in a bilingual edition from the University of New Mexico Press, and Gonzales-Berry is preparing a translation of *Paletitas* into English for a bilingual edition.

11. As I have suggested elsewhere ("The Act of Reading," note 1), Iser's approach is somewhat disappointing in dealing with bilingual and bicultural texts. In that earlier work of mine, I outlined Iser's response to a paper I presented on this topic (at the 1995 conference of the Modern Language Association of America) in which the German theoretician suggested that the reading of bicultural texts entails a sort of double reading process, as the text is interpreted first against one culture and then against the other. My own understanding of the issue is rather different, since I see the process of reading a bilingual or bicultural text as one of noncumulative transcultural intervention by the reader, as I will explore in detail below.

12. The concept of "blank" is applied by the German theoretician to indeterminacies of the text (182), whereas "negation" is understood by him as a process that "situates the reader halfway between a 'no longer' and a 'not yet'" (213) by altering or decontextualizing the extraliterary norms that the repertoire brings to the text.

13. The term "contact zone" was coined by Mary Louise Pratt to convey the idea of a space "where cultures meet, clash, and grapple with each other, often in contexts of highly asymmetrical relations of power" (34).

14. [We believe that the term *transculturation* is more suitable to express the different phases of the process of passing from a culture to another, because this process does not only involve acquiring a culture, which is what the Anglo-American term *acculturation* properly expresses, but also the loss or the uprooting of a previous culture, which could be termed a partial *deculturation*, and also the ensuing creation of new cultural phenomena which we could call *neoculturation*] (my translation).

15. [occupies the role of mediator, one of the roles typical of transculturation processes: a cultural legacy is deposited on him, and it takes shape in him in order to be transmitted to a new phase (a modernized one now) of development] (my translation).

16. On Cazemajou's "distant reader," see chapter 1.

17. In this sense, I believe that the use of children characters in transcultural fiction goes beyond the self-analysis that Goodenough, Heberle, and Sokoloff discuss in their introduction to *Infant Tongues*. According to these editors, "[f]or authors, of course, the return to childhood through writing enables a revisiting of the time when they first began to establish meaning through words. Putting children into texts is thus a way of getting to the truth of oneself as well, and the author's self-recapitulation may be shared by the reader, who was also a child, if never an author" (11). In the case of transcultural literature, as I am proposing in this chapter, the main premise when it comes to a reader's reception is not that the reader was never an author but rather that s/he was never part of the cultural group to which the child character belonged.

18. Antonio's middle name is Juan, as the reader learns shortly before this scene, on p. 85.

19. The ensuing cultural perspectivism, particularly as it applies to ethnic literatures, has been analyzed by Naomi B. Sokoloff, who concentrates on the analysis of Jewish literature.

20. Even the title refers to the pre-Hispanic god Tlaloc, one of the most important Mesoamerican deities. Among its attributes was that of reigning over the Tlalocan, one of the places where the souls of the dead could go for their final rest.

21. See G. M. Padilla, *My History,* especially pp. 70–73. In an earlier, more limited work, Padilla had already analyzed this "double-voice" effect in his introduction to *The Short Stories of Fray Angélico Chávez,* xviii–xix.

22. See Rosaura Sánchez and Beatrice Pita's introduction to the Arte Público Press reprint, as well as my "Textual and Land Reclamations."

23. See Rebolledo, *Women Singing,* 30–34.

24. Needless to say, there are many other possibilities in a particular reader's interaction with this kind of text, including aesthetic displeasure when encountering an unneeded cultural explanation.

25. A recent study by Ernst Rudin (*Tender Accents of Sound,* 1996) attempts a typology of the uses of Spanish in Chicano/a novels written in English. For an earlier, more concise assessment of this question see my "Lenguaje y poder."

26. See Keller, "The Literary Stratagems," 290 ff.

27. It should be remembered at this point that *The Mixquiahuala Letters* as a whole is constructed as a transcultural novel, in the sense that it employs a partly Anglo narratee, Alicia, as we saw in chapter 3. The fact that Alicia is familiar with Mexican and Chicano/a culture, therefore, may account for the lack of explanations I am discussing.

28. Interestingly, Caló is seldom followed by translation of any kind. This is likely the case because most texts employing Caló appear to be written with a Chicano/a reader in mind and the texts assume cultural and linguistic competence in their readers. Transcultural texts employing (and translating) Caló exist, nonetheless, for instance in the case of Mary Helen Ponce's *The Wedding.* Her transcultural use of Caló, among other things, has been the source of harsh criticism by at least one fellow Chicano writer, Alejandro Morales ("A Chicana Stereotypes").

29. Keller analyzes this strategy at length in his "Toward a Stylistic Analysis of Bilingual Texts."

30. Akers considers the differences between the versions as the product of "how Hinojosa is evolving as writer" ("From Translation," 92). While Akers's essay focuses on authorial intention and thus attributes the changes to Hinojosa's better control of his craft, my reading here stresses the reader's response as the reason for Hinojosa's versions.

31. For further analysis of Hinojosa's series see my *Rolando Hinojosa y su "cronicón" chicano,* where this particular example was also discussed along similar lines as those employed here.

32. In the same sense, the label works to reduce the differences between Chicano/a, U.S. Puerto Rican (or Nuyorican), and Cuban American literatures (as well as those literatures written by newer groups of Latinos/as in the United States), thereby erasing historical,

political, social, and even linguistic differences between these groups. Albert Memmi's notion of the "mark of the plural," that is, the process by which "[t]he colonized is never characterized in an individual manner" (85), may help in conceptualizing the homogenization of various communities and cultures into a single entity that I am exploring here.

33. *The New York Times Book Review*, 78 (February 28, 1993): 20.

34. In this, I concur with Ellen McCracken, who notes the following on *Dreaming in Cuban* and magical realism: "The common thread in several of the reviews is the implicit or explicit comparison of *Dreaming in Cuban* to the work of Gabriel García Márquez and Latin American magical realism, two of the most reductive modes by which the U.S. cultural mainstream has appropriated Latin American fiction of recent decades as a palatable Third World commodity" (*New Latina Narrative*, 22).

35. Needless to say, many Chicano/a authors and readers are familiar with García Márquez's work, as they are with the literature of other Latin American authors. My point is not to deny possible connections between Chicano/a and Latin American texts but rather to analyze the way the marketing of Chicano/a books in mainstream vehicles is subjected to a carefully orchestrated plan of culturally distorted affiliation.

36. *The New York Times* 21 June 1993: C18.

37. García Márquez's *Cien años de soledad* has been translated into forty-six languages. Over thirty million copies of this novel have been sold worldwide. Source: *El Pais Digital*, 21 September 2001 (Sección: Cultura): http://www.elpais.es/articulo.html?anchor =elpepicul&xref=20010921elpepicul_1&type=Tes&date=.

38. As explored in chapters 1 and 3, pressure of one kind or another is inevitable in the publishing industry and it tends to result in either "mild" incidents of editorial intervention in shaping up the final product or in more serious instances of censorship. The difference since the 1990s is that Chicano/a presses are no longer alone in signaling the path as they were in the 1970s and 1980s, for even if certain books by Chicanos/as were then printed by mainstream presses, very few of them have survived the test of time, whereas that is unlikely to be the case for some of the books now printed or reprinted by mainstream presses.

39. Perhaps coincidentally, Pineda is the author of a hilarious parody of the Latin American boom in her recent *The Love Queen of the Amazon*.

40. "Even as they are being canonized, these texts continue to evoke 'the presence of an absence' (de Certeau, [Practice of Everyday Life], 155), for the minorities they metonymically stand for have yet to achieve full equality in U.S. society" (McCracken, *New Latina*, 14).

41. On covers and other semiotic materials as preconditions of reading, see Mary Louise Pratt's *Toward a Speech Act Theory of Literary Discourse*, particularly chapter 1. For a similar discussion on a Latino/a context, see McCracken, introduction and chapter 1.

42. The same could be said of African American and other ethnic literatures, although their analysis falls beyond the limits of this book. For an analysis on a similar reductionism in presenting literature by women, see Petersen, 73. Petersen's chapter 6 is also very useful for the study of book covers.

43. I am using this term in a roughly similar way to that in which George Ritzer speaks

of the McDonaldization of society in his book by that title.

44. Cisneros's status as a literary icon is such that W. Clark aptly noted the irony in the fact that R. Anaya's "discovery" by the mainstream was conditioned to the possibilities opened by Cisneros's earlier success: "With nice poetic justice, the success of several younger Latino writers, such as Ana Castillo and Sandra Cisneros, for whom Anaya provided inspiration and a role model, has helped create the climate for their mentor's breakthrough" (24).

45. See, for instance, Juan Rodríguez's review in *The Austin Chronicle.*

46. The cover was designed by Eric Baker.

47. By the thirteenth Anchor Books printing of *Mixquiahuala* the cover just analyzed was substituted for one by Debra Lill (based on a photograph by Tatsuhiko Shimada). The upper part of this new cover represents a page on which we can see the handwritten lyrics of a lullaby sung by one of the characters in the book. The bottom part, under the novel's title, is a picture of a Mexican sarape. The word "Mixquiahuala" is written in old-fashioned calligraphy, not entirely unlike Zorro's famous signature mark.

48. As I was finishing revising this chapter, a Spanish translation published in Spain by Bassarai appeared. The cover of this Spanish edition features a cubist rendition of a village and the sky above it. The colors used in this drawing are dark blue, red, black, brown, and white. The drawing is surrounded, in turn, by a dark blue frame.

49. My (unpublished) research on Latinos/as and Latin Americans in U.S. children's books reveals as one of the most common plots (from, roughly, the 1930s to the 1960s) the story of a boy whose greatest aspiration is to own his own burro. Burros, furthermore, are present in the illustrations accompanying most of the children's books from this period, whether or not they center around variations on that plot line.

50. For two rather extensive descriptions and analyses of this plot see Eliud Martínez's "Ron Arias" and my "Border Crisscrossing."

51. Arias's novel is written in English, as its title implies.

52. The novel's "Postscript," taken from Francis Toor's *New Guide to Mexico,* clearly identifies the geographical reference for the reader who has finished the novel: "TAMAZUNCHALE . . . , former Huastec capital, is a tropical village in Moctezuma River Valley on C.N. 85; its sixteenth-century church has been disfigured by recent renovation. A naturalists' and sportsmen's Eden—river fishing from dugouts, mountain game. Moderate hotels are Texas, San Antonio, Quinta Chilla, Mirador" (107).

53. The only exception of note to this rule was Ron Arias's *The Road to Tamazunchale.* For further discussion on how the magical realist label was applied to this novel, see my "Border Crisscrossing."

54. [[*One Hundred Years of Solitude*] unearths Alejo Carpentier's term "the marvelous real," to the benefit of Eurocentrism, and it starts circulating the term "magical realism," which is nothing but the surprise of the "civilized" vis-à-vis the findings of primitivism] (my translation).

55. An anthology of his poems was published in 1992 by Chusma House under the title *Information: 20 Years of Joda.*

56. Arte Público Press published in 2000 an anthology of his poetry, titled *Selected Poetry.*

57. Editorial Pocho-Che reprinted the poems from the chapbook *Viaje/Trip* along with new works by Salinas in the anthology *Un Trip Through the Mind Jail y Otras Excursions*.

Chapter Five

1. *La Raza: The Mexican Americans*, 218.

2. "Mexican American Literature: A Historical Perspective," 32.

3. [And how is it possible . . . that such rich writings have been ignored for so many years? . . . How many Ulicas might there be buried on the dusty shelves of libraries or on the yellowish pages of newspapers? Until they are discovered, as Ulica has been, we would not be able to speak of a definitive history of Chicano literature] (my translation from the back cover of Jorge Ulica's *Crónicas diabólicas*).

4. All this is in addition and unrelated to earlier reprints of colonial and precolonial texts by publishing enterprises such as the Quivira Society in the United States, along with presses in Spain and Mexico that have printed from early on texts by Spanish soldiers and friars as well as from Mexican (American) politicians and writers such as Lorenzo de Zavala.

5. Source: www.arte.uh.edu.

6. "'A Net Made of Holes.'" An even earlier, slightly more limited formulation of these ideas is found in my "Textual and Land Reclamations."

7. Among the most recent manifestations of the chronological model, see Jesús Rosales, "A Sojourn of Desire" (2001), and the reprint in Dennis J. Bixler-Márquez et al., eds., *Chicano Studies* (second edition in 2001), of Francisco A. Lomelí's 1984 essay "An Overview of Chicano Letters: From Origins to Resurgence." Chronological histories have a (largely pedagogical) role to play, and I myself have participated in the past in such reconstructions of the Chicano/a literary past (see Leal and Martín-Rodríguez, "Chicano Literature"). However, there are certain limitations to this approach that make it not as suitable beyond an immediate introductory or didactic role, as we will see.

8. On Chicano/a *indigenismo*, see Gary D. Keller's "Alurista, Poeta Antropólogo" and my "Aesthetic Concepts."

9. ["the tripes" and "the counts" / "the tequilas" and "the reds" / today in the barrio / my people's clans / incarnate gangs of caciques / with feathers and knifes / eagle and tiger knights] (my translation). *Floricanto en Aztlán* is unpaginated, but the poems (at times two per page) are numbered.

10. The idealization of marginal figures in contemporary Chicano/a literature has generated debate among critics. A representative critique of this poetical license is found in Richard García's critique of Luis Valdez's reappropriation of the figure of the pachuco. See García's "Chicano Intellectual History."

11. For an assessment of the parameters of inclusion and exclusion in early Chicano/a literary historiography, see Juan Bruce-Novoa's "Canonical and NonCanonical Texts."

12. [Other than limited attempts and fractional essays, a history of the evolving estimation of the great authors in the popular and the critical mind is yet to be written in Spain. Menéndez y Pelayo's *Historia de las ideas estéticas* is something else altogether. What we ask for is a study in which we could follow—century after century, period after period—the formation and transformation of a particular author's reputation. . . . In reading that

(exemplary) book, we could get rid of many prejudices and ambiguities] (my translation).

13. The jarchas were first brought to public attention by S. M. Stern in "Les vers finaux en espagnol dans les *muwassahs* hispano-hébraïques."

14. My translation from the Spanish "las prehistorias siempre se descubren *ex eventu como prehistoria* de *una post-historia*" (H. R. Jauss, "El lector como instancia de una nueva historia de la literatura," in José Antonio Mayoral, ed., *Estética de la recepción*, 61 (original emphasis). The Spanish text is, in turn, a translation by Adelino Alvarez from the German original: "Der Leser als Instanz einer neuen Geschichte der Literatur" (*Poetica* 7, 1975: 325–44).

15. On positionality, see Homi Bhabha, *The Location of Culture;* on strategic essentialism, see Gayatri C. Spivak, *The Post-Colonial Critic;* on differential consciousness, see Chela Sandoval, *Methodology of the Oppressed.*

16. See Sánchez and Pita, 376, note 27.

17. Even such less confrontational critics as Lomelí and Urioste were hardly appreciative of the Chicano/a literary past in the 1970s. Although their *Chicano Perspectives* discussed Eusebio Chacón's work, their introduction dubbed Chicano/a literature "basically a contemporary phenomena" (10, *sic*) while decrying how prior to the Chicano/a Movement "literary expression remained an amorphous body written by a few" (10). Their concluding evaluation of the Chicano/a literary past is an eloquent testimony to the horizon of expectations of the 1970s: "These circumstances, then, tended to produce lyrical-escapist, unpublished protest, nostalgia-filled prose and poetry which too often disintegrated in old family chests. In accordance with the spirit of the times, literature was viewed as part of a social ritual and not as an instrument for understanding society" (10). Subsequently, Lomelí has made substantial contributions to the recovery effort, thus reflecting the general shift in the critical understanding of the Chicano/a literary past that I have illustrated with quotes from G. Padilla and from Sánchez and Pita.

18. In this sense, and back to the idea of how the mediation between present and past conditions our ability to read the past, it is impossible not to note that already in 1973 Luis Leal was calling for the reconstruction of the Chicano/a literary past in his seminal essay "Mexican-American Literature: A Historical Perspective," a true landmark in Chicano/a erudition from which I take my second epigraph for this chapter. While individual efforts of historical recovery took place between Leal's article and the current movements, as noted, it is clear that historians during the 1970s, the context in which Leal wrote, were not ready to look for and reclaim figures such as Ruiz de Burton and others who are now unquestionably part of the Chicano/a literary past.

19. See Bruce-Novoa's "Canonical and NonCanonical Texts" for further discussion of these authors' reception.

20. For the complete quote, see p. 43.

21. I am giving 1996 as the date on which my analysis was published under the title "Textual and Land Reclamations." In fact, I had presented variations of this analysis in several earlier forums, first within a paper titled "Reclaiming California: Land and Labor in Early Chicano Literature," at the 1992 annual convention of the Modern Language Association of America, then in a lecture at the University of Washington (February 2, 1994), and finally during the plenary session of the third annual conference of the Recov-

ery Project, at the University of Houston (December 2–3, 1994), under the title "Textual Reclamation and the Critical Reception of Early Chicano/a Literature."

22. Incidentally, such a fabrication of the past may lie at the very mythical origins of Chicanos/as. As Daniel Cooper Alarcón has summarized, "Many Mesoamerican scholars, for example, believe that the Aztecs rewrote their ancestral records in order to erase their nomadic past and to legitimize their presence in the Valley of Mexico by claiming direct descent from the Toltecs" (58). Alarcón then goes on to analyze the fabricated aspects of the Aztecs' historical records (first purposefully burned and then rewritten) and of the myth of Aztlán (58–59).

23. As suggested by David Perkins, and as I will analyze in more detail below, this is also characteristic of most histories of literature by minorities (137).

24. Commenting on the reconstruction of the New Mexican literary past, Erlinda Gonzales-Berry has also cautioned against the problems in overlooking differences when creating a new literary canon from recovered texts ("Two Texts," 129–30).

25. Spain, Mexico, the Republic of Texas, and the United States of America, not to mention the pre-Hispanic and pre-British peoples.

26. [Mahgrebian history is characterized by breaks and lacunae, discontinuity, cultural ruptures of the sources and of the Roman, Byzantine, Arab, Turkish, French, and nationalist phases. The most urgent task now is to consider these discontinuities, in particular those that affect Islamic and Arabic thought, rather than to continue constructing the illusory continuity that the nationalist elites desire] (my translation).

27. Perkins defines a "conceptual history as a discursive construction that "exhibits the interrelation of events as the logical relation of ideas" (49).

28. A first "recovered" edition was printed in 1984 by Mexico's Secretaría de Educación Pública with an introduction by Kanellos. The introduction to the 1984 edition was reprinted without significant changes in the 1999 Arte Público Press Spanish-language edition (as part of the Recovering the U.S. Hispanic Literary Heritage series). Interestingly, the English-language translation of *Don Chipote*, also published by Arte Público in 2000 as *The Adventures of Don Chipote*, includes a new introduction by Kanellos. In it, Kanellos qualifies his assertion as follows, indicating a more nuanced approach to internal differences and (dis)continuities: "[*Don Chipote*] may be considered the first 'Chicano' novel—or, at least, a precursor to the Chicano novel of the 1960s and 1970s, which also identifies with the working class, albeit the *Mexican American* working class" (9, original emphasis). On the issue of the "first" Chicano/a novel, see chapter 2, pp. 42.

29. [offers a new indication of the continuity of cultural production by Mexicans north of the border] (my translation).

30. Kanellos mentions *Ladrona* (1925), by Miguel Arce, and *El sol de Texas* (1927), by Conrado Espino[s]a, in his introduction (5).

31. The tension between continuity and cultural transformation is also observable outside the field of literature. As suggested by Mario T. García, for instance, "[c]ultural continuity as well as cultural change, the two in time developing in a Mexican border culture, can be detected in the family, recreational activities, religion, and voluntary associations" (72).

32. See, for example, the multicolumned, genre-based chronological sequence accompanying Julio A. Martínez and Francisco Lomelí's *Chicano Literature.*

33. For further discussion of this type of encyclopedic history, see Perkins, 53–60. Perkins explores encyclopedism as a manifestation of the postmodern, at odds with narrative models of literary history; Chicano/a literary "encyclopedism," though, does not read as incompatible with the conceptual type of history I analyzed at the end of the previous section. On the contrary, it has served as an argument for reinforcing a totalizing sense of continuity, based on the permanence of cultural traditions and societal practices.

34. Recall, in this respect, the ending of Miguel Méndez's *Peregrinos de Aztlán,* in which the narrator concludes: "Así la historia, de pronto, como en un mal sueño nos dejó varados en la isla del olvido, presos. No sólo eso, han quedado encadenados los genes que guardan la cultura, esencia de nuestra historia, vedando las arterias que como ríos traen el ímpetu de la sangre que anima la voz y el alma de nuestro pueblo. Ni dignidad ni letras para los esclavos, dijeron los dominadores, solamente la ignominia, la burla y la muerte; si acaso, la trágica baba de la demagogia, falsa moneda de los perversos" (183–84). For an English translation of this quote, see note 52 in chapter 2.

35. The metaphor, taken from a poem in the 1528 *Manuscript of Tlatelolco,* gives title to my essay "'A Net Made of Holes,'" which I am referencing here. These are the relevant lines from the poem: "On the roads lie broken arrows, / our hair is in disarray. / Without roofs are the houses, / and red are their walls with blood. . . . / We have struggled against the walls of adobe, / but our heritage was a net made of holes" (Miguel León Portilla, *Pre-Columbian Literatures of Mexico,* 150–51).

36. Following Homi Bhabha, Clifford speaks of how "[e]xperiences of unsettlement, loss, and recurring terror produce discrepant temporalities—broken histories that trouble the linear, progressive narratives of nation-states and global modernization" (317).

37. See my essay "'A Net Made of Holes,'" 17. These cultural continuities are also manifested in how contemporary authors engage in a figuration of the past in order to establish a cultural economy of linkages. The *Manuscript of Tlatelolco,* for instance, echoes in the mind of the informed reader when approaching Raúl R. Salinas's poem "About Invasion and Conquest," in which the poetic voices of the embattled indigenous (a Taino and a Mexica, in separate stanzas) ask, "Who will be left / to tell of what happened to us . . . ?" (*East,* 90); the response in both cases is similar, and it points toward the role of the poets as connectors in the "net made of holes": "Among those who survive, / there will be poets to recount / that which happened to us" (*East,* 90).

38. One of the earliest manifestos of the Chicano/a Movement, El Plan Espiritual de Aztlán, repeatedly stated the idea that Chicanos/as are a nation as it stressed the political usefulness of nationalism: "Nationalism is the common denominator that all members of La Raza can agree upon" (2).

39. Cf. Luis Leal, "Cuatro siglos de prosa aztlanense."

40. In an attempt to tackle this issue, Lomelí and Urioste first coined the term "literatura chicanesca" ("Chicanesque Literature") in 1976 to account for that literature that "only appears to be Chicano" [*Chicano Perspectives,* 12] to differentiate it from "Chicano literature [which] is written by Chicanos" (12). While those authors Lomelí and Urioste listed un-

der their Chicanesca label were clearly extraneous to the Chicano/a cultural experiences, other writers (e.g., Jim Sagel, Amado Muro) presented a different challenge when it came to their classification. By the time that Roberto C. Trujillo and Andrés Rodríguez adopted the term for their 1985 *Literatura chicana,* the label had become much more suspicious, to the point that Trujillo refers to it in the volume's introduction as those works written by "non-Chicanos" (original quotation marks, ii).

41. By the same token, others could question the status of *Caballero,* a novel written by Jovita González and Eve Raleigh (pseudonym of Margaret Eimer), particularly since the extent of their collaboration remains unclear. In fact, as discussed by L. G. Mendoza, such cross-cultural collaborations have been common in the history of Chicano/a political and literary activities (171). My contention is that Chicano/a literary history needs to open itself up to such instances of transnational and transcultural communication, not only by looking at authorial issues but by including matters of readership as well.

42. For more on these debates see J. Bruce-Novoa, "Canonical and NonCanonical," and R. Gutiérrez, "Nationalism," 247–48.

43. See also L. G. Mendoza, pp. 102 ff, for the blurring of national borders in turn-of-the-century newspapers in Texas.

44. This is not to be confused with José David Saldívar's effort to construct a pan-American literary history in *The Dialectics of Our America.* Rather than Saldívar's internationalism, which connects different cultures across borders, I am proposing a culturally specific (i.e., Chicano/a) literary history that, for historical reasons, has been produced in territories belonging to more than one present-day nation.

45. During the 1980s, Chicano/a-Latino/a presses such as San Francisco's El Pocho Che published books by authors residing in the Bay Area, including both Chicanos/as and Central Americans (and some South Americans as well). El Pocho Che's books often consisted of two different works bound together, as if to reinforce solidarity among Latino/a writers from different (or similar, depending on the volumes) backgrounds.

46. The volume was edited by R. A. Gutiérrez and G. M. Padilla.

47. Tatum is quoting from Rosaura Sánchez's "The History of Chicanas."

48. Juan Francisco de Cárdenas was the Spanish ambassador to the United States when the book was published in 1933. The full title of Arte Público Press's reprint of Cabeza de Vaca's *Relación* is *The Account: Alvar Núñez Cabeza de Vaca's Relación.*

49. Lorde's idea is expressed verbatim in the title of one of her two contributions to C. Moraga and G. Anzaldúa's anthology *This Bridge Called My Back.*

50. Padilla studies the period after the Mexican-American war, while I briefly study Chicano reactions to the Spanish-American War.

51. In 2000, Arte Público published the volume *Selected Poetry* by García-Camarillo, with an introduction by Enrique Lamadrid. Most of the author's poems were scattered in numerous chapbooks and journals prior to this edition.

Works Cited

Acuña, Rodolfo. *Occupied America: A History of Chicanos*. 1972. New York: Harper & Row, 1988. 3rd ed.

Akers, John C. "Fragmentation in the Chicano Novel: Literary Technique and Cultural Identity." *Revista Chicano-Riqueña* 13.3–4 (1985): 121–36.

——"From Translation to Rewriting: Rolando Hinojosa's *Estampas del Valle* and *The Valley*." *The Americas Review* 21.1 (1993): 91–102.

Alarcón, Daniel Cooper. "The Aztec Palimpsest: Toward a New Understanding of Aztlán." *Aztlán* 19.2 (1988–90): 33–68.

Alarcón, Justo S. "Lo esperpéntico en Miguel Méndez M." *The Americas Review* 17.1 (1989): 84–99.

Alarcón, Norma. "Chicana's Feminist Literature: A Re-vision Through Malintzin/or Malintzin: Putting Flesh Back on the Object." In Moraga and Anzaldúa, *This Bridge Called My Back*: 182–90.

——"The Sardonic Powers of the Erotic in the Work of Ana Castillo." In *Breaking Boundaries*, ed. A. Horno Delgado et al., 94–107.

——"Traddutora, Traditora: A Paradigmatic Figure of Chicana Feminism." *Cultural Critique* (fall 1989): 57–87.

Alurista. *Floricanto en Aztlán*. Los Angeles: Chicano Studies Center–University of California Press, 1976.

——*Nationchild Plumaroja*. San Diego: Toltecas en Aztlán, 1972.

Anaya, Rudolfo A. *Bless Me, Ultima*. 1972. New York: Warner, 1994.

——*Heart of Aztlán*. Berkeley, CA: Justa, 1976.

——"Rudolfo A. Anaya: An Autobiography." In *Rudolfo A. Anaya*, ed. C. A. González-T., 359–88.

——And Francisco A. Lomelí, eds. *Aztlán: Essays on the Chicano Homeland*. Albuquerque: El Norte Publications, 1989.

Anzaldúa, Gloria. *Borderlands/La frontera: The New Mestiza*. San Francisco: Spinsters/ Aunt Lute, 1987.

——"Speaking in Tongues: A Letter to 3rd World Women Writers." In *This Bridge Called My Back*, eds. C. Moraga and G. Anzaldúa, 165–74. "To(o) Queer the Writer—Loca, escritora y chicana." In *Living Chicana Theory*, ed. C. Trujillo, 263–76.

——ed. *Making Face, Making Soul. Haciendo Caras: Creative and Critical Perspectives by Women of Color*. San Francisco: Aunt Lute Foundation, 1990.

Argüello, Luis Antonio. *The Diary of Captain Luis Antonio Argüello*. Berkeley, CA: Friends of the Bancroft Library, 1992.

Arias, Ron. *El camino a Tamazunchale*. Trans. Ricardo Aguilar Melantzón and Beth Pollack. Vitoria-Gasteiz, Spain: Bassarai, 2002.

——*The Road to Tamazunchale.* Reno, NV: West Coast Poetry Review, 1975.

——*The Road to Tamazunchale.* Albuquerque: Pajarito Publications, 1978.

——*The Road to Tamazunchale.* Tempe, AZ: Bilingual Review/Press, 1987.

——*The Road to Tamazunchale.* New York: Doubleday, 1992.

Arkoun, Mohammed. "Lenguas, sociedad y religión en el Magreb independiente." In
     Las culturas del Magreb: Antropología, historia y sociedad, ed. Maria-Àngels
     Roque, 97–127. Barcelona: Icaria, 1996.

Arteaga, Alfred, ed. *An Other Tongue: Nation and Ethnicity in the Linguistic Borderlands.*
     Durham, NC: Duke University Press, 1994.

Atherton, Gertrude. *Rezánov.* New York: The Authors and Newspapers Association,
     1906.

Austin, J. L. *How to Do Things with Words.* Ed. J. O. Urmson. New York: Oxford
     University Press, 1962.

Azorín [José Martínez Ruiz]. *Lope en silueta.* Buenos Aires: Losada, 1960.

Bachelard, Gaston. *The Poetics of Space.* Trans. María Jolas. Boston: Beacon, 1969.

Bakhtin, Mikhail M. *The Dialogic Imagination.* Ed. Michael Holquist. Trans. Caryl
     Emerson and Michael Holquist. Austin: University of Texas Press, 1986.

Bancroft, Hubert H. *The Works of Hubert Howe Bancroft: Vol. 29, Essays and Miscellany.*
     San Francisco: The History Company, 1890.

Bandini, José. *A Description of California in 1828.* Berkeley, CA: Friends of the Bancroft
     Library, 1951.

Beck, Mary Ann, et al., eds. *The Analysis of Hispanic Texts: Current Trends and
     Methodology.* Jamaica, NY: Bilingual Press, 1976.

Berceo, Gonzalo de. *La vida de Santo Domingo de Silos.* Ed. Brian Dutton. London:
     Tamesis, 1978.

Bhabha, Homi K. *The Location of Culture.* New York: Routledge, 1994.

Bixler-Márquez, Dennis J., et al., eds. *Chicano Studies: Survey and Analysis.* 1997.
     Dubuque, IA: Kendall/Hunt, 2001. 2nd ed.

Booth, Wayne C. *The Rhetoric of Fiction.* Chicago: University of Chicago Press, 1988.

Bornstein de Somoza, Miriam. "Peregrinos de Aztlán: Dialéctica estructural e
     ideológica." *Revista Chicano-Riqueña* 8.4 (1980): 69–78.

Brito, Aristeo. *El diablo en Texas: The Devil in Texas.* Trans. David W. Foster. 1976.
     Tempe, AZ: Bilingual Review/Press, 1990.

——"El lenguaje tropológico en *Peregrinos de Aztlán.*" *La Luz* 4.2 (1975): 42–43.

Brox, Luis María. "Los límites del costumbrismo en *Estampas del Valle y otras obras.*"
     Mester 5.2 (1975): 101–4.

Broyles, Yolanda Julia. "Hinojosa's *Klail City y sus alrededores:* Oral Culture and Print
     Culture." In *The Rolando Hinojosa Reader,* ed. J. D. Saldívar, 109–32.

Broyles-González, Yolanda. *El Teatro Campesino: Theater in the Chicano Movement.*
     Austin: University of Texas Press, 1994.

Bruce-Novoa, Juan. "Canonical and NonCanonical Texts." *The Americas Review* 14.3–4
     (fall-winter 1986): 119–35.

——*Chicano Authors: Inquiry by Interview.* Austin, TX: University of Texas Press, 1980.

——"Dialogical Strategies, Monological Goals: Chicano Literature." In *An Other Tongue,* ed. A. Arteaga, 225–45.

——"Miguel Méndez: Voices of Silence." 1977. In *Contemporary Chicano Fiction,* ed. V. E. Lattin, 206–14.

——"Portraits of the Chicano Artist as a Young Man: The Making of the 'Author' in Three Chicano Novels." In *Flor y Canto II: An Anthology of Chicano Literature,* ed. Arnold C. Vento et al., 150–61.

——"'La Prensa' and the Chicano Community." *The Americas Review* 17.3–4 (1989): 150–6.

——"Righting the Oral Tradition." *Denver Quarterly* 16.3 (1981): 78–86.

Bus, Heiner. "'i too was of that small corner of the world': The Cross-Cultural Experience in Ana Castillo's *The Mixquiahuala Letters* (1986)." *The Americas Review* 21:3–4 (1993): 128–38.

Cabeza de Baca, Fabiola. *We Fed Them Cactus.* 1954. Albuquerque: University of New Mexico Press, 1989.

Calderón, Héctor. "The Novel and the Community of Readers: Rereading Tomás Rivera's *Y no se lo tragó la tierra.*" In *Criticism in the Borderlands,* ed. H. Calderón and J. D. Saldívar, 97–113.

——"Rudolfo Anaya's *Bless Me, Ultima:* A Chicano Romance of the Southwest." In *Rudolfo A. Anaya,* ed. C. A. González-T., 64–99.

——and José David Saldívar, eds. *Criticism in the Borderlands: Studies in Chicano Literature, Culture, and Ideology.* Durham and London: Duke University Press, 1991.

Candelaria, Cordelia. *Chicano Poetry: A Critical Introduction.* Westport, CT: Greenwood Press, 1986.

Cantú, Norma. "Women, Then and Now: An Analysis of the Adelita Image versus the Chicana as Political Writer and Philosopher." In *Chicana Voices,* 8–10.

Cantú, Roberto. "Apocalypse as an Ideological Construct: The Storyteller's Art in *Bless Me, Ultima.*" In *Rudolfo A. Anaya,* ed. C. A. González-T., 13–63.

Cárdenas, Juan Francisco de. *Hispanic Culture and Language in the United States.* New York: Instituto de las Españas en los Estados Unidos, 1933.

Cárdenas, Lupe. "La ciudad como arquetipo de la madre terrible en *Peregrinos de Aztlán.*" *La palabra* 3.1–2 (1981): 33–47.

Castillo, Ana. Interview with Elsa Saeta. *MELUS* 22.3 (1997): 133–49.

——*Massacre of the Dreamers: Essays on Xicanisma.* New York: Penguin, 1995.

——*The Mixquiahuala Letters.* Binghamton, NY: Bilingual Press, 1986.

——*The Mixquiahuala Letters.* New York: Doubleday, 1992.

——*My Father Was a Toltec.* Novato, CA: West End, 1988.

——*Women Are Not Roses.* Houston: Arte Público Press, 1984.

——"Yes, dear critic, there really is an Alicia." In *Máscaras,* ed. L. Corpi, 153–60.

Castillo, Debra A. "Reading Over Her Shoulder: Galdós/Cortázar." *Anales Galdosianos* 21 (1986): 147–60.

——*Talking Back: Toward a Latin American Feminist Literary Criticism.* Ithaca, NY: Cornell University Press, 1992.

Cavallo, Guglielmo, and Roger Chartier, eds. *Historia de la lectura en el mundo occidental.* 1997. Madrid: Taurus, 1998.

Cazemajou, Jean. "The Search for a Center: The Shamanic Journey of Mediators in Anaya's Trilogy, *Bless Me, Ultima; Heart of Aztlán,* and *Tortuga.*" In *Rudolfo A. Anaya,* ed. C. A. González-T., 254–73.

Cervantes, Lorna Dee. *Emplumada.* Pittsburgh, PA: University of Pittsburgh Press, 1981.

Chabrán, Rafael, and Richard Chabrán. "The Spanish-Language and Latino Press of the United States: Newspapers and Periodicals." In *Handbook of Hispanic Cultures,* ed. F. A. Lomelí, 360–83.

Chacón, Eusebio. *El hijo de la tempestad. Tras la tormenta la calma.* Santa Fe, N.Mex.: Tipografía El Boletín Popular, 1892.

Chávez, Angélico. *La Conquistadora: The Autobiography of an Ancient Statue.* Patterson, NJ: St. Anthony Guild, 1954.

——*The Short Stories of Fray Angélico Chávez.* Ed. Genaro M. Padilla. Albuquerque: University of New Mexico Press, 1987.

Chicana Voices: Intersections of Class, Race and Gender. Austin: Center for Mexican American Studies–University of Texas Press, 1986.

Cisneros, Sandra. *Bad Boys.* San Jose, CA: Mango, 1980.

——"Do You Know Me?: I Wrote *The House on Mango Street.*" *The Americas Review* 15.1 (1987): 77–79.

——"From a Writer's Notebook." *The Americas Review* 15.1 (1987): 69–79.

——"Ghosts and Voices: Writing from Obsession." *The Americas Review* 15.1 (spring 1987): 69–73.

——*The House on Mango Street.* Houston: Arte Público Press, 1984.

——*The House on Mango Street.* 1984. New York: Vintage, 1991.

——Interview with Pilar E. Rodríguez Aranda. *The Americas Review* 18.1 (1990): 64–80.

——*Loose Woman.* 1994. New York: Vintage, 1995.

——*My Wicked Wicked Ways.* Bloomington, IN: Third Woman, 1987.

——"Notes to a Young(er) Writer." *The Americas Review* 15.1 (1987): 74–76.

Cixous, Hélène. "The Laugh of the Medusa." 1976. In *New French Feminisms,* ed. Elaine Marks and Isabel de Courtivron, 245–264. New York: Schocken, 1981.

Clark, William. "The Mainstream Discovers Rudolfo Anaya." *Publishers Weekly* (21 Mar. 1994): 24.

Clifford, James. "Diasporas." *Cultural Anthropology* 9.3 (1994): 302–38.

Colahan, Clark. "Chronicles of Exploration and Discovery: The Enchantment of the Unknown." In *Pasó por aquí,* ed. E. Gonzales-Berry, 15–46.

Corominas, Joan. *Breve diccionario etimológico de la lengua castellana.* Madrid: Gredos, 1983.

Corpi, Lucha, ed. *Máscaras.* Berkeley: Third Woman, 1997.

Cortázar, Julio. *Hopscotch.* Trans. Gregory Rabassa. New York: Pantheon, 1966.

——*Rayuela.* 1963. Barcelona: Bruguera, 1982.

Cota-Cárdenas, Margarita. *Noches despertando inconciencias.* Tucson: Scorpion, 1977.
——*Puppet.* 1985. Albuquerque: University of New Mexico Press, 2000.
Cotera, Martha P. *Diosa y hembra: The History and Heritage of Chicanas in the U.S.*
    Austin, TX: Information Systems Development, 1976.
Culler, Jonathan. *On Deconstruction: Theory and Criticism after Structuralism.* Ithaca,
    NY: Cornell University Press, 1982.
——"Prolegomena to a Theory of Reading." In *The Reader in the Text,* ed. Suleiman
    and Crosman, 46–66.

Davidson, Cathy N. "The Life and Times of Charlotte Temple: The Biography of a
    Book." In *Reading in America,* ed. C. N. Davidson, 157–79.
——ed. *Reading in America: Literature and Social History.* Baltimore: Johns Hopkins
    University Press, 1993.
de Casas, Celso A. *Pelón Drops Out.* Berkeley, CA: Tonatiuh International, 1979.
Del Castillo, Adelaida R. "Malintzin Tenépal: A Preliminary Look into a New Perspec-
    tive." In *Essays on la Mujer,* ed. R. Sánchez and R. Martínez Cruz, 124–49.
Deleuze, Gilles, and Félix Guattari. *A Thousand Plateaus: Capitalism and Schizophrenia.*
    Trans. Brian Massumi. Minneapolis: University of Minnesota Press, 1987.

Eco, Umberto. *The Open Work.* Trans. Anna Cancogni. Cambridge: Harvard University
    Press, 1989.
——*The Role of the Reader: Explorations in the Semiotics of Texts.* Bloomington:
    Indiana University Press, 1979.
"Encuentro entre escritoras chicanas y mexicanas: Coloquio Literatura Escrita por
    Mujeres Chicanas (25 de junio de 1993)." In *Las formas de nuestras voces,* ed. C.
    Joysmith, 209–32.
Escarpit, Robert. *Sociology of Literature.* Trans. Ernest Pick. London: 1971. 2nd ed.
Eysturoy, Annie O. *Daughters of Self-Creation: The Contemporary Chicana Novel.*
    Albuquerque: University of New Mexico Press, 1996.

Fernández, Roberta. "Depicting Women's Culture in *Intaglio: A Novel in Six Stories.*" In
    Máscaras, ed. L. Corpi, 73–96.
Fetterley, Judith. "Reading about Reading: 'A Jury of Her Peers,' 'The Murders in the
    Rue Morgue,' and 'The Yellow Wallpaper.'" In *Gender and Reading,* ed. E. A.
    Flynn and P. P. Schweickart, 147–64.
——*The Resisting Reader: A Feminist Approach to American Fiction.* Bloomington:
    Indiana University Press, 1978.
Fish, Stanley. *Is There a Text in This Class? The Authority of Interpretive Communities.*
    Cambridge, MA: Harvard University Press, 1980.
Flores, Lauro. "The Discourse of Silence in the Narrative of Tomás Rivera." *Revista
    Chicano-Riqueña* 13.3–4 (1985): 96–106.
Flynn, Elizabeth A., and Patrocinio P. Schweickart, eds. *Gender and Reading: Essays on
    Readers, Texts, and Contexts.* Baltimore: Johns Hopkins University Press, 1992.

Foucault, Michael. *The Archaeology of Knowledge.* 1969. Trans. A. M. Sheridan Smith. New York: Pantheon, 1972.

Fuentes, Carlos. *La nueva novela hispanoamericana.* 1969. Mexico City: Joaquín Mortiz, 1980.

Galarza, Ernesto. *Todo mundo lee.* San Jose, CA: Almadén, 1973.

García, Cristina. *Dreaming in Cuban.* New York: Ballantine, 1993.

García, Mario T. "Border Culture." In *From Different Shores: Perspectives on Race and Ethnicity in America,* ed. Ronald Takaki, 72–81. New York: Oxford University Press, 1994.

García, Richard A. "Chicano Intellectual History: Myths and Reality." *Revista Chicano-Riqueña* 7.2 (1979): 58–62.

García-Camarillo, Cecilio. *Selected Poetry.* Houston: Arte Público Press, 2000.

García Márquez, Gabriel. *Cien años de soledad.* 1967. Buenos Aires: Sudamericana, 1990.

Gaspar de Alba, Alicia. *Chicano Art: Inside/Outside the Master's House.* Austin: University of Texas Press, 1998. "The Politics of Location of the Tenth Muse of America: An Interview with Sor Juana Inés de la Cruz." In *Living Chicana Theory,* ed. C. Trujillo, 136–65.

Gilbert, Sandra, and Susan Gubar. *The Madwoman in the Attic: The Woman Writer and the Nineteenth-Century Literary Imagination.* New Haven, CT: Yale University Press, 1979.

Gonzales, Rodolfo. "Corky." *I Am Joaquin.* n.p.: n.p., 1967.

Gonzales-Berry, Erlinda. *Paletitas de guayaba.* Albuquerque: El Norte, 1991.

——"The [Subversive] Mixquiahuala Letters: An Antidote for Self-Hate." In *Chicana (W)Rites,* ed. M. Herrera-Sobek and H. M. Viramontes, 115–24.

——"Two Texts for a New Canon: Vicente Bernal's *Las Primicias* and Felipe Maximiliano Chacón's *Poesía y prosa.* In *Recovering the U.S. Hispanic Literary Heritage,* ed. R. A. Gutiérrez and G. M. Padilla, 129–51.

——ed. *Pasó por aquí: Critical Essays on the New Mexican Literary Tradition, 1542–1988.* Albuquerque: University of New Mexico Press, 1989.

——and Tey Diana Rebolledo. "Growing Up Chicano: Tomás Rivera and Sandra Cisneros." *Revista Chicano-Riqueña* 13.3–4 (fall-winter 1985): 109–19.

González, Deena J. "Speaking Secrets: Living Chicana Theory." In *Living Chicana Theory,* ed. C. Trujillo, 46–77.

González, Jovita. *Dew on the Thorn.* Ed. José Limón. Houston: Arte Público Press, 1997.

—— *The Woman Who Lost Her Soul and Other Stories.* Ed. Sergio Reyna. Houston: Arte Público Press, 1997.

——and Eve Raleigh. *Caballero: A Historical Novel.* College Station: Texas A&M University Press, 1996.

González-T., César A., ed. *Rudolfo A. Anaya: Focus on Criticism.* La Jolla, CA: Lalo Press, 1990.

Goodenough, Elizabeth, Mark A. Heberle, and Naomi B. Sokoloff, eds. *Infant Tongues: The Voice of the Child in Literature.* Detroit: Wayne State University Press, 1994.

Griswold del Castillo, Richard. *The Treaty of Guadalupe Hidalgo: A Legacy of Conflict.* Norman: University of Oklahoma Press, 1990.

Gutiérrez, Ramón A. "Nationalism and Literary Production: The Hispanic and Chicano Experiences." In *Recovering the U.S. Hispanic Literary Heritage,* ed. R. A. Gutiérrez and G. M. Padilla, 241–50.

——and Genaro M. Padilla, eds. *Recovering the U.S. Hispanic Literary Heritage.* Houston: Arte Público Press, 1993.

Gutiérrez-Jones, Carl. *Rethinking the Borderlands: Between Chicano Culture and Legal Discourse.* Berkeley: University of California Press, 1995.

Gutiérrez Martínez-Conde, Juan. *Literatura y sociedad en el mundo chicano.* Madrid: De la Torre, 1992.

Gutiérrez-Revuelta, Pedro. "Género e ideología en el libro de Sandra Cisneros: *The House on Mango Street. Crítica* 1.3 (1986): 48–59.

——"Peregrinos y humillados en la épica de Méndez." *La palabra* 3.1–2 (1981): 58–66.

Hadley-Garcia, George. *Hispanic Hollywood: The Latins in Motion Pictures.* 1990. New York: Carol, 1993.

Heilbrun, Carolyn. "Millett's *Sexual Politics:* A Year Later." *Aphra* 2 (1971): 38–47.

Herrera, Juan Felipe. *Akrílica.* Santa Cruz: Alcatraz, 1989.

Herrera-Sobek, María. "The Street Scene: Metaphoric Strategies in Two Contemporary Chicana Poets." In *Chicana (W)Rites,* ed. M. Herrera-Sobek and H. M. Viramontes, 147–69.

——ed. *Beyond Stereotypes: The Critical Analysis of Chicana Literature.* Binghamton, NY: Bilingual Review/Press, 1985.

——ed. *Reconstructing a Chicano/a Literary Heritage: Hispanic Colonial Literature of the Southwest.* Tucson: University of Arizona Press, 1993.

——and Helena María Viramontes, eds. *Chicana (W)Rites on Word and Film.* Berkeley: Third Woman, 1995.

Híjar, Carlos N., Eulalia Pérez, and Agustín Escobar. *Three Memoirs of Mexican California as recorded in 1877 by Thomas Savage (or under his supervision).* Berkeley, CA: Friends of the Bancroft Library, 1988.

Hinojosa-Smith, Rolando. *Dear Rafe.* Houston, TX: Arte Público Press, 1985.

——*Estampas del Valle.* Berkeley, CA: Quinto Sol, 1973.

——*Klail City.* Houston: Arte Público Press, 1987.

——*Klail City y sus alrededores.* La Habana: Casa de las Américas, 1976.

——*Korean Love Songs.* Berkeley, CA: Justa, 1978.

——"'La Prensa': A Lifelong Influence on Hispanics in Texas." *The Americas Review* 17.3–4 (1989): 125–9.

——*Mi querido Rafa.* Houston, TX: Arte Público Press, 1981.

——*Rites and Witnesses.* Houston, TX: Arte Público Press, 1982.

——*This Migrant Earth.* Houston, TX: Arte Público Press, 1987.

——*The Useless Servants.* Houston: Arte Público Press, 1993.

——*The Valley.* Ypsilanti, MI: Bilingual Review/Press, 1983.

Horno-Delgado, Asunción, et al., eds. *Breaking Boundaries: Latina Writings and Critical Readings.* Amherst: University of Massachusetts Press, 1989.

Huerta, Jorge A. *Chicano Theater: Themes and Forms.* Ypsilanti, MI: Bilingual Press/
Editorial Bilingüe, 1982.
——"Looking for the Magic: Chicanos in the Mainstream." In *Negotiating Performance:*
37–48. Durham, NC: Duke University Press, 1994.

Iser, Wolfgang. *The Act of Reading: A Theory of Aesthetic Response.* 1976. Baltimore:
Johns Hopkins University Press, 1987.
Islas, Arturo. *The Rain God.* Palo Alto, CA: Alexandrian, 1984.

Jaramillo, Cleofas. *Romance of a Little Village Girl.* 1955. Albuquerque: University of
New Mexico Press, 2000.
Jauss, Hans R. *Aesthetic Experience and Literary Hermeneutics.* Trans. Michael Shaw.
Minneapolis: University of Minnesota Press, 1982.
——"El lector como instancia de una nueva historia de la literatura." In *Estética de la*
recepción, trans. Adelino Alvarez, ed. José Antonio Mayoral, 59–85. Madrid:
Arco/Libros, 1987.
——*Toward an Aesthetic of Reception.* Trans. Timothy Bahti. Minneapolis: University
of Minnesota Press, 1982.
Jiménez, Francisco, ed. *The Identification and Analysis of Chicano Literature.* Ypsilanti,
MI: Bilingual Press, 1979.
Joysmith, Claire, ed. *Las formas de nuestras voces: Chicana and Mexicana Writers in Mexico.*
Mexico City: UNAM-Centro de Investigaciones Sobre América del Norte, 1995.

Kanellos, Nicolás. "Daniel Venegas." In *Dictionary of Literary Biography,* vol. 82, ed.
Francisco A. Lomelí and Carl R. Shirley, 271–74. Detroit: Bruccoli Clark Layman, 1989.
——"Introducción." In *Las aventuras de don Chipote o: Cuando los periocos mamen,* D.
Venegas, 7–15.
——"Introduction." In *The Adventures of Don Chipote or: When Parrots Breast-Feed,* D.
Venegas, 1–17.
——"A Socio-Historic Study of Hispanic Newspapers in the United States." In
Recovering the U.S. Hispanic Literary Heritage, ed. R. A. Gutiérrez and G. M.
Padilla, 107–28.
——ed. *Nochebuena: Hispanic American Christmas Stories.* Oxford: Oxford University
Press, 2000.
——and Helvetia Martell. *Hispanic Periodicals in the United States, Origins to 1960: A Brief*
History and Comprehensive Bibliography. Houston: Arte Público Press, 2000.
——et al., eds. *Herencia: The Anthology of Hispanic Literature of the United States.*
Oxford and New York: Oxford University Press, 2002.
Keating, AnaLouise. *Women Reading Women Writing: Self-Invention in Paula Gunn*
Allen, Gloria Anzaldúa and Audre Lorde. Philadelphia: Temple University Press,
1996.
Keller, Gary D. "Alurista, Poeta-Antropólogo, and the Recuperation of the Chicano
Identity." In *Return: Poems Collected and New,* xi–xlix. Ypsilanti, MI: Bilingual
Press, 1982.

——"The Literary Stratagems Available to the Bilingual Chicano Writer." In *The Identification and Analysis of Chicano Literature*, ed. F. Jiménez, 263–316.

——"Toward a Stylistic Analysis of Bilingual Texts: From Ernest Hemingway to Contemporary Boricua and Chicano Literature." In *The Analysis of Hispanic Texts*, ed. M. A. Beck et al., 130–49.

Kerr, Lucille. "Leaps Across the Board." *Diacritics* 4.4 (1974): 29–34.

Kolodny, Annette. "Dancing through the Minefield: Some Observations on the Theory, Practice and Politics of a Feminist Literary Criticism." *Feminist Studies* 6 (1980): 1–25.

Lakritz, Andrew. "Identification and Difference: Structures of Privilege in Cultural Criticism." In *Who Can Speak? Authority and Critical Identity*, ed. Judith Roof and Robyn Wiegman, 3–29. Urbana: University of Illinois Press, 1995.

Lamadrid, Enrique. "The Dynamics of Myth in the Creative Vision of Rudolfo Anaya." In *Pasó por aquí*, ed. E. Gonzales-Berry, 243–54.

Lattin, Vernon E., ed. *Contemporary Chicano Fiction*. Binghamton, NY: Bilingual Press, 1986.

Lauter, Paul. "Race and Gender in the Shaping of the American Literary Canon." 1983. In *Feminist Criticism and Social Change: Sex, Class and Race in Literature and Culture*, ed. Judith Newton and Deborah Rosenfelt, 19–44. New York: Methuen, 1985.

Leal, Luis. "Cuatro siglos de prosa aztlanense." *La palabra* 2.1 (1980): 2–12.

——"En busca de Aztlán." *Aztlán y México: Perfiles literarios e históricos*. Binghamton, NY: Bilingual Review/Press, 1985, 21–28.

——"In Search of Aztlán." 1981. Trans. Gladys Leal. In *Aztlán*, ed. R. A. Anaya and F. A. Lomelí, 6–13.

——"Mexican-American Literature: A Historical Perspective." *Revista Chicano-Riqueña* 1.1 (1973): 32–44.

——and Manuel M. Martín-Rodríguez. "Chicano Literature." In *The Cambridge History of Latin American Literature*, vol. 2, ed. Roberto González Echevarría and Enrique Pupo-Walker, 557–86. Cambridge: Cambridge University Press, 1996.

León Portilla, Miguel. *Pre-Columbian Literatures of Mexico*. Trans. Grace Lobanov and Miguel León Portilla. Norman: University of Oklahoma Press, 1969.

Lesy, Michael. *Wisconsin Death Trip*. New York: Pantheon, 1973.

Lomelí, Francisco A. "Chicana Novelists in the Process of Creating Fictive Voices." In *Beyond Stereotypes*, ed. M. Herrera-Sobek, 29–46.

——"Contemporary Chicano Literature, 1959–1990: From Oblivion to Affirmation to the Forefront." In *Handbook of Hispanic Cultures in the United States*, ed. F. A. Lomelí, 86–108.

——"A Literary Portrait of Hispanic New Mexico: Dialectics of Perspective." In *Pasó por aquí*, ed. E. Gonzales-Berry, 131–48. "An Overview of Chicano Letters: From Origins to Resurgence." 1984. In *Chicano Studies*, ed. D. J. Bixler-Márquez et al., 309–17.

——ed. *Handbook of Hispanic Cultures in the United States: Literature and Art.*
Houston: Arte Público Press–Instituto de Cooperación Iberoamericana, 1993.
——and Donaldo W. Urioste. *Chicano Perspectives in Literature: A Critical and Annotated Bibliography.* Albuquerque: Pajarito Publications, 1976.

López, José Timoteo, Edgardo Núñez, and Roberto Lara Vialpando. *Breve reseña de la literatura hispana de Nuevo México y Colorado.* Ciudad Juárez, Mexico: Imprenta Comercial, 1959.

López, Miguel R. *Chicano Timespace: The Poetry and Politics of Ricardo Sánchez.* College Station: Texas A&M University Press, 2001.

López, Sonia A. "The Role of the Chicana Within the Student Movement." In *Essays on la Mujer,* ed. R. Sánchez and R. Martínez Cruz, 16–29.

Lorde, Audre. "The Master's Tools Will Never Dismantle the Master's House." In *This Bridge Called My Back,* ed. C. Moraga and G. Anzaldúa, 98–101.

Lyons, Martyn. "Los nuevos lectores del siglo XX: Mujeres, niños, obreros." In *Historia de la lectura,* ed. G. Cavallo and R. Chartier, 473–517.

Martín-Rodríguez, Manuel M. "The Act of Reading Chicano/a Texts: Strategies for Creating a Multicultural Readership." *Language and Literature* XXIV (1999): 17–29.

——"Aesthetic Concepts of Hispanics." In *Handbook of Hispanic Cultures in the United States,* ed. F. A. Lomelí, 109–33.

——"The Book on Mango Street: Escritura y liberación en la obra de Sandra Cisneros." In *Mujer y Literatura Mexicana y Chicana: Culturas en Contacto,* vol. 2, ed. Aralia López González et al., 249–54. Mexico City: El Colegio de México, 1990.

——"Border Crisscrossing: *The* (Long and Winding) *Road to Tamazunchale.*" In *Cross-Addressing: Discourse on the Border,* ed. John C. Hawley, 181–206. Buffalo: State University of New York Press, 1996.

——"En la frontera del lenguaje: Escritores y lectores en *Peregrinos de Aztlán.*" *Bilingual Review/Revista Bilingüe* 19.3 (Sept.-Dec. 1994): 57–70.

——"En la lengua materna: Las escritoras chicanas y la novela en español." *Latin American Literary Review* 23.45 (1995): 64–84.

——"Lenguaje y poder: El español en la literatura chicana." In *El poder hispano,* ed. Alberto Moncada Lorenzo et al., 487–97. Madrid: Universidad de Alcalá, 1994.

——"'A Net Made of Holes': Towards a Cultural History of Chicano Literature." *Modern Language Quarterly* 62.1 (Mar. 2001): 1–18.

——"The Raw and Who Cooked It: Food, Identity, and Culture in U.S. Latino/a Literature." In *U.S. Latino Literatures and Cultures: Transnational Perspectives,* ed. Francisco A. Lomelí and Karin Ikas, 37–51. Heidelberg, Germany: Universitätsverlag C. Winter, 2000.

——*Rolando Hinojosa y su "cronicón" chicano: Una novela del lector.* Sevilla, Spain: Universidad de Sevilla, 1993.

——"Textual and Land Reclamations: The Critical Reception of Early Chicano/a Literature." In *Recovering the U.S. Hispanic Literary Heritage,* vol. 2, ed. Charles Tatum and Erlinda Gonzales-Berry, 40–58. Houston, TX: Arte Público Press, 1996.

———"Voces, gestos y signos: de la oralidad a la escritura en *". . . y no se lo tragó la tierra"* de Tomás Rivera." *Revista Española de Estudios Norteamericanos* 8.14 (1997): 9–19.

———ed. *La voz urgente: Antología de literatura chicana en español.* 1995. Madrid: Fundamentos, 1999.

Martínez, Eliud. "Ron Arias' *The Road to Tamazunchale:* A Chicano Novel of the New Reality." 1977. In *Contemporary Chicano Fiction,* ed. V. E. Lattin, 226–38.

Martínez, Julio A., and Francisco A. Lomelí. *Chicano Literature: A Reference Guide.* Westport, CT: Greenwood, 1985.

Martínez, Max. *Schoolland.* Houston: Arte Público Press, 1988.

Mayoral, José Antonio, comp. *Estética de la recepción.* Madrid: Arco/Libros, 1987.

McCracken, Ellen. *New Latina Narrative: The Feminine Space of Postmodern Ethnicity.* Tucson: University of Arizona Press, 1999.

———"Sandra Cisneros' *The House on Mango Street:* Community-Oriented Introspection and the Demystification of Patriarchal Violence." In *Breaking Boundaries,* ed. A. Horno-Delgado et al., 62–71.

McHale, Brian. *Postmodernist Fiction.* New York and London: Methuen, 1987.

McWilliams, Carey. *North from Mexico: The Spanish Speaking People of the United States.* New York: Greenwood Press, 1948.

Meier, Matt S., and Feliciano Ribera. *Mexican Americans/American Mexicans: From Conquistadors to Chicanos.* New York: Hill & Wang, 1999.

Meléndez, A. Gabriel. *So All Is Not Lost: The Poetics of Print in Nuevomexicano Communities, 1834–1958.* Albuquerque: University of New Mexico Press, 1997.

Memmi, Albert. *The Colonizer and the Colonized.* London: Souvenir, 1974.

Mena, Jennifer. "Women on the Verge: Four Brash Latinas Writers Transform the Literary Landscape." *Hispanic* (Nov. 1995): 2.

Mena, María Cristina. *The Collected Stories of María Cristina Mena.* Ed. Amy Doherty. Houston: Arte Público Press, 1997.

Méndez, Miguel M. *Los criaderos humanos (épica de los desamparados) y Sahuaros.* Tucson, AZ: Peregrinos, 1975.

———Interview. *In Chicano Authors: Inquiry by Interview,* J. Bruce-Novoa, 83–93. Austin: University of Texas Press, 1980.

———*Peregrinos de Aztlán.* 1974. Tempe, AZ: Bilingual Review/Press, 1991.

———*Pilgrims in Aztlán.* Trans. David W. Foster. Tempe: Bilingual Review/Press, 1992.

———*Tata Casehua y otros cuentos.* Berkeley, CA: Justa Publications, 1980.

Mendoza, Louis Gerard. *Historia: The Literary Making of Chicana and Chicano History.* College Station, TX: Texas A&M University Press, 2001.

Merleau-Ponty, Maurice. *L'oeil et l'esprit.* Paris: Gallimard, 1964.

Meyer, Doris. *Speaking for Themselves: Neomexicano Cultural Identity and the Spanish-Language Press, 1880–1920.* Albuquerque: University of New Mexico Press, 1996.

Mexicanos pintados por sí mismos, Los. Mexico City: M. Murguía, 1885.

"Mitólogos y mitómanos: Mesa redonda con Alurista, R. Anaya, M. Herrera-Sobek, A. Morales y H. Viramontes." *Maize* 4.3–4 (1981): 6–23.

Monsiváis, Carlos. *Aires de familia: Cultura y sociedad en América Latina.* Barcelona: Anagrama, 2000.

Montoya, José. *Information: 20 Years of Joda.* San Jose: Chusma, 1992.

Mora, Pat. *Tomás and the Library Lady.* New York: Alfred A. Knopf, 1997.

Moraga, Cherríe. "Algo secretamente amado." *Third Woman* 4 (1989): 151–56.

——*The Last Generation.* Boston: South End, 1993.

——and Gloria Anzaldúa, eds. 1981. *This Bridge Called My Back: Writings by Radical Women of Color.* New York: Kitchen Table, 1983.

Morales, Alejandro. *Caras viejas y vino nuevo.* Mexico City: Joaquín Mortiz, 1975.

——"A Chicana Stereotypes Her Own People." *Los Angeles Times Book Reviews* 19 (1989): 10.

——"Dynamic Identities in Heterotopia." In *Alejandro Morales: Fiction Past, Present, Future Perfect,* ed. José A. Gurpegui, 11–27. Tempe, AZ: Bilingual Review/Press, 1996.

——*The Rag Doll Plagues.* Houston: Arte Público Press, 1992.

——*Reto en el paraíso.* Ypsilanti, MI: Bilingual Review/Press, 1983.

——"'Y no se lo tragó la tierra': palabra y estructura en una cultura postmoderna." In *Culturas hispanas de los Estados Unidos de América,* ed. María J. Buxó Rey and Tomás Calvo Buezas, 494–500. Madrid: Cultura Hispánica, 1990.

Munguía, Rubén. "'La Prensa': Memories of a Boy . . . Sixty Years Later." *The Americas Review* 17.3–4 (1989): 130–5.

Myers, Oliver T., and Rodolfo J. Cortina. "The Language of *El Mutualista* and *La Guardia:* A Diachronic Study of Chicano Vocabulary." *Revista Chicano-Riqueña* 13.2 (1985): 55–64.

Nell, Victor. *Lost in a Book: The Psychology of Reading for Pleasure.* New Haven, CT: Yale University Press, 1988.

Nietzsche, Friedrich. "On the Utility and Liability of History for Life." In *Unfashionable Observations,* ed. Ernst Behler, trans. Richard T. Gray, 83–167. Stanford, CA: Stanford University Press, 1995.

Nord, David Paul. "A Republican Literature: Magazine Reading and Readers in Late-Eighteenth Century New York." In *Reading in America,* ed. C. N. Davidson, 114–39.

Núñez Cabeza de Vaca, Alvar. *The Account: Alvar Núñez Cabeza de Vaca's Relación.* Ed. and trans. José Fernández and Martin Favata. Houston: Arte Público Press, 1993.

Olivares, Julián. "Sandra Cisneros' *The House on Mango Street* and the Poetics of Space." *The Americas Review* 15.3–4 (1987): 160–70.

——"The Search for Being, Identity and Form in the Work of Tomás Rivera." *Revista Chicano-Riqueña* 13.3–4 (1985): 66–80.

Ong, Walter J. *Orality and Literacy: The Technologizing of the Word.* London and New York: Methuen, 1982.

Ornelas, Berta. *Come Down from the Mound.* Phoenix, AZ: Miter, 1975.

Ortega, Eliana, and Nancy Saporta Sternbach. "At the Threshold of the Unnamed: Latina Literary Discourse in the Eighties." In *Breaking Boundaries,* ed. A. Horno-Delgado et al., 2–23.

Otero, Miguel Antonio. *The Real Billy the Kid.* 1936. Houston: Arte Público Press, 1998.

Padilla, Genaro M. "Imprisoned Narrative? Or Lies, Secrets, and Silence in New Mexico Women's Autobiography." In *Criticism in the Borderlands,* ed. H. Calderón and J. D. Saldívar, 43–60.

——"Introduction." In *The Short Stories of Fray Angelico Chavez,* ed. G. M. Padilla, vii–xx. Albuquerque: University of New Mexico Press, 1987.

——*My History, Not Yours: The Formation of Mexican American Autobiography.* Madison, WI: University of Wisconsin Press, 1993.

Padilla, Raymond V. "A Critique of Pittian History." *El Grito* 6.1 (fall 1972): 3–44.

Paredes, Américo. *Between Two Worlds.* Houston: Arte Público Press, 1991.

——*Folklore and Culture on the Texas-Mexican Border.* Austin: University of Texas Press, 1993.

——*George Washington Gómez.* Houston: Arte Público Press, 1990.

——*The Hammon and the Beans and Other Stories.* Houston: Arte Público Press, 1994.

——*The Shadow.* Houston: Arte Público Press, 1998.

——*With His Pistol in His Hand: A Border Ballad and Its Hero.* 1958. Austin: University of Texas Press, 1986.

Parle, Dennis J. "The Novels of the Mexican Revolution Published by the Casa Editorial Lozano." *The Americas Review* 17.3–4 (1989): 163–8.

Pérez, Emma. *The Decolonial Imaginary: Writing Chicanas into History.* Bloomington, IN: Indiana University Press, 1999.

——"Irigaray's Female Symbolic in the Making of Chicana Lesbian Sitios y Lenguas (Sites and Discourses)." In *Living Chicana Theory,* ed. C. Trujillo, 87–101.

Pérez, Luis. *El Coyote the Rebel.* 1947. Houston: Arte Público Press, 2000.

Pérez de Villagrá, Gaspar. *Historia de la Nueva México.* Ed. Miguel Encinias, Alfred Rodríguez, and Joseph P. Sánchez. Albuquerque: University of New Mexico Press, 1992.

Perkins, David. *Is Literary History Possible?* Baltimore: Johns Hopkins University Press, 1992.

Petersen, Clarence. *The Bantam Story: Thirty Years of Paperback Publishing.* New York: Bantam, 1975. 2nd ed.

Pettit, Arthur G. *Images of the Mexican American in Fiction and Film.* College Station: Texas A&M University Press, 1980.

Pineda, Cecile. "Deracinated." In *Máscaras,* ed. L. Corpi, 57–70.

——*The Love Queen of the Amazon.* Boston: Little, Brown, 1992.

Pitt, Leonard M. *The Decline of the Californios: A Social History of the Spanish-Speaking Californians, 1846–1890.* Berkeley: University of California Press, 1966.

Plan Espiritual de Aztlán, El. In *Aztlán: Essays on the Chicano Homeland,* ed. R. A. Anaya and F. A. Lomelí, 1–5.

Ponce, Mary Helen. *The Wedding.* Houston: Arte Público Press, 1989.

Portillo-Trambley, Estela. *Rain of Scorpions and Other Writings.* Berkeley, CA: Tonatiuh, 1975.

Pratt, Annis. *Archetypal Patterns in Women's Fiction.* Bloomington, IN: Indiana
    University Press, 1981.
Pratt, Mary Louise. "Arts of the Contact Zone." *Profession (MLA)* (1991): 33–40.
——*Toward a Speech Act Theory of Literary Discourse.* Bloomington, IN: Indiana
    University Press, 1977.

Quintana, Alvina E. "Ana Castillo's *The Mixquiahuala Letters:* The Novelist as Ethnog-
    rapher." *In Criticism in the Borderlands,* ed. H. Calderón and J. D. Saldívar, 72–83.

Rabinowitz, Peter J. "'What's Hecuba to Us?' The Audience's Experience of Literary
    Borrowing." In *The Reader in the Text,* ed. S. R. Suleiman and I. Crosman, 241–63.
Radway, Janice. *Reading the Romance: Women, Patriarchy, and Popular Literature.*
    London: Verso, 1987.
Rama, Angel. *Transculturación narrativa en América Latina.* Mexico City: Siglo
    Veintiuno, 1982.
Ramírez, Elizabeth C. *Chicanas/Latinas in American Theatre: A History of Performance.*
    Bloomington, IN: Indiana University Press, 2000.
Real Academia de la Lengua Española. *Diccionario de la lengua española.* Madrid:
    RALE, 1992. 2 vols.
Rebolledo, Tey D. *Women Singing in the Snow: A Cultural Analysis of Chicana Litera-
    ture.* Tucson: University of Arizona Press, 1995.
——and M. Teresa Márquez, eds. *Women's Tales from the New Mexico WPA: La Diabla
    a Pie.* Houston: Arte Público Press, 2000.
Rechy, John. *The Miraculous Day of Amalia Gómez.* New York: Little, Brown, 1991.
Ríos, Isabella. *Victuum.* Ventura, CA: Diana-Etna, 1976.
Ríos-McMillan, Nora. "A Biography of a Man and His Newspaper." *The Americas
    Review* 17.3–4 (1989): 136–49.
Ritzer, George. *The McDonaldization of Society.* London: Sage, 1992.
Rivera, Tomás. *The Complete Works.* Ed. Julián Olivares. Houston: Arte Público Press,
    1991.
——*. . . y no se lo tragó la tierra/And the Earth Did Not Devour Him.* 1971. Trans.
    Evangelina Vigil-Piñón. Houston: Arte Público Press, 1992.
Robinson, Cecil. *With the Ears of Strangers: The Mexican in American Literature.*
    Tucson: University of Arizona Press, 1963.
Rodríguez, Juan. "The Problematic in Tomás Rivera's *. . . And the Earth Did Not Part.*"
    Revista Chicano-Riqueña 6.3 (summer 1978): 42–50.
——"Review of *The House on Mango Street* by Sandra Cisneros." *Austin Chronicle* 10
    Aug. 1984.
Rodríguez del Pino, Salvador. *La novela chicana escrita en español: Cinco autores
    comprometidos.* Ypsilanti, MI: Bilingual Press, 1982.
Rojas, Guillermo. "La prosa chicana: tres epígonos de la novela mexicana de la
    Revolución." In *The Identification and Analysis of Chicano Literature,* ed. F.
    Jiménez, 317–28.

Romano-V., Octavio I., ed. *El espejo–The Mirror: Selected Mexican-American Literature.* Berkeley: Quinto Sol, 1969.

Romano-V., Octavio I., and Herminio Rios-C. "Quinto Sol and Chicano Publications: The First Five Years, 1967–1972." *El Grito* 5.4 (1972): 3–6.

Rosaldo, Renato. *Culture and Truth: The Remaking of Social Analysis.* Boston: Beacon, 1989.

Rosales, Jesús. "A Sojourn of Desire, Cuando lleguemos: Chicano/a Literature, A Historical Reflection." *Aztlán* 26.2 (2001): 125–51.

Rudin, Ernst. *Tender Accent of Sounds: Spanish in the Chicano Novel in English.* Tempe: Bilingual Review/Press, 1996.

Ruiz de Burton, María Amparo. *Conflicts of Interest: The Letters of María Amparo Ruiz de Burton.* Eds. Rosaura Sánchez and Beatrice Pita. Houston: Arte Público Press, 2001.

——*The Squatter and the Don: A Novel Descriptive of Contemporary Occurrences in California.* 1885. Eds. Rosaura Sánchez and Beatrice Pita. Houston: Arte Público Press, 1993.

——*Who Would Have Thought It?* 1872. Eds. Rosaura Sánchez and Beatrice Pita. Houston: Arte Público Press, 1995.

Salazar Parr, Carmen, and Genevieve M. Ramírez. "The Female Hero in Chicano Literature." In *Beyond Stereotypes,* ed. M. Herrera-Sobek, 47–60.

Saldívar, José David. *The Dialectics of Our America: Genealogy, Cultural Critique, and Literary History.* Durham, NC: Duke University Press, 1991.

——"Rolando Hinojosa's *Klail City Death Trip:* A Critical Introduction." In *The Rolando Hinojosa Reader,* ed. J. D. Saldívar, 44–63.

——ed. *The Rolando Hinojosa Reader.* Houston: Arte Público Press, 1984.

Saldívar, Ramón. *Chicano Narrative: The Dialectics of Difference.* Madison: University of Wisconsin Press, 1990.

Salinas, Raúl R. *East of the Freeway.* Austin, TX: Red Salmon, 1995.

——*Un Trip Through the Mind Jail y Otras Excursions.* San Francisco: Pocho-Che, 1980.

San Miguel, Guadalupe Jr. *"Let All of Them Take Heed": Mexican Americans and the Campaign for Educational Equality in Texas, 1910–1981.* Austin: University of Texas Press, 1987.

Sánchez, Rosaura. "The History of Chicanas: Proposal for a Materialist Perspective." In *Between Borders: Essays on Mexicana/Chicana History,* ed. Adelaida del Castillo, 1–29. Encino, CA: Floricanto Press, 1989.

——*Telling Identities: The Californio Testimonios.* Minneapolis: University of Minnesota, 1995.

——and Rosa Martínez Cruz, eds. *Essays on la Mujer.* Los Angeles: Chicano Studies Center–University of California, Los Angeles, 1977.

——and Beatrice Pita. "Introduction." In *The Squatter and the Don,* M. A. Ruiz de Burton, 5–51.

Sandoval, Chela. *Methodology of the Oppressed.* Minneapolis: University of Minnesota Press, 2000.

Santamaría, Francisco J. *Diccionario de mejicanismos.* Mexico City: Porrúa, 1983.

Schweickart, Patrocinio P. "Reading Ourselves: Toward a Feminist Theory of Reading." In *Gender and Reading,* ed. E. A. Flynn and P. P. Schweickart, 31–62.

Segade, Gustavo. "Chicano Indigenismo: Alurista and Miguel Méndez." *Xalmán* 1.4 (spring 1977): 4–11.

Segel, Elizabeth. "'As the Twig Is Bent . . .': Gender and Childhood Reading." In *Gender and Reading,* ed. E. A. Flynn and P. P. Schweickart, 165–86.

Shell, Marc, and Werner Sollors, eds. *The Multilingual Anthology of American Literature: A Reader of Original Texts with English Translations.* New York: New York University Press, 2000.

Sokoloff, Naomi B. *Imagining the Child in Modern Jewish Fiction.* Baltimore: Johns Hopkins University Press, 1992.

Spivak, Gayatri C. *The Post-Colonial Critic: Interviews, Strategies, Dialogues.* Ed. Sarah Harasym. New York: Routledge, 1990.

Steiner, Stan. *La Raza: The Mexican Americans.* New York: Harper Colophon, 1970.

Stern, S. M. "Les vers finaux en espagnol dans les *muwassahs* hispano-hébraïques. Une contribution à l'histoire du *muwassah* et à l'étude du vieux dialecte espagnol mozarabe." *Al-Andalus* XIII (1948): 299–346.

Suleiman, Susan R., and Inge Crosman, eds. *The Reader in the Text: Essays on Audience and Interpretation.* Princeton: Princeton University Press, 1980.

Svenbro, Jesper. "La Grecia arcaica y clásica: La invención de la lectura silenciosa." In *Historia de la lectura,* ed. G. Cavallo and R. Chartier, 57–93.

Tatum, Charles. "Some Considerations on Genres and Chronology for Nineteenth-Century Hispanic Literature." In *Recovering the U.S. Hispanic Literary Heritage,* ed. R. A. Gutiérrez and G. M. Padilla, 199–08.

Testa, Daniel. "Extensive/Intensive Dimensions in Anaya's *Bless Me, Ultima.*" *Latin American Literary Review* 5.10 (1977): 70–78.

Thiebaux, Marcelle. "Foucault's Fantasia for Feminists: The Woman Reading." In *Theory and Practice of Feminist Literary Criticism,* ed. Gabriela Mora and Karen Van Hooft, 45–61. Ypsilanti, MI: Bilingual Press, 1982.

Todorov, Tzvetan. *The Poetics of Prose.* 1977. Trans. Richard Howard. Ithaca, NY: Cornell University Press, 1992.

Tonn, Horst. "*Bless Me, Ultima:* Fictional Response to Times of Transition." In *Rudolfo A. Anaya,* ed. C. A. González-T., 1–12.

Trujillo, Carla, ed. *Living Chicana Theory.* Berkeley: Third Woman, 1998.

Trujillo, Roberto C., and Andrés Rodríguez. *Literatura Chicana: Creative and Critical Writings Through 1984.* Oakland, CA: Floricanto Press, 1985.

Ulica, Jorge. *Crónicas diabólicas.* Ed. Juan Rodríguez. San Diego: Maize, 1982.

Valdez, Luis. "Bernabé." *Early Works.* Houston: Arte Público Press, 1990, 134–67.

Valentine, Robert Y. "Cortázar's Rhetoric of Reading Participation." In *The Analysis of Literary Texts: Currents Trends in Methodology,* ed. Randolph D. Pope, 212–23. Ypsilanti, MI: Bilingual Press, 1980.

Venegas, Daniel. *The Adventures of Don Chipote or When Parrots Breast-Feed.* Trans. Ethriam C. Brammer. Houston: Arte Público Press, 2000.

——*Las aventuras de don Chipote o cuando los pericos mamen.* 1928. Mexico City: Secretaría de Educación Pública and Centro de Estudios de la Frontera Norte, 1985.

Vento, Arnold, et al., eds. *Flor y Canto II : An Anthology of Chicano Literature.* Albuquerque, N.Mex.: Pajarito Publications, c. 1979.

Vigil, Evangelina. *Thirty an' Seen a Lot.* Houston: Arte Público Press, 1985.

Villarreal, José Antonio. *Pocho.* Garden City, NY: Doubleday, 1959.

Villegas de Magnón, Leonor. *The Rebel.* Ed. Clara Lomas. Houston: Arte Público Press, 1994.

Webb, Walter P. *The Texas Rangers: A Century of Frontier Defense.* 1935. Austin: University of Texas Press, 1965.

White, Hayden. *Metahistory: The Historical Imagination in Nineteenth Century Europe.* Baltimore: Johns Hopkins University Press, 1973.

——*Tropics of Discourse.* Baltimore: Johns Hopkins University Press, 1978.

Yarbro-Bejarano, Yvonne. "The Multiple Subject in the Writing of Ana Castillo." *The Americas Review* 20.1 (1992): 65–72.

Zamora, Bernice. "Silence at Bay." In *Máscaras,* ed. L. Corpi, 21–34.

Zavala, Adina de. *History and Legends of the Alamo and Other Missions in and Around San Antonio.* Ed. Richard Flores. Houston: Arte Público Press, 1996.

Zboray, Ronald J. "Antebellum Reading and the Ironies of Technological Innovation." In *Reading in America,* ed. C. N. Davidson, 180–200.

Zill, Nicholas, and Marianne Winglee. *Who Reads Literature? The Future of the United States as a Nation of Readers.* Cabin John, MD: Seven Locks, 1990.

Index of Names

Index